Layman's BIBLE Commentary

Daniel thru Malachi

Volume 7

Contributing Editors:

JOHN HANNEMAN
REV. STEPHEN C. MAGEE
DOUG MCINTOSH
DR. ROBERT RAYBURN

Consulting Editor:

DR. TREMPER LONGMAN

BARBOUR
PUBLISHING

© 2010 by Barbour Publishing

ISBN 978-1-62029-780-3

Produced with the assistance of Christopher. D. Hudson & Associates. Contributing writers include: Gordon Lawrence, Heather Rippetoe, Laura Coggin, Stan Campbell, and Carol Smith.

Published by Barbour Publishing, Inc., P.O. Box 719, Uhrichsville, Ohio 44683 www.barbourbooks.com

Our mission is to publish and distribute inspirational products offering exceptional value and biblical encouragement to the masses.

Member of the
Evangelical Christian
Publishers Association

Printed in the United States of America.

TABLE OF CONTENTS

DANIEL

INTRODUCTION TO DANIEL

The book of Daniel contains some of the best-known stories in the Bible, but it also provides some of the most challenging and intriguing passages to attempt to comprehend. Some of the prophets had sent warning of a judgment of God's people to come; others are present at the end of the captivity to help encourage and empower the beleaguered exiles. But Daniel goes into exile along with his countrymen and provides an insider's view of Judah's experiences in the faraway land of Babylon.

AUTHOR

Daniel came from a royal family. He is compared with Noah and Job in terms of faithfulness to God and righteousness (see Ezekiel 14:14). Daniel also demonstrates great wisdom, always giving God complete credit. Unlike Solomon, who started life strong as a young man but strayed from God as an adult, Daniel's faith and wisdom are consistent and evident throughout his long lifetime.

OCCASION

Daniel describes events that occur during one of the worst situations the people of God ever experienced. The nation of Israel had fallen to the Assyrians more than one hundred years earlier, but Judah survived. Yet Judah continues to refuse to heed God's warning and soon faces humiliating defeat themselves. The Babylonians breach the walls of Jerusalem, ransack the temple, and carry off most of the population in a series of deportations. Daniel is among the first group taken. His writing offers much assurance in that even though circumstances are bad, God is still with His people.

THEMES

From start to finish, the theme of the book of Daniel is the sovereignty of God. This theme is detected in the way the Lord interacts with individuals, controls nations, and shares with Daniel plans for the long-range future of His people.

HISTORICAL CONTEXT

Babylon was considered to be one of the most glorious and powerful kingdoms of the world at the time that Daniel was written. The palace and gardens are listed among the seven wonders of the ancient world. God uses Babylon's strong armies to conquer Judah after the people refuse to serve Him. In the process, the Babylonians kill many Judeans and take many into captivity. Yet by the end of Daniel, the Babylonian Empire has already fallen to Cyrus, leader of the Medes and Persians.

CONTRIBUTION TO THE BIBLE

In addition to some of the Bible's most beloved stories (including the fiery furnace and the lions' den), the book of Daniel is an invaluable source of information concerning various events of future history. Coupled with John's writing in Revelation, many of the symbols of the apocalyptic literature begin to cohere and make sense. Certainly, there are numerous ways to interpret the same information, and it can be difficult to do more than speculate in many places. However, Jesus quotes Daniel as a source for what to look for in the future (see Matthew 24:15–16), giving the prophet's writing the highest degree of credibility.

OUTLINE

DANIEL 1:1–21

DANIEL TAKEN TO BABYLON

Setting Up the Section

The book of Daniel describes some of the same era as 2 Kings and 2 Chronicles, yet Daniel describes this era from within the Babylonian exile. Due to persistent disregard for God's laws and other sins throughout Judah, the Lord had allowed His people to be conquered. The Babylonian armies had shown little mercy as they marched into Judah, laid siege to Jerusalem, and eventually left the city and the surrounding territory in ruins. Many people died while fighting; many others starved to death. Most of those who survived were deported to Babylon—Daniel among them. The people feel as though God has deserted them. However, Daniel repeatedly attests to the power of the one true God at work, even while His people are exiled in the idolatrous land of Babylon.

q 1:1–2

A DISTRESSING BEGINNING

Daniel has one of the bleakest openings of any book of scripture. Within the first two verses, the beloved city of Jerusalem falls into the hands of one of the most terrifying empires on earth. The temple's holy items are carted away and placed among the idols of Babylon. To make things worse, it is the Lord who has given Jerusalem over to her enemies. The captivity that results is a God-designed plan to chastise His people for their ongoing rebellion. The year is 605 BC. Judah's king at the time is Jehoiakim.

This is one of the worst experiences in the history of Judah. (The northern kingdom of Israel had faced a similar end more than a century earlier at the hands of the Assyrians.) Yet despite this potentially depressing beginning, Daniel never ceases to be encouraging and optimistic. Right from the start, the theme of his book is the sovereignty of God. The Lord is in control of the nations and is working out His plan in this world. He is absolutely in control.

Critical Observation

The prophet Habakkuk confirms that God permitted the brutal Babylonian invasion as a result of the wickedness of His people (Habakkuk 1:5–11). In fact, Habakkuk tries to talk God out of impending disaster (Habakkuk 1:12–2:1). He learns, however, that the plans of God are God's alone, and that the best he can do is walk by faith, no matter what happens.

Other sources describe various horrific events associated with the fall of Jerusalem, so it is interesting to notice what Daniel focuses on in his record. Of all the dreadful and repulsive things taking place around him, he singles out the degradation of the temple (1:2). Israel's worship had become ritualistic rather than genuine, so God took worship away from them. He allowed all of the gold previously used in temple worship to be used to mock Him in the presence of false gods. It is humiliating to Judah and to the Lord.

Israel's mind-set and practice of worship as ritual had no effect on their day-to-day lives. Placing their so-called holy objects among the idols of other nations is God's way of giving them a picture of what is in their hearts. Their "worship" is no different than that of the Babylonians.

God wants to see His people redeemed. He wants Judah to repent and fall before Him in complete devotion. Therefore, He allows them to endure much heartache and lose their temple temporarily so that ultimately they might be saved.

q 1:3-7

THE BEST IN A BAD SITUATION

After Jerusalem falls, Babylonian King Nebuchadnezzar conducts a search for some of Judah's top young people—a common practice of the time by victorious rulers. By indoctrinating the up-and-coming leaders of the defeated nation, Nebuchadnezzar hopes to ensure that new generations will settle into the Babylonian way of life rather than attempting escape or revolt.

Daniel is one of four young men from Judah mentioned by name who are taken (1:6). At the time, they are probably about fifteen or sixteen years old. Nothing is said of their parents, but the Babylonians wouldn't have thought twice about breaking up families to carry off anyone they wished.

Being handsome and without defect (1:4), Daniel and his three peers clearly have genetics working for them. But they also are noted for their quickness to learn and their aptitude for accumulating wisdom. They are expected to quickly assimilate into Babylonian culture by absorbing the language and literature of their new home. They are also given Babylonians names.

Demystifying Daniel

A change in names had spiritual as well as cultural significance. The Hebrew names all acknowledged characteristics of the awesome God of Judah:

Daniel meant, "God is my Judge."

Hananiah meant, "Yahweh is gracious."

Mishael meant, "Who is like God?"

Azariah meant, "Yahweh is my helper."

The newly assigned names, in contrast (Belteshazzar, Shadrach, Meshach, and Abednego), acknowledged various Babylonian deities: Bel, Aku, and Nego/Nebo.

Theirs was a demanding, three-year program (1:5). Nebuchadnezzar changed their names, clothes, language, home, and culture, yet he was not successful in changing their hearts.

📖 1:8–21

PASSING THE FIRST TEST

However, there are benefits in addition to the demands for these men. The young trainees are entitled to a daily allotment of food from the king's own table—the best of the best (1:5). This is intended to be a privilege, but Daniel and his friends do not see it that way. Daniel is probably well aware of the numerous dietary restrictions in Jewish law, and the gourmet food of Babylon did not meet those standards. Also, the Babylonian food was associated with their idols.

Regardless of his motivation, Daniel determines not to defile himself with Nebuchadnezzar's choice food or fine wine (1:8). This verse is key in understanding who Daniel truly is. He is a young man, away from home and family, plunged into a new and potentially mesmerizing culture, and offered the best of everything. Many young people would quickly succumb to exotic opportunities and temptations, especially in a setting where it appears that righteous behavior does not matter. Yet Daniel never loses his resolve to live a holy life for the Lord.

He acts on his belief, and the way he does so also attests to his character. He doesn't make a big scene, attempt to manipulate anyone, or tell little white lies. He realizes this is a delicate situation—one that can get his supervisor killed if things go badly (1:10). So Daniel goes behind the scenes and makes an agreement with the delivery boy, suggesting a ten-day test period.

Daniel acts wisely, yet the text makes it clear that it is God who is at work to resolve the problem (1:9). Even as God's people are being disciplined, the Lord is at work among them, still preserving and protecting them. All the other trainees in Nebuchadnezzar's program are given the rich foods, while Daniel and his three friends stick to a vegetable and water diet (1:11–14).

After ten days, Daniel and his three friends are noticeably healthier and better nourished than their peers. Their supervisor breaths a sigh of relief and continues their vegetable diet, and they feel no more pressure to defy their religious convictions in order to fit in (1:15–16).

But the diet test is just a beginning. God gives Daniel, Hananiah (Shadrach), Mishael (Meshach), and Azariah (Abednego) great understanding and wisdom in all areas of learning and philosophy (1:17). Daniel is given a special ability to understand dreams and visions. Daniel and his friends aren't actively seeking special favor from God, yet the Lord responds to their devotion and obedience.

Critical Observation

In the midst of destruction and misery for Judah, God is still blessing His people. And through them, others will be blessed. In this case, Daniel's supervisor comes out looking good. Before long, the young men of Judah will be influencing kings.

At the end of the three-year training period, Nebuchadnezzar interviews each of the young men who have gone through his program. Again, Daniel and his three friends are clearly exceptional. The king deems them ten times better in terms of wisdom and understanding than any of the magicians and enchanters from whom he seeks advice (1:20).

Ten times better (1:20) is not a quantitative term. Just as people today think in terms of "a perfect 10" at an Olympic event, or judge an extremely attractive person as "a 10," the number had similar meaning in ancient times. *Ten* was a number that represented fullness or completeness.

Considering their young age and circumstances, the faithfulness of Daniel and his friends is particularly amazing. And yet, both Daniel and his three friends will face far greater challenges (and successes) ahead.

Take It Home

Daniel demonstrates that the battle for holiness is either won or lost in the small areas of life. Instead of attempting to change circumstances that are beyond his control, he shifts his focus to simply obeying God. In fact, sometimes the desire to maintain control is the polar opposite of faith. Can you think of any areas in your life where you might need to relinquish control in order to let God act on your behalf instead?

DANIEL 2:1–49

DANIEL INTERPRETS NEBUCHADNEZZAR'S DREAM

Setting Up the Section

After going through Nebuchadnezzar's three-year training period and excelling among his fellow participants (1:3–5, 18–20), Daniel is soon put to the test. In an account that demonstrates how eccentric and brutal Babylonian leadership could be at times, the king makes a demand of his advisors that seems impossible, yet their failure will result in their deaths. As the Lord had done previously, He again provides a way out for Daniel—an act that delivers not only Daniel but also spares the entire group of Nebuchadnezzar's advisors.

📖 2:1–13

NEBUCHADNEZZAR'S CHALLENGE

Before delving into the crux of the passage, a matter of interpretation needs to be addressed. Daniel 2:1 records that this account occurs during the second year of the reign of Nebuchadnezzar, yet Daniel and his friends are put into the king's service after three years of training (1:5, 18). Because of this apparent discrepancy, some people have actually sought to dismiss the book of Daniel as unauthentic or even fictional.

However, in the Babylonian system, a king's years of service are counted the same way people today number birthdays. Even though Nebuchadnezzar might have been well into his third year chronologically, the record would have shown it as his second. This observation should be coupled with another one that explains why Daniel uses the Babylonian counting system. At this point in his narrative (from 2:4–7:28), Daniel shifts from Hebrew to Aramaic in his writing. Aramaic was a widespread language, understood by many diverse peoples. (Nebuchadnezzar's advisors, for example, were probably from different nations, and according to 2:4, they spoke in Aramaic.) Daniel reverts to Hebrew for chapters 8–12.

So in a common language, Daniel writes of a dream that had troubled Nebuchadnezzar. It is a divine dream that creates a divine disturbance, driving Nebuchadnezzar to reconcile the disturbance that he feels. He needs to make sure that the dream is interpreted correctly, so he sets forth a challenge that rattles his entire staff. Not only does Nebuchadnezzar demand an interpretation to his dream; first he wants his magicians and astrologers to tell him what he has dreamed! If they do, he will reward them handsomely with wealth and honor. But if they don't, he will have them cut into pieces and their houses destroyed (2:5–6). They attempt to negotiate a better deal, but Nebuchadnezzar will not back down from his ultimatum, and he accuses them of stalling (2:7–9).

When Nebuchadnezzar remains adamant, his usual counselors attempt to plead and reason with him. They tell him that in the known history of the world, no one has ever expected such a thing. It is an impossible task. They say only the gods can do such a thing, and that the gods do not dwell with people (2:10–11).

The response of Nebuchadnezzar's magicians reveals their worldview. They perceive a distinct separation between gods and people. From their perspective, gods stay in their world, and it is the responsibility of humans to reach out to them. The magicians' statement sets the stage for the rest of the book of Daniel, which explains the gospel message in terms that can be understood by the Gentile world of the Babylonian culture. Daniel will go on to describe how God enters the world of humanity to rescue people. Every story told from this point forward demonstrates how God interacts with this world. The second half of Daniel's book describes more specifically how and when God will come to the world in the person of the Messiah.

The court magicians' pleas to Nebuchadnezzar are to no avail. The infuriated king immediately gives the order to have all the wise men of Babylon put to death—an order that includes Daniel, Shadrach, Meshach, and Abednego (2:12–13). This apparent crisis is divinely orchestrated to create a supposedly impossible situation through which God's plan for the world will be revealed.

📖 **2:14–23**

DANIEL'S RESPONSE

The captain of the king's guard is sent to inform Daniel of the grim news. Daniel, however, responds with discretion and discernment. He asks for a bit more time so that he might do what the king has asked (2:14–16). Even though Nebuchadnezzar had just accused his court magicians and sorcerers of attempting to stall for time (2:8), it seems that he respects Daniel's request (2:16).

Daniel gathers his three Hebrew friends, and the four of them pray (2:17–18). They realize this is a divine challenge that they face, so they turn to God for clarity. They appeal to Him for mercy and wisdom, and He provides the solution.

Daniel has a vision during the night in which God gives him the answer that Nebuchadnezzar desires (2:19). But after receiving the solution, Daniel doesn't immediately go running to the king. First he takes time to praise God, appropriately ascribing all wisdom and power to the Lord.

It appears that Daniel's prayer is also influenced by the content of the dream God reveals (a dream not yet revealed in scripture). It is God who determines times and seasons, who sets up and deposes kings as he sees fit (2:21)—all in anticipation of a Messiah to come. Daniel acknowledges God's sovereign hand in the world. Unlike the gods of the Babylonians, the Lord *does* interact with this world. Not only does He interact, but He also controls the world.

The Lord is a God of light, who exposes the things of darkness. He also reveals hidden things. God enables Daniel to be wise and discerning, and Daniel uses his wisdom to seek God's help. In return, God makes known to Daniel something that Daniel couldn't possibly discern on his own. Daniel's knowledge of Nebuchadnezzar's dream will allow many people to live who otherwise would have been put to death. So Daniel also praises God for revealing Nebuchadnezzar's dream to him (2:22–23).

📖 **2:24–43**

DANIEL'S INTERPRETATION

Daniel's praise to God is not limited to the privacy of prayer. When he is called back in to speak to Nebuchadnezzar, he gives God full credit before the king. Daniel makes it patently clear that no human—not wise men, enchanters, magicians, or diviners—could have given Nebuchadnezzar the answer he sought. Yet his God is in heaven and can reveal mysteries (2:26–28). Daniel elevates the focus from humanity to God.

Only a revelation from God could enable anyone to understand Nebuchadnezzar's dream. Through Daniel, God is letting Nebuchadnezzar know that God is at work in the world, revealing His glory. This is the Lord's world, the future is in the Lord's control, and even the ability to see and understand what the Lord is saying requires divinely inspired insight.

Demystifying Daniel

The entire book of Daniel is a revelation of the gospel. God has just demonstrated to Nebuchadnezzar the seed plot to the teaching of justification by faith. To interact with the wisdom of God and understand what He is doing, one must go to God and seek His kingdom, wisdom, and righteousness. Later portions of Daniel will reveal even more about God's plan.

Then Daniel begins to relate the specifics of what Nebuchadnezzar had dreamed. The king had seen a great statue (2:31). Even though Nebuchadnezzar is the mightiest king in the world, who had conquered every nation in his path, he is not the center of the dream; the statue is. Nor is he in control of the events in his dream; he is merely an observer. Perhaps it is the sense that someone or something is more powerful than he is that had created all the fear and anxiety behind his threats toward those who serve him.

The statue is made of different kinds of metal. The head is gold, the chest and arms are silver, the middle portions are bronze, the legs are iron, and the feet are iron mixed with baked clay (2:31–33). As Nebuchadnezzar continues to observe, he sees a rock that is cut out, but not by human hands (2:34). The rock smashes into the statue. The statue topples over and breaks into pieces, which are quickly swept away by the wind like chaff at threshing time. The rock, however, grows into a huge mountain that fills the whole earth (2:34–35).

This dream both humbled and frightened Nebuchadnezzar. This was no mere nightmare that resulted from indigestion or an active imagination. Daniel will soon make it clear that this is a divine revelation that Nebuchadnezzar had received (2:45). God is allowing Nebuchadnezzar to come face-to-face with a future not under his control, but the Lord's. As Daniel goes on to interpret the dream, Nebuchadnezzar will receive the first of several lessons concerning the sovereignty of God.

Daniel's explanation foretells four world empires. Each section of the statue represents a different nation. He starts with Nebuchadnezzar and Babylon.

For modern readers with New Testament awareness, it may sound peculiar to read that Daniel refers to Nebuchadnezzar as "king of kings" (2:36–37). Literally, the phrase refers to a king that all other kings are subject to, which is why it becomes such a meaningful messianic title for Jesus. But Daniel uses the term to affirm that Nebuchadnezzar is a dominant figure. From Babylon's inception (Genesis 10:8–12), it had always stood for defiance of God. In time, the kingdom of Nebuchadnezzar came to symbolize the kingdom of this world. So in a literal sense, Nebuchadnezzar is indeed king of kings over those who are opposed to God.

Critical Observation

During the decline of the Roman Empire, Augustine wrote a monumental work called *City of God*. His observation was that there are really only two kingdoms: the kingdom of man and the kingdom of God. Those in the kingdom of man live to serve themselves, while those in the kingdom of God live to serve the Lord.

The head of gold on the statue in Nebuchadnezzar's dream (2:32, 36–38) symbolizes Babylon. Nebuchadnezzar is the leader of the most glorious of all the kingdoms in the world. Yet it will not be a lasting kingdom.

Next on the statue are the chest and arms of silver (2:32, 39). The nations that conquer Babylon (the Medes and Persians) will be inferior to Babylon. They will be stronger, but not as glorious. Daniel is letting Nebuchadnezzar know that his days are numbered. The kingdom he has established will fall to another.

But then a third kingdom will arise after the second. The statue's belly and thighs of bronze (2:32, 39) represent Greece. Just as bronze is stronger than silver, Alexander the Great will dominate the leaders of the Medes and Persians. Yet the Greek Empire will be less glorious than the Persian Empire had been.

Stronger still will be the Roman Empire, the statue's legs of iron (2:33, 40). At a point in the future, the Romans will arise and conquer all the surrounding kingdoms. Yet again there will be a diminishing of the glory of the kingdom. In addition, this fourth kingdom will be divided. Portions will be as strong as iron, but other parts will be like clay—and iron and clay certainly don't mix well (2:43). The imagery is most appropriate. As it turns out, the mighty Roman Empire will lack unity as it is plagued by civil wars, social unrest, and moral relativism.

Demystifying Daniel

Daniel speaks only of a series of specific kingdoms to come and doesn't identify them by name. Yet history shows that the series of Babylonian, Medo-Persian, Greek, and Roman world domination provide a fitting fulfillment of Daniel's prophecy. The rock (the establishment of the kingdom of God) also seems to fit the historic scenario very well with the birth of Jesus Christ during the time of the Roman Empire.

📖 2:44–49

THE FINAL KINGDOM

The imagery in Nebuchadnezzar's divinely inspired dream is important. Even though four great nations are mentioned in Daniel's interpretation, they comprise a single statue. The series of nations, even though distinct from one another, represent one world system.

As Daniel continues to interpret the dream for Nebuchadnezzar, he explains that the cut rock (2:34) represents the kingdom of God (2:44). The stone smashed into the feet of the image (the Roman Empire) and the entire statue (the human world system) come crashing down. God's kingdom, ruled by Jesus, will destroy the kingdom of the world. All the combined glory and strength of humanity will not be able to stand before the kingdom of God.

Modern readers need to remember that Daniel wrote this account to remind the Jews that God is sovereign, and therefore nothing is beyond His control. Specifically, even Judah's domination by the Babylonians is part of God's plan. Nations that rise do so because God allows it. Nations that fall do so because God brings them to an end. All nations are temporary until the final kingdom of God. The rock in Nebuchadnezzar's dream produces a mountain that fills the whole earth (2:35), and it will last forever. In demonstrating to Judah that God is still in full control of their future, Daniel is also warning Babylon that they are not eternal and will see their kingdom fall one day.

Daniel's accurate recall of Nebuchadnezzar's dream, and his insightful interpretation of what it means, impresses the king. Nebuchadnezzar becomes very appreciative and accommodating. He even acknowledges the superiority of Daniel's God above all other gods and kings (2:46–47). However, Nebuchadnezzar's contrition will be short-lived. In the following section, his ego will be back in full bloom, and God will humble him again. In fact, Nebuchadnezzar will have numerous encounters with the humbling arm of God.

Meanwhile, Daniel is rewarded with many gifts and elevated to a position of power above all the other wise men of the court. At Daniel's request, Nebuchadnezzar also promotes Shadrach, Meshach, and Abednego (2:48–49). God is at work to place His people in positions of influence over the entire Babylonian world at that time.

Throughout this section, Daniel refers to God as a *revealer of mysteries* (2:19, 22, 28–29, 47). Certainly, there may be mysteries of life that people will not or cannot understand in this world. Other deep truths, however, are available to those who seek God's wisdom as Daniel did. Sometimes you might find yourself in Daniel's position, providing valid answers for someone else. Other times you may find yourself like Nebuchadnezzar—confused and seeking help. What are some of the mysteries that persistently pique your curiosity? What are some sources you might consult (people, reference materials, etc.) to help gather information as you continue to seek God's answers for your hardest questions?

DANIEL 3:1–30

THE FIERY FURNACE AND GOD'S DELIVERANCE

Nebuchadnezzar's Statue	3:1–7
The Hebrews' Dilemma	3:8–18
Nebuchadnezzar's Lesson	3:19–30

Setting Up the Section

Four men of Judah are mentioned by name as being taken from Judah to Babylon to be trained to serve King Nebuchadnezzar (1:6–7). The primary focus so far has been on Daniel. In this section, however, the attention is placed on his three friends, better known by their Babylonian names: Shadrach, Meshach, and Abednego.

📖 3:1–7

NEBUCHADNEZZAR'S STATUE

To get a proper perspective on this account, one must relate it to the events of Daniel 2. In chapter 2, King Nebuchadnezzar dreams of a great statue and is eventually told that he is the head. So when Nebuchadnezzar subsequently has a huge statue built of his image, there can be little doubt that the statue expresses his desire to see his dream not only fulfilled but surpassed.

Nebuchadnezzar has been told that he is the king of kings—the head of gold (2:37–38). It is commonly thought that the king's pride leads him to then make a statue of himself in complete gold. Perhaps he is so prideful that he misses the point of the dream and hears only that he is the king of kings. The statue, then, communicates that his kingdom is beautiful and will last forever.

It is not only an ambitious project but also a huge expense. The golden figure is ninety feet high and nine feet wide (3:1). It is the ultimate expression of human ego; Nebuchadnezzar is so enthralled with himself that he brings his entire staff together and has them listen to a new decree (3:2–6). A close reading reveals that the unveiling of Nebuchadnezzar's statue is shrouded in religious overtones. He is not just introducing the image as a token of remembrance; he is presenting a new religion.

The unveiling ceremony involves much religious symbolism: a dedication (3:2); music and a desire to create a worship ritual (3:5); and the act of bowing down in honor, reverence, and worship (3:5). It seems safe to presume that the image is of Nebuchadnezzar. If so, then the people are required to bow down to worship his image every time the music is played. Apparently the king believes that he is the sovereign lord of the earth and the leader of the world, and therefore he deserves worship. But in order to think in such a manner, he has to disregard the interpretation of his dream that Daniel provided—that Nebuchadnezzar's kingdom is a gift of the true God.

Demystifying Daniel

This section of Daniel introduces some obscure words. But since translations vary, it is enough to say for our purposes that the list of terms in 3:3 (*satraps*, *prefects*, and so forth) is of government leaders at various levels. And the list in 3:5 is an assortment of musical instruments of the era.

It is easy to be critical of Nebuchadnezzar's haughty attitude, but it is far more common than many might like to admit. It is a temptation for all humankind to take credit for the things with which God has blessed them. People tend to never be satisfied with what God provides and feel that they deserve more. Then, when they get more, they lose sight of the fact that every blessing is a result of the kindness and mercy of God. Nebuchadnezzar is only one example.

It seems that most people have no problem with Nebuchadnezzar's new ruling. When the music plays, they bow as they have been ordered (3:7). This naturally exposes anyone who doesn't bow, as is the case with Shadrach, Meshach, and Abednego.

Demystifying Daniel

The question that usually comes up at this point is, "Where is Daniel while all this is going on?" His three friends are left to themselves to deal with a high-pressure situation. It seems likely that Daniel would have been required to travel in his position as Nebuchadnezzar's top assistant. He might well have been in another part of the kingdom. One should also note that considerable time has probably passed between Daniel 2 and Daniel 3. Ninety-foot-tall gold statues are not quickly constructed.

📖 3:8–18

THE HEBREWS' DILEMMA

It takes little time for a group of Babylonians to go running to Nebuchadnezzar and tell him that certain Jews have not bowed down like everyone else. Their specific accusations bear close attention. They accuse Shadrach, Meshach, and Abednego of: (1) disregarding

Nebuchadnezzar; (2) not serving his gods; and (3) not worshiping the golden image he has set up. Nowhere in Nebuchadnezzar's decree did he stipulate that everyone had to serve his gods, but these men add it to their list of charges.

It is likely that the accusers are jealous of the prior success of Shadrach, Meshach, and Abednego, because the charges are certainly exaggerated. In reality, the three Hebrews have not disregarded the king or defied his position. They are three of Nebuchadnezzar's greatest assets and more than willing to serve on his staff. But in that culture, no king could afford to easily dismiss accusations of treason against those close to him.

Nebuchadnezzar's response to the news is immediate rage. He sends for Shadrach, Meshach, and Abednego. He personally repeats for them the mandate that had previously been announced publicly. Then he gives them an ultimatum: Either bow down and worship him now or be thrown into the fiery furnace and die (3:13–15).

Nebuchadnezzar's final comment during this brief conversation is telling. If they refuse to bow to the image, he wants to know, "What god will be able to rescue you from my hand?" (3:15 NIV).

The king has dismissed everything Daniel told him. He has established himself as a god again. He presumes his form of torture is the maximum punishment in both this world and the heavenly world. And in the greatest offense of all, he believes that the Hebrew God is impotent in comparison to him.

Despite the unreasonable hostility of Nebuchadnezzar, the response of Shadrach, Meshach, and Abednego remain fearless and well-reasoned. They don't feel compelled to answer him because his threats are empty in light of the power of their God. Still, they *choose* to respond and explain themselves. In doing so, they reveal four important points.

First, they fully trust God's sovereignty. Even in this difficult and threatening situation, they do not consider it foolish to trust God. Nebuchadnezzar's power pales in comparison to God's. Second, they remain true to the scriptures. This isn't just a difference of opinion between them and the king. They only disobeyed Nebuchadnezzar because they were following a higher law by refusing to bow down to any image or idol (Exodus 20:3–6). Third, they are willing to die for their faith. They know God is powerful enough to rescue them, whether or not He chooses to do so. And fourth, they remain completely submissive to God's will. Their faith is not conditional, based on a prescribed outcome. At issue is not their comfort; it is their obedience to God.

NEBUCHADNEZZAR'S LESSON

The response of Shadrach, Meshach, and Abednego is not what Nebuchadnezzar wants to hear. His very countenance changes (3:19). He had trusted these men and placed them on his elite team. Now he feels betrayed and wants to see nothing less than their total destruction. In his great fury, he orders the furnace to be heated to seven times its usual temperature—most likely, to its maximum heat (3:19–20). He has the three traitors bound (3:20), which serves no good purpose other than the psychological strategy of removing control from them, preventing them from even minimally shielding themselves from the heat. Doing his work for him are his strongest soldiers.

Critical Observation

Nebuchadnezzar is parading his strength for all to see. He wants the totality of his power to be made known so that the three young men and everyone observing will know that he is the most powerful man on earth.

The punishment for Shadrach, Meshach, and Abednego is intended to be most cruel, as is proven when a number of their captors die just from tossing the three into the flames (3:22–23). The judgment intended for the Hebrews falls instead on some of Nebuchadnezzar's most valiant warriors. As for the three who have so deeply angered the king, they are about to astonish him.

Peering into the furnace, Nebuchadnezzar sees the men walking around, but there are four figures instead of three (3:24–25). He asks his advisors for confirmation, and they assure him that only three people had gone into the furnace. But the king can clearly see four men walking around unbound and unharmed.

Not only does God preserve Shadrach, Meshach, and Abednego; He joins them in the furnace. Some people think the fourth figure may be the preincarnate Christ. Nebuchadnezzar can only speculate as to the fourth figure, calling him a son of the gods, but he definitely wants to know more.

He approaches the furnace and calls for the three to come out (3:26–27). As they do, all the Babylonian leaders gather around to inspect them. No one would even suspect the men had been near fire. Not only is their skin, clothes, and hair unaffected, but they don't even smell of smoke! Apparently all the flames had done was burn off the ropes with which they had been bound.

As a result, Nebuchadnezzar has a complete change of heart (3:28–30). At this point, he is both impressed that they have defied him and overwhelmed that their faithfulness to their God is stronger than their physical security. He correctly reaches the conclusion that no other god can deliver someone in the manner that their God has just done. Moreover, Nebuchadnezzar amends his previous mandate. From now on, he says, anyone who speaks out against the God of Shadrach, Meshach, and Abednego will receive the worst punishment conceivable.

As for the three young Hebrew men, they are again promoted (2:49; 3:30). Even though they haven't sought any tangible result from their display of faith, God allows them to prosper. Their steadfastness during great crisis is rewarded.

Take It Home

People of faith can expect occasional debates, disagreements, or conflicts with people who don't believe in God, and they can learn much from Shadrach, Meshach, and Abednego. Even at risk of their lives, the Hebrew trio refuses to compromise their beliefs. Although under great pressure, they remain remarkably calm and even understated. They don't attempt to overpower or outshout Nebuchadnezzar, or maneuver their way out of a tricky situation. They simply explain what they believe to be true and leave the outcome to God. Can you think of current examples where Christians and nonbelievers are at odds over important issues? In each instance, how well do you think the believers involved represent their God and their faith? On a personal level, what can you learn from this narrative that will help you be a better spokesperson for God?

DANIEL 4:1–37

NEBUCHADNEZZAR'S HUMBLING EXPERIENCE

Setting Up the Section

The previous two chapters of Daniel have shown how God is dealing with the pride of King Nebuchadnezzar, first through Daniel and then through Shadrach, Meshach, and Abednego. This section is the final segment concerning Nebuchadnezzar, as the king recounts what he has learned. Even Nebuchadnezzar has come to realize that God is the Lord of the universe, and he opens and closes the section with a declaration about the sovereign power and glory of God.

📖 4:1–18

NEBUCHADNEZZAR'S SECOND DREAM

Daniel 4 is a letter to the nations that Nebuchadnezzar composes after he is finally convinced of the sovereignty of God. Coming from the pen of a Gentile king, this chapter provides some incredible transforming insights about the Lord.

The positive opening temporarily shields the fact that Nebuchadnezzar has been through a horrendous experience. However, the experience has taught him about his own sin and the nature of God, so he records the lesson for all the governors in his kingdom so they will not make the same mistake he has (4:1–2).

Nebuchadnezzar opens by acknowledging four aspects of God that he has discovered (4:3). First are the great *signs* he has observed. The Lord has communicated with the king through dreams and then provided Daniel to interpret the dreams. God even enabled Daniel to know what Nebuchadnezzar had dreamed without being told (2:5-6, 19). God had specifically communicated with Nebuchadnezzar, and the king praises Him for such an extraordinary experience.

Next Nebuchadnezzar praises God for His mighty *wonders*—God's intervention in this world. God literally changes the course of life for Nebuchadnezzar, as the king will soon explain. The story he tells will confirm the great wonders God can perform. As previously noted, the Babylonian gods were not known to step into the world of humanity, but Judah's God is undoubtedly active among His people.

Third, Nebuchadnezzar praises God's *eternal kingdom*. For the first time, the reader sees the Babylonian leader acknowledge a greater kingdom. Babylon will not be a lasting empire, but God's kingdom will have no end. Such acknowledgment reflects a significant change in Nebuchadnezzar, demonstrating the extent of his humility.

Finally, the king concedes God's *rule* over the earth. The Lord's dominion extends throughout all generations. God is the only authentic ruler of the world because no kingdom, past or present, is beyond His control.

Nebuchadnezzar begins his story by explaining that everything in his life and kingdom was going well—or so he thought (4:4). He was prosperous, contented, and happy. And then he has another dream.

The previous dream of Nebuchadnezzar's—the image made of different metal (2:31–35)—had no small effect on the king. But this one is apparently even more influential. This dream terrifies him, and he can't get it out of his mind (4:5).

Seeking some kind of clarity or insight, Nebuchadnezzar calls for his staff of wise men and describes his dream to them. But they are no more helpful in this case than they had been before (2:10–11). When they fail to understand and interpret the dream, the king calls for Daniel, who again comes through for him. Why Nebuchadnezzar always waits to ask Daniel is unknown, although his tendency to do so repeatedly proves that the Lord enlightens Daniel in ways that none of the other magicians, enchanters, astrologers, and diviners (4:6–7) can come close to matching.

Critical Observation

The Hebrew captives who had been drafted into Nebuchadnezzar's service have been given Babylonian names. Daniel's three friends—Hananiah, Mishael, and Azariah—are better known by their new names: Shadrach, Meshach, and Abednego. Daniel's name is also changed. Since Daniel 4 is from Nebuchadnezzar's perspective, Daniel's Babylonian name (Belteshazzar) is used (4:8–9, 18–19). However, in most other cases, Daniel's Hebrew name is used, and that is the name by which he is best known.

Nebuchadnezzar has made two key observations about Daniel. First, he realizes that "the spirit of the holy gods" is in him (4:9). It is not likely that Nebuchadnezzar is giving the one true God full credit here, although some translations use the upper case *G* for *gods*. This passage is within the portion of Daniel that is written in Aramaic (2:4–7:28), and translators face some difficulty putting the original language into English. Yet at the heart of the king's expression is his certainty that Daniel has been given insight by some divine source.

The second observation about Daniel is that no mystery baffles the young man. Daniel has already proven himself beyond doubt, and the king has great confidence that Daniel can interpret any dream—even one that has stumped all his peers on Nebuchadnezzar's court.

So Nebuchadnezzar lays out his dream for Daniel to hear (4:10–18). It is indeed a strange account of a great tree that flourishes for a time until a heavenly voice commands it to be chopped down. The stump and roots are left in the field, bound with iron and bronze. Then the tree appears to become a beast, sentenced to live in the field for a period of time. Finally, a declaration is made about a person being removed from power so that everyone will know that the One speaking is the Most High Lord of the universe.

It is likely that Nebuchadnezzar has a sense of what the dream means, which is probably why it troubles him so much. He may even have enjoyed the first part of the dream as he saw himself as the great tree that touched the sky and provided shelter and sustenance for so many. If so, he is surely unsettled as the dream unfolds and strange events begin to occur.

📄 **4:19–37**

THE DREAM'S INTERPRETATION AND FULFILLMENT

After Daniel hears the dream, he is unsettled himself—not because he doesn't understand the meaning, but because he *does*. He is reluctant to look the king in the eye and deliver bad news, yet Nebuchadnezzar encourages him to speak truthfully.

The last time the king had dreamed about the future, Daniel identified Nebuchadnezzar as king of kings (2:37) and the head of gold (2:38). Shortly afterward, Nebuchadnezzar built a ninety-foot statue in honor of himself (3:1). This time, however, Daniel has the responsibility of telling Nebuchadnezzar that God is going to take his kingdom away, and the king will suffer in even worse ways as well.

Daniel confirms that the tree in the dream is indeed a symbol for Nebuchadnezzar (4:20–22). He has become the most powerful man in the world, and the rest of the world is subject to him. More than being merely strong and mighty, Babylon is known for its glory. Yet as dominant as Nebuchadnezzar has become, he is still merely a human. Heavenly forces are at work over which he has no control. At a single command by a holy messenger, the great tree is cut down.

The future of the king is grim. He is going to go mad and then be driven from Babylon. God's action will be the result of the king's refusal to recognize that it is the Lord who rules. Nebuchadnezzar has acknowledged that Daniel's God is a strong God, and he notes that Daniel and his friends benefited from serving their God. But Nebuchadnezzar has always stopped short of *submitting* to Daniel's God.

Demystifying Daniel

When Daniel tells Nebuchadnezzar that the king needs to acknowledge that "heaven rules" (4:26), he is using a figure of speech that substitutes a place for a person. Similarly, someone today might say that an action made by the president is made by Washington, or the White House. Daniel isn't attempting to soften what he is saying. Indeed, he has been quite bold when speaking about God to King Nebuchadnezzar (2:27–28).

Daniel exhorts Nebuchadnezzar to cease his sin and start practicing righteousness (4:27), supposing that he might be able to avoid the judgment predicted by the dream. Daniel's approach is tactful and humble. He still respects the office of Nebuchadnezzar. He doesn't leap right to accusations and judgment; he starts with the opportunity of repentance. He lays out the option for the king to start right away to cease his wickedness and serve God by showing mercy to the weak. In that case, maybe the king's prosperity will continue.

Perhaps Nebuchadnezzar takes Daniel's words to heart for a while, but not for the long run. A year later, the king is walking on a royal rooftop and starts looking out over his kingdom. With Daniel's warning forgotten, in a moment of unrestricted pride and arrogance, Nebuchadnezzar boasts of how he is responsible for the success of Babylon (4:28–30). The words aren't completely out of his mouth before a heavenly voice decrees the removal of his royal authority. In addition, the voice says Nebuchadnezzar will spend a length of time (probably seven years) with beasts, living as an animal (4:31–32).

His sentence begins immediately. The once-arrogant king is driven away from people. He eats grass like cattle. He stays outside in the dew as his hair grows long (like the feathers of an eagle) and his nails become like bird claws (4:33).

Critical Observation

A fragmentary cuneiform tablet in the British Museum refers to Nebuchadnezzar, apparently during this part of his life. It states that "life appeared of no value to" Nebuchadnezzar, that "he does not show love to son and daughter," and that "family and clan does not exist" for him any longer.

Animals don't reason as humans do, and perhaps Nebuchadnezzar suffers in that respect as well. But eventually he raises his eyes toward heaven. In that action, he evidently submits to God, and his sanity is restored (4:34).

When he is able, he praises, honors, and glorifies God. He acknowledges God's eternal dominion and kingdom, as well as God's complete sovereignty over both the powers of heaven and the people of earth (4:34–35).

Afterward, God does indeed allow Nebuchadnezzar to prosper again. In fact, the king says he becomes even greater than before (4:36). And this time he doesn't make any attempt to take credit for his fame. Instead, he exalts and glorifies the King of heaven (4:37). Had he done so earlier, in response to Daniel's advice, he might have avoided a lot of misery.

Take It Home

Perhaps one reason that Nebuchadnezzar's strange experiences were recorded for posterity as well as for his peers at that time is to caution everyone of the importance of fully submitting to God as the Lord of the universe. It's rather easy to verbally acknowledge God, to claim to know God, or even to express love for God. However, such actions mean nothing if not accompanied by complete and humble submission to Him. On a scale of 1 (least) to 10 (most), how would you rate your submission to God in recent days? Can you tell a difference in your life when your obedience begins to lessen a bit?

DANIEL 5:1–31

DANIEL AND BELSHAZZAR

Setting Up the Section

At least six years have passed between the previous section and this one. In that time, King Nebuchadnezzar has been replaced by Belshazzar. It appears that Daniel's high-profile position in the king's court has also come to an end. Although the previous section highlights a public letter from Nebuchadnezzar warning his fellow Babylonian leaders what can happen if they defy the God of Judah, Belshazzar is either oblivious or defiant. Either way, he will suffer for it.

📖 5:1–4

BELSHAZZAR'S BANQUET

After the death of Nebuchadnezzar, his successor is his son Evil-Merodach. This son rules for two years until he is assassinated by Labashi-Marduk and replaced by Neriglissar. After Neriglissar, Evil-Merodach's brother-in-law, an Assyrian named Nabonidus takes control of the kingdom. As new king, Nabonidus establishes a home in the oasis that is now the location of Saudi Arabia. He appoints his son Belshazzar to reign as vice-regent and handle the business of Babylon.

The first thing the Bible records about Belshazzar is that he throws a banquet. It is no small affair, attended by a thousand of the leaders of Babylon along with their wives and concubines (5:1–3). This event may have been a kind of preparation for war, since Babylon was already under the attack of the Persians.

The banquet became the backdrop for a major misstep on the part of Belshazzar—his callous disregard for the holy Jewish objects stored in his treasury. When he sees that his wine is of a good vintage, he sends for the golden goblets that had been taken from the Jerusalem temple. They were originally set aside to be used exclusively for the worship of God. Even after Nebuchadnezzar seized Jerusalem and took the temple furnishings, he had several encounters with the God of Daniel and eventually came to have a respect for the King of heaven (4:37), decreeing that the Lord should not be mocked under penalty of death (3:29).

As Daniel will eventually make clear, Belshazzar cannot plead ignorance. He knew about Nebuchadnezzar's decrees and the holiness attached to the Jewish goblets (5:22–23). He just doesn't care. In the ultimate mockery of God, he uses the temple's sacred vessels for his party, passing out wine to impress his nobles as well as their female companions. Even worse, as they drink they praise their gods (5:4).

📄 **5:5–12**

THE WRITING ON THE WALL

Belshazzar considers Judah's God a trivial matter, but his casual and carefree attitude changes in an instant when a disembodied hand suddenly appears and begins to write on the palace wall. The king's defiance of God has been public; so, too, is God's condemnation of Belshazzar. In front of all his guests, the king turns pale, goes limp, and is gripped by fear to the point of terror. Then, after the experience of seeing the hand come and go, Belshazzar is left with a message he can't comprehend (5:5–6).

Critical Observation

Clearly, Belshazzar doesn't know what (who) he is dealing with. Yet his response of such intense fear indicates that he acknowledges something more powerful than he is. His initial fears will soon be confirmed.

He brings together all of the spiritual leaders of his cabinet to attempt to interpret the words left on the wall, promising to promote anyone who can do so to third place in the entire kingdom. (Belshazzar is responsible to Nabonidus, so the top two places are already filled.) It is a magnificent offer, yet no one is able to decipher the message (5:7–9). The sum total of the religious wisdom of the day is unable to read or understand the words, and the king has no peace.

Belshazzar thinks he is out of options. God has spoken to him, yet the leaders of Babylon can't determine what God has said. God has extended Belshazzar beyond his limits, just as he had for Nebuchadnezzar. And the answers will come from the same source: God's servant, Daniel.

The queen at the time may well have been the queen mother—possibly the widow of Nebuchadnezzar, or perhaps his daughter (5:10). In any case, she is well aware of the recent goings on within the palace. In particular, she knows of Daniel and his reputation of divine knowledge and understanding, and also his ability to interpret dreams, explain riddles, and solve difficult problems (5:12). It is the exact job description Belshazzar needs, so he takes the queen's advice and summons Daniel.

In addressing Belshazzar, the queen refers to "your father the king" (5:11). The usage of *father* cannot be assumed to mean a biological relationship or even a relationship in terms of one generation to the next. The word was sometimes used in referring to a person's lineage. The Jews often spoke of Abraham as their father. Similarly, Nebuchadnezzar could be considered a father by any number of offspring, not merely his biological children.

📖 5:13–31

THE WRITING'S INTERPRETATION

Daniel had risen to the top of Nebuchadnezzar's group of advisors (2:48–49), yet he must have been sidelined when the new king came into power. Clearly, Belshazzar doesn't even know who Daniel is. Ironically, Belshazzar will get to know him the same way Nebuchadnezzar had—by bringing him in only after every other option has failed.

Belshazzar goes through the proper protocol of flattering Daniel, briefly summarizing the situation for him and offering him great rewards for his much-needed help (5:13–16). Daniel agrees to help, but not because of the proffered rewards. He is more confrontational with Belshazzar than he had been with Nebuchadnezzar, and for good reason. Nebuchadnezzar had left the world a letter outlining his sin of pride and the ultimate result. He had learned that God—not the leader of Babylon—deserved the glory for whatever good happened in the world. But Belshazzar had ignored the lesson of the past and in a matter of a few years openly defied God. Daniel will do as the king asks, but he has no desire to work for this new regime (5:17). (Of course, it will turn out that in interpreting God's message, Daniel is foretelling the fall of the existing king anyway.)

Daniel begins with a short history lesson that will put God's message into context. Nebuchadnezzar had been bestowed with the most powerful and glorious kingdom of the world—not because of anything special he had done, but because it was part of God's plan. When pride became an issue, God had removed the kingdom from Nebuchadnezzar and had driven the king out to live like an animal. Eventually, after Nebuchadnezzar lifted his eyes to heaven and acceded that God was the sovereign ruler of the world, he was reinstated into his position as king with a much clearer understanding of who God is (5:18–21).

And here is Daniel's point: He isn't telling Belshazzar anything the king doesn't already know (5:22). A mighty ruler who leaves the throne for a while to live in the fields, eat grass, and grow animal-like hair and nails is not quickly forgotten. Belshazzar knows the story, but he hasn't heeded the lesson of Nebuchadnezzar. Because Belshazzar refuses to honor God, his defiant party is the last one he will ever have.

The words the hand had written on the wall—*Mene, Mene, Tekel, Parsin* (5:25)—essentially mean, "Number," "Weigh," and "Divide." The message that no one else could determine is quite clear to Daniel: The days of Belshazzar are numbered, his life has been weighed (evaluated) by God, and because he is found deficient, his kingdom will be divided as the Medes and Persians take over. Simply put, the end is at hand for the king.

Belshazzar's response is telling. He certainly must have believed Daniel, because he restores the authority and prosperity that had been taken away from him (5:29). Yet this appears to be his *only* response. He hears a disturbing message that has been divinely delivered in an astounding manner, and he does nothing. He shows no hint of remorse, repentance, confession, or desire to change. Perhaps this is why God's punishment is much swifter than it had been with Nebuchadnezzar. It is this very night that the Medes breach the walls, take over the city, and put Belshazzar to death (5:30).

The new ruler of the kingdom is Darius the Mede. In the next section, he, too, will learn a lesson about God because of his experience with Daniel.

Take It Home

The fall of Belshazzar is particularly brutal because he failed to learn from the experience of Nebuchadnezzar who had come before him. Can you think of any spiritual lessons, either positive or negative, that you have observed in the lives of other people? To what extent do those lessons influence your personal faith? What lessons do you hope to pass on to others who might be observing the way you live?

DANIEL 6:1–28

DANIEL AND DARIUS

Setting Up the Section

The previous section ends with the demise of Babylonian King Belshazzar and his replacement by Darius the Mede. This section continues with the establishment of Darius as king and how he comes to experience the power of Daniel's God.

📄 6:1–4

DANIEL'S EXEMPLARY CHARACTER

Throughout the book of Daniel so far, kings have come and gone while Daniel's service to God, as well as to his human rulers, has remained consistent. It seems clear that the godly wisdom demonstrated by Daniel in his youth has carried into his senior years as well. He serves as one of three key leaders to whom another 120 officials report. This leadership structure is used by Darius so that he can protect his interests (6:2). In other words, Darius is wisely attempting to avoid losing his kingdom to a rebel group or having the wealth of his kingdom pilfered by an unscrupulous, unsupervised overseer. He is aware of the temptations inherent with power and control.

It is in this environment that Daniel's character shines. In a competitive setting with little regard for righteousness, Daniel continues to faithfully follow God. Before long, Darius has plans to reward Daniel's exceptional qualities and promote him to the top position over the entire kingdom (6:3).

Critical Observation

Daniel's integrity becomes evident in a close comparison between verses 2 and 3. At first King Darius is cautious about placing too much power in the hands of any one person (6:2). But when he sees how Daniel lives and works, he trusts him to have even more power without fear that he will misuse it (6:3).

Not surprisingly, there is a good deal of resentment when the other leaders hear that Daniel is in line to become their boss. They decide to work together, watch him closely, and get some dirt on him that they can take to Darius. But the closer they monitor his behavior, the more evident it becomes that he isn't doing anything he shouldn't do, nor is he neglecting to do anything he should be doing (6:4).

📄 6:5–12

THE CONSPIRACY AGAINST DANIEL

When Daniel's jealous peers can't find a single problem with his integrity, they change their strategy. When they closely examine his life, they see his bold faith in God and realize his spiritual consistency is all they can use against him (6:5).

Apparently *they* have no problem operating without integrity. They devise a plan to present Darius with a proposal for a law requiring his subjects to pray to no one but him for a thirty-day period. Furthermore, the law will make it clear that anyone who disobeys the injunction will be thrown into the lions' den (6:6–8). Scripture doesn't say that Darius is flattered at their proposal, but he doesn't appear to need much coaxing. It is said simply that he puts the decree into writing, which makes it an unalterable law (6:9). Not even Darius can revoke it.

Although it is a despicable attempt to get rid of Daniel, the plan is an intelligent one. Darius had structured his leadership team to protect the kingdom from disloyal people, and at face value it appears that this proposal will support the king in his desire.

Daniel is well aware of the king's signing of the decree. He understands the consequences of breaking it. He goes to pray to God in his usual place at his usual time (6:10). He has other options, such as waiting thirty days or praying in a more private location. But Daniel truly believes what he has been communicating to Nebuchadnezzar and Belshazzar: God is sovereign and in control. God's kingdom is a priority for him, and if death is a result of his commitment, so be it.

Evidently the conspirators have Daniel's home staked out. It takes little time for them to witness him in prayer and go running to Darius. First they clarify the essence of the decree that has been passed and ensure that it cannot be revoked. *Then* they inform the king that Daniel has defied the law.

Note how expertly they pervert the truth (6:11–13). They had found nothing wicked or illicit for which they could accuse Daniel. So they manipulate the legal system to pass a binding, unrighteous law. When Daniel maintains his integrity and ignores the law, his accusers present him as a wicked person, disloyal to the king.

📖 6:13–28

DANIEL SURVIVES THE LIONS' DEN

It appears that Darius is not fooled by their manipulation, but there is nothing he can do about it. He searches for legal loopholes but can find no way to avoid sentencing Daniel to the punishment as set forth in the decree (6:14). So when Daniel's accusers return as a group, the king has little recourse but to order Daniel thrown into the lions' den (6:15). Yet in that moment it becomes clear how much Daniel's faithfulness to his God has influenced Darius. It is admirable that Daniel displays faith that God will deliver him, whether in life or in death. But as a result of his consistent faith, even *Darius* suggests that Daniel's God might deliver him (6:16).

The lions' den is an enclosure with no visual access. Daniel is apparently lowered into it, a stone is laid over the top, and the king seals it with his signet ring. It is a fretful night for Darius. He can't sleep, won't eat, and refuses any kind of entertainment (6:17–18). He is up at dawn to return to the lions' den, and he is surprisingly optimistic. He doesn't just call out to Daniel; he asks a question that demands a response (6:19–20). And Daniel's voice assures him that, yes, God has indeed delivered him from the lions. He also sets the record straight by averring, "I have not wronged you, Your Majesty" (6:21–22 NLT).

Demystifying Daniel

Daniel has defied a Persian law and submitted to what was intended to be the Persian death penalty. So God's deliverance of Daniel is more than simply a reward for his steady faith. It is also God's divine declaration of Daniel's innocence based on the law of the Lord and an emphatic demonstration that God's law is to be feared over any human law.

Daniel is freed from the den unharmed. He has no bite marks and no scratches (6:23). God's rule of the world includes both corrupt political systems and the animal kingdom.

The people who had attempted to destroy Daniel are then rounded up and thrown to the lions, along with their wives and children (6:24). Their scheme is revealed for what it is: a malicious attempt to murder an innocent man. Historians have learned that Persian law dictated the destruction of entire families of people who were harmful to the kingdom. It may be that in a culture of violence and vengeance, it was believed that the children of an offender might attempt vengeance when they grew up.

For whatever reason the men and their families are condemned, their deaths make a certain point: The lions are hungry. Before the wicked conspirators even hit the bottom of the den, the lions overpower them and crush them (6:24). It becomes clear that Daniel had not escaped death because the animals had been overfed or drugged the night before. The king's seal is affixed to the only entrance/exit to the den. Any attempt to explain away a divine solution to Daniel's dilemma is met with a biblical counterargument.

The section concludes with a new decree, written by King Darius and sent throughout the land to people of all languages (6:26–27). The king mandates that everyone in his kingdom must show reverence to Daniel's God. Just as the Lord made Himself known to Nebuchadnezzar and Belshazzar in phenomenal ways, so, too, He persuades Darius of His unequalled power.

Critical Observation

The decree that had been designed to entrap Daniel supposedly could not be repealed (6:12, 15) and was supposed to be in effect for thirty days (6:7, 12). Perhaps King Darius waited a month before issuing his new order, although it appears to have been sent out immediately after Daniel's release. It might have been that Darius came to the conclusion that God's law effectively superseded any contradictory human law, and he repealed the first decree after all.

After his return trip from the lions' den, Daniel does quite well throughout the reign of Darius (6:28). In fact, his service continues into the rule of the next king, Cyrus.

Take It Home

In previous situations, Daniel had wisely used compromise to keep from doing something that would have gone against his beliefs (1:11–16). In this case, he wisely trusts God to see him through, and he refuses to alter his prayer habits in any way. It can be difficult to know when to yield a bit and when to stand firm. What do you think determined how Daniel decided to respond in various circumstances? Can you think of similar examples from your own life? How do you decide when it is appropriate to seek compromise and when you need to be completely unwavering in the exercise of your beliefs?

DANIEL 7:1–28

DANIEL'S FIRST VISION

Setting Up the Section

The first half of the book of Daniel (chapters 1–6) is a mostly chronological narrative of Daniel's service to various kings of Babylon and Medo-Persia. The second half (chapters 7–12) contains more personal accounts of some of Daniel's dreams and visions.

📖 **7:1–14**

DANIEL'S DREAM OF FOUR STRANGE CREATURES

The book of Daniel was written during a time when the Jews had just been conquered, their temple destroyed, and most of the potential leaders taken captive and carried away. It appears that aggressive human forces are in control and that God either no longer cares or is unable to do anything to deliver His people.

But Daniel has repeatedly highlighted the ongoing sovereignty of God throughout the first half of his book. God makes it clear that even though human kingdoms are being allowed some temporary successes, they will not reign forever. The kingdom of God will arrive, it will succeed, and God will be the eternal King.

Beginning in chapter 7, Daniel shares a series of revelations to explain how God plans to bring about the end of the human kingdoms. The prophecies deal with the destruction of arrogant human rulers and the coming of the Messiah, who will sit on the throne to rule forever. Chapter 7 provides an overview of what is going to happen in the world, setting up the prophecies that follow.

The chronological progression of Daniel is interrupted at this point as the author returns to the reign of Belshazzar (7:1). In Daniel 5, the observation is made that Daniel appears to be sidelined when Belshazzar replaces Nebuchadnezzar. Perhaps Belshazzar didn't make use of Daniel during that time, but here it is evident that God did. It also appears that Daniel saw more than he recorded but only wrote down all the high points.

His vision begins with an image of the great sea (the Mediterranean) being greatly disturbed by "the four winds of heaven" (7:2). Those who sail for a living pay close attention to wind direction, partly because the direction helps determine what kind of storm to expect. In Daniel's vision, God stirs up the waters to bring about various storms of discord and confusion.

Critical Observation

For those living in the Middle East, the only great sea they knew was the Mediterranean Sea. It was the territory that all the kingdoms of the world sought to control. The Mediterranean provided a path for international shipping, sustenance for living, and protection from invading forces. It was both literally and figuratively a "great sea."

As Daniel continues to observe, four different types of "great beasts" come out of the sea (7:3). He will later be told that the beasts represent kingdoms (7:17), so his description is more to differentiate their qualities and characteristics than to detail their specific physical appearances.

The first creature is like a lion with wings like an eagle—both powerful and swift (7:4). But then its wings are plucked, and it is placed on the ground with two feet instead of four, with a human's power to reason. The implication is that the figure began as a wicked being, fell from earthly glory, and was restored to normal. Nebuchadnezzar immediately comes to mind after his account provided in Daniel 5, although some people believe this will be a king yet to come. At this point, more information is needed.

The second creature is compared to a bear—powerful and vicious, but with a tendency to be slow and lazy (7:5). It is raised up on one of its sides, perhaps indicating a walking position. And it has been feeding on another animal, having been given permission to conquer.

The third beast is described as a four-headed, four-winged leopard, meaning it is swift, fierce, and has the ability to cover a lot of territory quickly (7:6). The biblical concept of multiple heads frequently symbolizes different kingdoms or regions, so the creature is perhaps a single kingdom with four regions.

Comparisons fail Daniel while he attempts to describe the fourth creature (7:7). He can only say it is dreadful, powerful, and frightening. Its large iron teeth crush and devour its victims. It is different from any of the others in that it has ten horns. Animal horns are symbols of power, and ten is a number of completeness, so this final creature appears to have all rule and power.

This fourth beast is captivating. Daniel continues to watch it as yet another horn emerges, uprooting three of the existing ones. This new horn is different from the others. For one thing, it is smaller. Even stranger, however, is that it has eyes and a mouth, and the mouth is boasting (7:8).

Yet as fascinating as this bragging, multi-horned beast is, Daniel's eyes are drawn to an even more intriguing sight. He sees God (the "Ancient of Days") taking His seat among a number of thrones. His garments are white, symbolizing purity, as is His hair. His throne is ablaze. Fire flows from Him like a river, representing God's judgment poured out over all the earth (7:9–10). His is the throne of a judge; the other thrones are set up for those who will be watching the proceedings. (The book of Revelation speaks of great multitudes who will witness God's final judgment [Revelation 7:9–10; 19:1–3].)

Demystifying Daniel

The books that Daniel sees opened in 7:10 may be the same books mentioned in Revelation 20:11–15. God's judgment is based on the deeds recorded in these books. God notices the injustices done in this world, and they will not go unpunished.

Despite the presence of the Ancient of Days, the little horn continues its boasting. As Daniel watches, the fourth beast is killed as it speaks, and its body is thrown into a roaring fire. The other beasts are still around, but all their authority has been removed (7:11–12).

Then, in stark contrast to the boasting beast, Daniel sees another figure, whom he describes "like a son of man" (7:13–14). All the previous rulers of the world have been described as various animals (symbols of strength and power). It is clear from the text that this new figure is a special ruler, and he is somehow related to the Ancient of Days, yet he is perceived in human form. The concept of God ruling the earth in the form of a man is a profound thought, and would have been especially so to the religious leaders of Babylon and Persia.

The new ruler is given authority and power over all nations and peoples. The scope of his rule is unlimited, as is its length. His position as ruler is everlasting (7:13–14).

🖹 7:15–28

THE INTERPRETATION OF THE DREAM

Even within his dream, Daniel is troubled. It must have been overwhelming to realize he was seeing what is in the future yet not fully understanding his visions. So he asks for clarification, and one of the heavenly figures (angels) helps him interpret the symbols and meaning (7:15–16).

The various beasts are kingdoms. Four of them will arise from the natural order of the earth. They will threaten and persecute the people of God, but God's kingdom will never be in doubt.

Critical Observation

The word interpreted *saints* in 7:18 can mean a couple of different things. It may be instinctive to see the word and think of people who are devoted to the lordship of God and who willingly submit to Him. However, Daniel is still writing in Aramaic throughout this section, and in that language *saints* could also mean "angels." This possibility is bolstered by later sections of Daniel that indicate an intense heavenly conflict taking place beyond what is visible on earth.

Not surprisingly, Daniel is particularly eager to learn more about the fourth beast (7:19–22). It is the most vicious and terrifying. The numerous horns, of shifting number, are mysterious. Even as he continues to watch, the boastful, outspoken horn is warring against the saints and is actually winning until the Ancient of Days puts an end to the matter by pronouncing judgment in favor of His saints.

The angel's response to Daniel reveals that the fourth creature is a cruel beast that will control ten kingdoms and conquer the world (7:23–27). Another king would arise after the others, displacing three of the existing kingdoms and supporting the beast in speaking out against God and His followers. He will even work through the legal system to change laws in his oppression of God's people. His reign of terror will last for "a time, times, and half a time" (7:25). In Aramaic, the use of the word *time* refers to the passing of one year (4:16). A common interpretation of the phrase, then, is to consider *a time* as one year, *times* as two years, and *half a time* as half a year, yielding a total of three and a half years.

Demystifying Daniel

The four beasts in Daniel's dream appear to correspond with the four sections of the great statue of Nebuchadnezzar's first dream (2:31–35). The descriptions of the four creatures lend credence to their representation of Babylon, Medo-Persia, Greece, and Rome. Much debate takes place as to the significance of the ten horns and the final, boastful horn. Many people connect this section of Daniel with John's writing in Revelation and believe that Daniel's dream describes the end-times Antichrist (called the "beast" in Revelation) and the false prophet who serves as a type of prime minister for him.

After the violent reign of this figure, God's heavenly court will assemble to strip him of power and destroy him once and for all. The people of God will then be given control of all the kingdoms of the world. God will be acknowledged as the true King, ensuring everlasting peace and contentment (7:26–27).

It is a satisfying ending, to be sure, yet the dream completely overwhelms Daniel. It is quite a burden to not only be informed of the end of the world as he knows it but to witness and experience it to a certain extent. He is deeply troubled, but he doesn't say anything about it to anyone.

Take It Home

Sometimes people feel they have witnessed the worst that humanity has to offer. In Daniel's case, he could make that claim with confidence, and he was physically shaken by the experience. Yet every time a prophet confronts his readers/listeners with bad news, it is coupled with the assurance that beyond the bad times, God will step in to restore and reward those who are faithful to Him. What are some distressing events you have recently experienced? If you could be absolutely sure that God is in control of those events, how would your perception of them change? What can you do to strengthen your awareness of God's sovereignty?

DANIEL 8:1–27

DANIEL'S SECOND VISION

Setting Up the Section

This section follows the previous one as another account from the private life of Daniel, in contrast to his interactions with various kings in chapters 1–6. This vision of Daniel's is also filled with symbols, as is his dream in chapter 7.

📄 8:1–14

A RAM AND A GOAT

In this chapter, Daniel returns to writing in Hebrew. The section between 2:4 and 7:28 was written in Aramaic and was a message of God's sovereignty over all nations. In chapter 8, the focus of Daniel's writing shifts to what God is planning to do *to* and *through* the nation of Israel.

Another notable observation of Daniel 8 is that it is a description of rage. The nations rage as they seek control of the world. One figure in particular rages in his attempt to take over the world. And, ultimately, the rage of God is witnessed as He punishes those who have rejected Him to embrace the world. The chapter should be approached as a description of events that are difficult to accept. However, an interpretation is provided for the vision that is specific and helpful for properly understanding its meaning.

This vision occurs during the third year of Belshazzar's reign (8:1), which is about two years after the dream Daniel previously described (7:1). The location in the vision is Susa, a city in the heart of the Medo-Persian Empire that will later become a common vacation spot for King Darius. So during the final years of the Babylonian Empire, Daniel is shown a vision of the destruction of the Persian Empire that will follow (8:1–2).

The citadel in Susa is synonymous with the success of the Persians, and the ram in the vision (8:3–4) is later identified as the Medo-Persian Empire (8:20). The ram dominates all other animals in every direction. The variance in the size of its two horns is most likely a prediction that the Medes will be the stronger of the two allied nations at first, although the Persians later gained power.

The land acquisitions of the Medo-Persians were not typically peaceful. They frequently resulted in war, death, destruction, pain, and misery. A raging ram is an appropriate symbol to represent their approach to surrounding nations.

The geographic spread of the Medo-Persian Empire was one step in preparation for the Roman Empire to eventually unite diverse areas in language and customs. In the first century AD, the gospel will be taken throughout the world with great efficiency. In this way, the unity formed (forced) by the Persians could be seen as laying the foundation for the early church.

But the ram finally meets its match in the form of a goat that shatters its two horns (8:5-7). Daniel will soon be informed that the goat represents Greece (8:21). It has a single prominent horn between its eyes (a single leader) and moves across the earth without touching the ground (indicating great speed).

The goat strikes the ram and quickly overpowers it. And when Persia comes up against Alexander the Great, it falls hard and fast. Alexander will go on to conquer most of the populated world before he is thirty. His combination of strength, speed of conquest, and youth will stand out in history. Napoleon and George Patton are two of many military leaders who studied the strategies of Alexander in designing their own battle plans.

Daniel's vision continues as he sees the goat grow in fame, but it suddenly has its large horn broken off. In place of the severed horn grows four other horns (8:8). History confirms that Alexander became quite proud and exalted himself. Yet by the age of thirty-three, he had died (the cause of which is widely disputed). After his death, the Greek nation is split into four states, each with a different leader.

God is not revealing these events to Daniel simply to give him preview of what will occur in history. These events will have a direct impact on the Jewish people. One of the four horns from the goat (Greece) starts small but quickly becomes great. Among the territories to which he turns his attention is *the Beautiful Land*—the name the Jews use for Jerusalem (8:9; Psalm 48:2).

The language that follows (Daniel 8:10-12) includes war imagery. "The host of heaven" is the army of heaven, a term sometimes applied to angels. Stars can represent large numbers of people. The horn strives to set himself up as an equal to God ("Prince of the host") by eliminating other religious ceremonies. He is associated with rebellion and a disregard for truth.

Again, history sheds light on this prophetic vision. One of the leaders who rises to power after Alexander the Great is a man named Antiochus Epiphanes. He has an intense dislike of the Jews, persecuting them, killing their high priest, and entering their temple to have pigs sacrificed to him because he believes he is the Messiah. In the ultimate insult, he corrupts and twists the entire religious system of the Jews so that it serves him.

Critical Observation

The religious corruption initiated by Antiochus Epiphanes will actually turn out to be a worse experience for the Jews than their exile. In Babylon, they mourned because they knew their temple and city were being neglected. But later, when they see their religion perverted and a false Messiah desecrating their temple, it is heart-wrenching.

Daniel overhears a heavenly conversation taking place regarding the length of time the rebellious horn will be allowed to trouble God's people (8:13–14). The answer has created a bit of confusion. It seems reasonable that 2,300 evenings and mornings should be 2,300 days, or almost six and a half years. Another possibility is that it means 2,300 *sacrifices*, with one each morning and one each evening for a total time of only half as long. But since the daily sacrifices are suspended during this time, this option doesn't seem as likely.

📖 8:15–27

THE INTERPRETATION OF THE VISION

Modern readers who are confused by passages such as this may be comforted to realize that Daniel also struggled to understand what he was seeing (8:15–16). First he is confused. As the angel Gabriel begins to explain the vision to him, he becomes terrified. Then when he discovers that the vision concerns a time of the end, he is so physically afflicted—almost comatose—that he needs help standing (8:17–18).

Gabriel's reference to the "time of the end" (8:19 NIV) should be interpreted from Daniel's perspective, not a modern one. The Jewish people are undergoing a time of God's discipline. They are currently exiled in Babylon, and Daniel is discovering that this won't be the worst of it. It is a couple of centuries before the horrors of Antiochus Epiphanes falls on them, but soon thereafter the consequences for the sins of Israel will come to an end.

Demystifying Daniel

When Daniel is addressed as *son of man* (8:17), it is not intended as a special title, as when it is applied to the Messiah. Rather, Daniel is among heavenly beings, so it is only logical that he would be singled out as the human in the group.

However, it is also fair to say that Antiochus Epiphanes is a picture of the end-times Antichrist (the beast in Revelation). The description in 8:23–25 is applicable to both figures: "completely wicked," "master of intrigue," and "very strong" (NIV). Both feel superior and spread deceit. Both are especially destructive because they establish their power while people feel secure. Only later do they reveal their true natures. And eventually, both will be destroyed, but not by human power (8:25). (Antiochus isn't killed; he eventually dies of tuberculosis.)

The wrath that Gabriel speaks of is God's response after God's people allow themselves to be fooled by the false religion of Antiochus (8:19). After they agree to the Greek leader's twisted religion, God will allow them to suffer the consequences. But as Daniel is about to be shown (in chapter 9), shortly afterward will come a Messiah to rescue God's people.

Daniel is assured that what he has seen is true (8:26). But then he is asked to seal the vision—not to discuss it with anyone. The reason, he will discover, is that he is about to receive another vision that will take precedence. Daniel can see some of the behind-the-scenes operations of God's kingdom, but the Lord doesn't want people motivated to come to Him out of fear. The next vision will reveal the coming of an anointed one, a Messiah, who acts out of compassion and offers salvation.

The knowledge of what is ahead for God's people overwhelms Daniel for a period of time. He is physically sick for several days. Even when he recovers and goes back to work, the vision continues to weigh on him. He will continue to struggle with what he has seen until God reveals more to him and puts his mind to rest.

Take It Home

Brazen leaders have defied God throughout history. Antiochus Epiphanes is certainly one of the worst, but there are many others. In fact, John warns God's people to watch out for antichrists who have already come (1 John 2:18). Such people need not have widespread influence. Anyone who persistently opposes God and attempts to sway others to that belief is, by definition, an antichrist. Do you know anyone whom you would place in that category? How do you tend to respond/interact with such people?

DANIEL 9:1-27

DANIEL'S THIRD VISION

Setting Up the Section

Continuing his record of various divine revelations he has received, Daniel describes a prayer for which he is given a most emphatic response. During his prayer, he is visited by the angel Gabriel, who tells Daniel what to expect in the future, although the symbolism used is challenging and difficult to properly interpret and understand.

📖 **9:1–19**

DANIEL'S PRAYER

The date that Daniel provides in 9:1 reveals that fourteen years have passed between his previous recorded vision (chapter 8) and this prayer. At the end of the previous section, Daniel is left exhausted, sick, and confused about what he has witnessed. He has been shown that God is going to bring the kingdoms of humanity to an end and that He is going to discipline the Jewish people. Seemingly, those fourteen years have been a time of searching for Daniel. He has not questioned that both discipline and judgment are deserved, yet God has promised that they will not last forever. So Daniel is seeking to discover when God will restore His glory.

Critical Observation

Jerusalem was an integral part of worship for the Jewish people. It symbolized the land God had given to His people, and the temple represented the presence of God amongst them. With the temple destroyed and the people scattered, Jerusalem was desolate at the time of Daniel's writing.

He has searched the scriptures available to him and found Jeremiah's prophecies, written prior to the invasion of Babylon, warning the people of what will come (Jeremiah 25:11–12). But along with the bad news of the coming captivity is the announcement that after seventy years the people will be allowed to return to Jerusalem.

This is encouraging news to Daniel, so he begins to pursue God in prayer. He realizes that the reason the Jews have fallen out of fellowship with God to begin with is because of their sin. So Daniel approaches God in prayer and petition, fasting, and sackcloth and ashes (9:3). His mind-set, habits, and dress are all designed to place his full focus on the Lord.

Daniel's prayer begins with confession, which is followed by a request for mercy (9:4–19). He first acknowledges the character of God (9:4). God is great and awe-inspiring because He can be counted on to keep His promises and care for His people.

God's people, however, have sinned in many ways (9:5–6). They have been wicked and rebellious, ignoring God's commandments. When God sent prophets to confront them about their sin, the people had rejected them. They had persistently lived for themselves, not for God.

Their rejection of God leads to their being scattered to various countries and their leaders driven from positions of responsibility. Daniel acknowledges that they deserve everything that has happened to them. However, in spite of the sins of the people, Daniel realizes that God remains merciful and forgiving (9:7–10).

The people have no excuse for their sinful rejection of God. The consequences of such sin are clearly spelled out in the Law of Moses (Leviticus 26:14–20). They had ignored Moses and a long series of prophets, and God had done what He said He would do (Daniel 9:11–14). The Lord's action in response to their sin is only proof of His righteousness.

Daniel then moves on to his request: He asks God to turn away His anger from Jerusalem (9:15–16). This is not a personal request. Rather, Daniel is asking God to reestablish His glory in the world. Ever since God allowed the Babylonians to conquer Jerusalem and take away the people, there has been no specific physical location where God is acknowledged and worshiped. Daniel's request is not just to get "home" but rather to see the glory of Jerusalem restored and an end to God's name being mocked by pagan nations.

Critical Observation

When Daniel (or any other Jewish person, for that matter) states that his God is more powerful than any other god, it appears to be a foolish statement to anyone outside of Judah. The Jews had been brutally defeated and were still living as captives. From all appearances, their God either doesn't care or is unable to do anything to improve the situation. Daniel's prayer is to correct such misperceptions about God.

📖 9:20–27

GOD'S RESPONSE TO DANIEL'S PRAYER

Daniel is still in prayer in the evening, when the angel Gabriel appears to him in swift flight. Daniel recognizes the angel from his previous vision (9:20–21). Ever since then, for fourteen years, Daniel must have wondered about the future. Gabriel had shared with him a description of punishment the Jews could expect in those days, but he had said nothing at the time about their salvation/deliverance (8:15–26). Finally, Gabriel has been instructed to provide Daniel with additional insight and understanding (9:22–23).

Still, what Daniel is about to hear has since been described as one of the most difficult passages in the Bible. Gabriel begins to depict a unit of time comprised of seventy sets of sevens, during which God will bring about redemption for His people (9:24). Numerous theories abound as to what this message really means. Some consider each "seven" to be a seven-year period. If so, much of what Gabriel says begins to fit a historic time line starting when a decree is passed to rebuild Jerusalem (which is described in Ezra 7:12–26) and carrying through to Jesus' ministry.

What is known for certain—what Gabriel tells Daniel—is that a ruler will appear who will again destroy the temple and the city of Jerusalem (Daniel 9:26). It will be a time of war. The destructive ruler to come will establish a covenant with the people for that final "seven" (9:27), but halfway through that period he will abolish all sacrifices and offerings, desecrating the temple with something called *an abomination that causes desolation* (NIV). But the ruler's end, already decreed, will occur shortly thereafter.

Demystifying Daniel

The *abomination that causes desolation* (NIV) means "the abomination that desolates or appalls" (9:27). It is a reference to something so detestable and repugnant that no decent, ethical, religious person will have anything to do with it. Such people will be nowhere near it, leaving that area desolate.

One understanding of this passage is that the destruction and desolation described in Daniel takes place in 70 AD, when the Romans overthrow a Jewish uprising by completely demolishing the temple. The ruler at the time is Titus. Those events fit a portion of what Daniel is told to expect, but not all.

More likely, the final "seven" is a still-future period of time. It seems logical to relate this new information that Daniel receives from Gabriel with the prophet's previous vision of the beast with the ten horns (7:19–27). If the ruler of 9:26–27 is the same as the boastful horn (7:20–22), the final "seven" will begin with the contract made by this malicious leader. He will break his covenant midway through, and great suffering will ensue for God's people. But after a period of time, God will remove him from leadership and make all things right.

Daniel's response to this new information is not recorded. However, it must have been encouraging to be assured that the predicted punishments he learned of in his previous vision will indeed come to an end and that God will make atonement for the sin of the people and provide everlasting righteousness (9:24).

Take It Home

Although the specific interpretation of future events as presented in this section may be confusing and debatable, one clear observation is that God has a plan. Events are moving toward the dates that He has specified. Even in the worst of times—especially in the worst of times—believers need to remain faithfully committed to Him. When are some recent times when your faith may not have been as strong as you wished? What are some specific truths about God that you might want to recall the next time you face similar situations?

DANIEL 10:1–12:13
DANIEL'S FOURTH VISION

Setting Up the Section

Daniel has recorded three visions so far: one of the destruction of human kingdoms and establishment of the kingdom of God (chapter 7), one of the punishment that will be inflicted on God's people because of their sin and rejection of God (chapter 8), and one of the coming Messiah who will conquer sin and provide a way of everlasting righteousness (chapter 9). In the rest of his book, Daniel records one final vision that encompasses, integrates, and further explains much of what he has already witnessed.

📖 **10:1–11:1**

THE FRAMEWORK FOR THE VISION

Daniel regularly dates his visions based on the reign of the leader at the time (7:1; 8:1; 9:1). This one is last chronologically. Darius (9:1) and Cyrus (10:1) rule Persia at the same time. Cyrus was the great king over the entire Persian Empire, which at this time included Israel. Darius may have been a subking under him as emperor. During Cyrus's first year, he passes a decree allowing the Jews to return to Judah and rebuild Jerusalem (Ezra 1:1–4). This final vision of Daniel's is two years later.

Critical Observation

Some people question why Daniel doesn't return to his homeland when he had the opportunity. No reason is given, although a couple of possibilities seem logical. First, he would have been at least in his mid-eighties, and a long journey could be difficult. Second, God had used Daniel as a consistently faithful voice in the midst of a people who had no knowledge of the Lord. Daniel had already demonstrated that he lived for the kingdom of God and not for his own well-being, advancement, or success. Perhaps his was a conscious decision to remain and serve where God had placed him.

Daniel's vision is nothing new, but it is more developed than his previous ones. As he begins to comprehend more clearly, he grows very troubled and goes into mourning, setting aside all the pleasantries of life such as wine, choice food, and lotions used to minimize the effects of the hot, arid climate (10:1–3). He is still troubled over the sin of God's people and the approaching punishment that will be the consequence. His emotions are probably heightened by the date as well, which would have coincided with the annual Passover to celebrate God's deliverance of His people in the past (10:4). Daniel is passionate about both the will of God and the people he loves on earth.

A biblical reference to the "great river" usually means the Euphrates, but Daniel clarifies that he is beside the Tigris (10:4). There he sees a heavenly figure whose description is similar to that of Jesus in Revelation 1:12–16. Some people have suggested that it is indeed a preincarnate appearance of Jesus, but the difficulty this figure faces in spiritual warfare would not have been true of the Lord (10:13). Daniel witnesses the splendor of one of God's angels, but not Jesus.

The figure is bedecked in linen (a sign of purity) and a gold belt (worn by royal leaders). His body is like beryl, a shiny and transparent gold-colored stone. His face is like lightning, his eyes like flaming torches. His arms and feet have a gleam like polished bronze. His voice is unusually powerful (10:5–6).

As impressive as this figure is, only Daniel is enabled to see him. Those with Daniel only realize something unexplainable is happening, and they run to hide (10:7). Daniel, too, is affected; he goes pale, feels entirely weak and helpless, and soon falls into a deep sleep (10:8–9). A touch of the angel helps him up, first to his hands and knees, and then to a standing position, although he is still quite wobbly (10:10–11).

The angel addresses Daniel as a man who is "highly esteemed" (10:11 NIV). God honors Daniel because his heart is not callous. The Lord values the pain that Daniel feels as a result of the people's sin.

Daniel has been fasting and praying for three weeks, and the angel had been quickly dispatched to respond to his prayers and desires. Daniel's prayers are heeded because he has set his heart on understanding and because he has humbled himself before God (10:12). Yet there has been a long delay between Daniel's petition and the angel's response, because the messenger sent to Daniel became involved in a fight with the prince of the Persian kingdom that lasted three weeks (10:12–13). Clearly this is a hostile and aggressive spiritual being, perhaps working to affect the kingdom of Persia for evil. Eventually the messenger of God, still struggling against the evil force, summons the help of Michael the archangel, the most powerful of the angels, and is able to continue on his way to Daniel.

Demystifying Daniel

This passage (10:12–14) alerts the reader to some of the truths about the unseen spiritual world. It is evident that angels are real, and both good angels and bad angels (demons) can influence the affairs of human beings.

Daniel has already heard what to expect for the Jews in the latter days, but he is about to receive another summary. Again, Daniel feels weak and unworthy to be part of such a divine moment (10:14–17). And again, he is touched by the heavenly messenger and encouraged to remain courageous and strong. As he listens, Daniel begins to regain his strength (10:18–19).

The angel is preparing to return and reengage in spiritual warfare, but first he wants to share with Daniel what is written in the Book of Truth (10:20–21). The messenger angel and the angel Michael stand opposed to the evil in the land, both in Persia and Greece. God had allowed those nations to thrive for a time, and His people had suffered. But here it is seen that God's protection is always in place. The sovereign Lord controls everything—including limiting the evil that occurs.

Demystifying Daniel

The Babylonians thought their gods had a Tablet of Destiny that supposedly foretold their history. Gabriel's reference to the Book of Truth in 10:21 may have suggested Daniel's awareness of such a Tablet, and it could have been the angel's way of assuring Daniel that God is sovereign and has the future in His hand. In any event, Gabriel is about to reveal some truth about the future to Daniel (11:2).

📄 11:2–35

THE VISION UNFOLDS

At this point, Gabriel begins to relate to Daniel a rather complex explanation of future events. It is helpful to keep in mind that as God orchestrates the events of the world, it is toward the purification of Israel and all of His followers. Some degree of purifying the nation will include punishment and persecution. God's plan includes the temporary emergence and dominance of various nations along with individual world leaders who exert a certain amount of control. Afterward, God's people will be purged and ready to serve Him.

Daniel has already been assured that no matter what takes place in world events, and as bad as things will become, God is always in control and permits evil to continue only for a limited time (9:24). With that in mind, he is then told that four more kings will arise in Persia, the fourth creating conflict against Greece (11:2). The three Persian leaders who follow Darius are Cambyses (530–522 BC), Smerdis (522 BC), and Darius I (522–486 BC). However, the Persian Empire had a total of thirteen leaders, and opinions vary as to whether the three referred to in Daniel 11:2 are the consecutive kings after Darius or the three most prominent leaders who succeed him.

Also debated is the identity of the fourth Persian king, although much evidence points to Xerxes I (486–465 BC). He is a strong king whose empire and wealth grow to large proportions. Eventually he seeks to attack Greece and incorporate the nation into his empire, but he fails miserably. His antagonism may have been the primary catalyst for the fall of Persia to Greece more than a century later.

However, almost everyone agrees that the "mighty king" who will appear and do as he pleases is Alexander the Great (11:3). The description in 11:4 fits Alexander precisely. His few family members are assassinated shortly after his death, and none of them inherit the great empire he had conquered and organized. Instead, rule goes to his four primary generals ("the four winds of heaven"), essentially segmenting the large empire into four separate kingdoms.

Two of those four kingdoms become prominent: Syria (the kingdom of the north) and Egypt (the kingdom of the south). The king of the south (Ptolemy I) and the king of the north (Seleucus I) begin as allies. Seleucus spends time with Ptolemy in Egypt while avoiding conflict with another power in the north. They fight together to defeat that opponent, and Seleucus returns to the north, settling in Babylon.

Tension forms between these two powers over the land in between them—the area of Palestine. It technically belongs to Seleucus, but Ptolemy occupies it. This tension appears to have continued to their successors, who attempt to resolve it with a marriage to unite the two kingdoms.

Ptolemy II (the successor of Ptolemy I) offers his daughter Berenice to Antiochus II Theos (the grandson of Seleucus). Antiochus agrees to the marriage, although he has to divorce his first wife, Laodice, to do so. Laodice had a son with him (Seleucus II). Antiochus and Berenice then have a son who appears to be next in line for the throne. In time, Antiochus reconciles with Laodice, which proves to be a mistake. She evidently doesn't like seeing another woman's son being groomed for leadership because she poisons Antiochus, Berenice, and their son. Laodice then occupies the throne until her son, Seleucus II, is ready to rule.

Needless to say, Laodice's actions are not well received in Egypt. Not long after the brother of Berenice (Ptolemy III Euergetes) takes the throne, he marches north to do battle against Seleucus II. He is initially successful and carries off the images of the northern gods, but subsequent battles continue between the two forces (11:5–8).

Critical Observation

This may sound like a complicated ancient history lesson. However, the details are important in demonstrating how accurate and succinct Daniel's account is, who recorded his prophecies two to four hundred years prior to the occurrence of the events.

Daniel's descriptions in 11:9–19 are pretty much self-explanatory, except for the names that are later provided for the participants. Laodice's son rules for twenty years before he dies and is replaced by his two sons, Seleucus III and Antiochus III. During the war described in 11:10, Seleucus III is murdered, leaving Antiochus III as sole leader of the northern kingdom. In the next battle that ensues, Antiochus assembles 62,000 infantry, 6,000 cavalry, and 102 elephants. He sends his army to Egypt, where they confront an opposing force of 70,000 infantry, 5,000 cavalry, and 73 elephants. The Egyptian army of Ptolemy IV Philopator is victorious, enacting a wholesale execution of the north and taking much land (including Palestine). Fifteen years later, Antiochus assembles an even larger army and begins to reacquire much of the territory he had lost (again, including Palestine). He presses on until he has gained control of Egypt. But for many years, the balance of power continues to go back and forth between the two nations.

The king of the north in Daniel 11:14–19 is still Antiochus III. The marriage of his daughter (Cleopatra I) to the king of the south (Ptolemy V) doesn't work as anticipated. Antiochus was hoping to win Ptolemy's favor. Instead, his daughter sides with her new husband rather than her father.

Stalled in his efforts against Egypt, Antiochus begins to tangle with the Roman army that is beginning to make some serious advancements in the area. The Romans first defeat Antiochus and then require him to pay heavy fines for his attacks, which place an economic strain on his country. When Antiochus returns home, he is killed by an angry mob who resents paying so much to Rome (11:18–19).

Demystifying Daniel

All the names and conflicts of this section definitely correlate with history. However, they serve the primary purpose of explaining the rise of one figure in particular: Antiochus IV Epiphanes. He is the ruler who most directly affects the people of God in their homeland.

After the death of Antiochus III, his son Seleucus IV takes over. He is the one who sends out a tax collector in an attempt to pay Rome the taxes they demanded (11:20). That tax collector, however, kills Seleucus in an attempted coup. He is unsuccessful, yet his actions leave the throne open to other contenders. The person who comes out on top is Antiochus IV Epiphanes. The rightful heir to the throne, a man named Demetrius, is being held hostage in Rome until his nation's taxes are paid. So Antiochus seizes the leadership role; he is not *given* the honor (11:21).

Still, Antiochus IV uses political savvy and false promises to gain and maintain power. When Egypt launches an unsuccessful attack attempting to regain Palestine, Antiochus takes their king captive. The brother of Egypt's king uses that opportunity to secure Egypt's throne for himself. The former king then proposes to Antiochus that they can work together to regain the Egyptian throne and rule the entire region together. Antiochus likes the idea. He signs an agreement and gives the Egyptian leader the title "prince of the covenant." But no sooner has the former Egyptian king been released than he breaks the covenant with Antiochus and forms an alliance with his brother to attempt to drive Antiochus out of Palestine. The forces of Antiochus are too strong, however, and the Egyptian attack fails (11:22–23).

In the peaceful interlude that follows, Antiochus begins to show his true colors. He begins to plunder the wealth of his own land, including the riches from the temple in Jerusalem. And when some of the Egyptians later betray their king, Antiochus is able to overpower that country as well, at the cost of many lives (11:24–26).

Yet another attempted alliance between Antiochus IV and the king of Egypt fails to work out. Antiochus returns home but then marches against Egypt again. However, this time ships from Rome are in the Mediterranean Sea with support for Egypt, and Antiochus is turned away (11:27–30).

He is not in a good mood as he returns home through Palestine, and he takes his anger out on the Jews. He not only kills Jewish people, but he seeks to destroy Judaism as well. (This is perhaps the time that Daniel had previously written about, when a figure would arrive under the pretense of peace and gain support, but would then break his promises, turn on the Jews, and sacrifice a pig to himself in their temple [9:27].)

Some Jews will be deceived and side with him. Some will be betrayed, but they will choose to remain silent rather than be confrontational. A few will resist Antiochus and fight back, many of whom will die as a result (11:31–34). This will be the beginning of the purging to purify God's people, although more is to come (11:35).

Critical Observation

One of the most notable opponents to the aggression of Antiochus IV Epiphanes is a man named Judas Maccabeus, who stands for God. He forms an army of dedicated fighters. They are unable to rid their land of Greek influence, but they do regain the temple.

📖 11:36–12:13

FURTHER INTO THE FUTURE

Up until this point in the vision, the events described appear to have been fulfilled by very specific events in history between Daniel's time and the modern day. In fact, the amazing accuracy has led some scholars to believe that Daniel must have lived in the second century BC and backdated his prophecy. The literary technique was not unusual at the time, but a close study of numerous additional aspects of Daniel's writing has convinced other scholars of its much earlier date, its reliability, and the reliability of his predictive prophecy. As Daniel repeatedly tells King Nebuchadnezzar, God is a revealer of mysteries (2:22, 28, 29). The precision of Daniel's visions only confirms this fact.

Beginning with 11:36, however, Daniel's prophecy makes an almost imperceptible shift. He continues to write about the king of the north and the king of the south, but the events no longer correlate to what has been recorded about Antiochus Epiphanes. In addition, his language adopts a grander scale than previously, and he begins to speak of end times.

It is difficult to state with certainty exactly what Daniel knew at the time and intended to communicate, but several scholars believe he must be writing of the last-days Antichrist, a figure who certainly can be compared with Antiochus Epiphanes in terms of deceit, hatred of God's people, and self-importance. The following comments will be based on that presumption. However, according to one school of thought, Daniel may not even have realized that his prophecy was jumping from a future Greek Empire to an even more distant future.

Many times people study the events concerning the end of the world and become scared when it seems that God cannot or will not stop the evil that is so strong and prevalent. Yet it is clear that God is always in control. In fact, He uses the events of the last days to bring about the cleansing and purging of evil that is necessary so He can establish His eternal kingdom. Just as He allowed the persecution of Israel during the reign of Antiochus IV Epiphanes, He will allow a similar purging during the final period of "seven" under the rule of the Antichrist (9:27).

The first thing revealed about this end-times figure is that he does as he pleases (11:36). He is able to carry out every notion and plan that comes to his mind. Antiochus had assumed the role of Messiah, but this figure goes one step further to position himself above *all* other gods, even the one true God (11:36-37). He will be successful, but only because God allows it.

Demystifying Daniel

Translations of 11:37 vary. Some say that the figure described has no desire for women, which would indicate that he is so consumed with himself that no other relationships matter. Other translations say that he has he has no desire for the god loved by women. In this case, the reference might be to a Babylonian fertility god named Tammuz. (The only overt biblical mention of this god is in Ezekiel 8:14.) His following was much like the one that would follow for the Greek god Adonis.

The only god that appeals to this individual is power (11:38-39). His religion is based on his ability to conquer. As he accumulates more and more power, it confirms his misassumption that he is the one and only god.

Sill, nations see the harm this figure can do, and they attempt to resist, even though they are not successful. He will go wherever he wishes. He will have strength like no king before him (11:40). Yet as he nears the land of Israel, for some reason he is unable to overtake the southeastern portions that include Edom, Moab, and Ammon. Why these areas are spared is not known. But other than the areas that God deems off-limits, the destructive leader will be allowed widespread conquest. Along with his territorial acquisitions comes economic strength as well (11:41-43). When he hears of threats, his intent is to annihilate (not merely stop) his opponents (11:44).

One observation that must have greatly disturbed Daniel's original readers is the location of this individual's headquarters. He sets up "between the glorious holy mountain and the sea" (11:45 NLT)—right in the heart of Israel. But as soon as this fact is revealed, it also confirms that his success will be limited. His time of conquest will quickly be concluded. When God finally takes action against him, his end is inevitable.

The period designated *at that time* in 12:1 is "the time of the end" (11:40). When the beast takes up residence in Israel, the great archangel Michael will depart. His presence has been to provide protection, and once that is removed, a time of unprecedented distress will occur. By this time, the Jewish people have already suffered through the rage of Antiochus IV Epiphanes and have been brutally murdered in great numbers by Hitler. But Daniel warns that what is yet to come will be even worse.

Critical Observation

It should not be presumed that Daniel is seeing *all* the events to take place in future times. More likely, he is shown the highlights in some semblance of order. Therefore, translators and interpreters have differing opinions as to many of the specifics involved.

However, God is aware of which people have placed their faith in Him, and He will deliver the believers (12:1). A resurrection will take place as well, one that includes both righteous people and those who died as unbelievers. The righteous will receive rewards, including everlasting life (12:2). Those who are rewarded are identified as wise, or insightful (12:3). They are the people who understand that the world is God's and through Him are saved and find their purpose. They also share with others what they have discovered about God. Such people live forever, shining like stars in a clear night sky (12:3).

In ancient times, an official document was concealed or put in a safe place after being sealed. Gabriel instructs Daniel to close and seal what he has seen and heard (12:4). When later generations are ready to increase their knowledge, this book will be available to them.

Daniel is still on the bank of the river (10:5). At this point, he overhears two angels, one on either bank of the Tigris. One asks how long it will take to fulfill these astonishing things and is told it will be a period of three and a half years (12:5–8). Furthermore, it will be a time when the power of the holy people has finally been shattered (12:7).

Since the inception of Israel as a nation, the people had not learned to steadfastly serve God, so the Lord is going to deal with their rebellion through this persecution. The result will be a final end to the people's rebellion.

Even after seeing and hearing so much, Daniel can't help but ask what the outcome will be of all these events (12:8). What will be the result of the separating and shattering of the people?

Most people are intrigued with what will happen in the future and end-of-the-world events. Daniel is no exception. Yet even Daniel, with all his wisdom and devotion, is told to go (12:9, 13). God will see to everything in His own way and His own timing. It is not always for people to try to figure out everything He will do and when it will be done.

However, wisdom will provide understanding for the things the Lord *does* want people to know (12:10). His people can be purified and acquire greater spiritual knowledge, but intentionally wicked people will never comprehend the plan of God.

Wisdom requires patience, and Daniel's patience results in a final bit of information: The evil end-times ruler will openly persecute God's people for 1,290 days (three and a half years), beginning with his cessation of Jewish temple rites and his desecration of the temple. This is a long time for people to remain faithful to God. And even beyond the 1,290 days is another forty-five-day period during which people are to patiently persevere (12:11–12).

Demystifying Daniel

No explanation is provided for the different lengths of time mentioned in Daniel 12:11–12 (1,290 days vs. 1,335 days). Conceivably, a forty-five-day period might pass between the time God puts an end to the suffering of His people and His ultimate destruction of the person responsible for it.

The best Daniel can do in response to all he has seen is to continue on until the end (12:13). He has faithfully served his God throughout his long life. In return, he is promised rest and eventual resurrection, after which he will receive everything God has in store for him.

Take It Home

Many times people are reluctant to discuss spiritual matters with others because there is so much they don't fully understand. It should be somewhat comforting, then, to see that even Daniel doesn't completely comprehend the things of God. Still, he is expected to continue serving and speaking out faithfully. Indeed, God's people have a challenge before them to lead many to righteousness (12:3). What is your opinion of evangelism? Do you feel it is everyone's responsibility, or is it best left to the experts (pastors, teachers, scholars, etc.)? When believers don't have all the answers to life's mysteries, do you think their testimony to others is adversely affected?

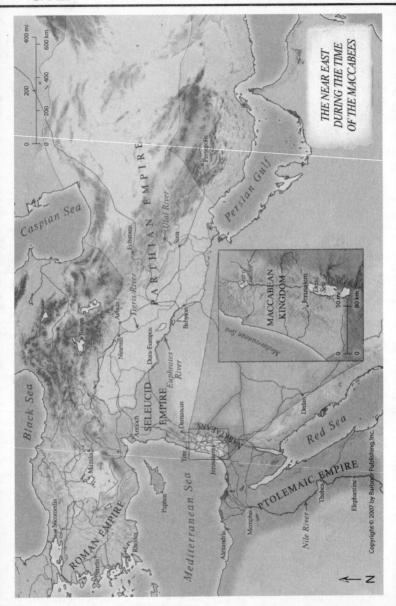

THE NEAR EAST
DURING THE TIME
OF THE MACCABEES

Caspian Sea

Black Sea

Mediterranean Sea

Red Sea

Persian Gulf

PARTHIAN EMPIRE

SELEUCID EMPIRE

ROMAN EMPIRE

PTOLEMAIC EMPIRE

NABATAEANS

MACCABEAN KINGDOM

Tigris River

Euphrates River

Ulai River

Nile River

Sea of Galilee

Dead Sea

Ecbatana
Susa
Persepolis
Nineveh
Arbela
Babylon
Dura-Europos
Tesiphon
Mazaka
Nicomedia
Sardis
Rhodes
Paphos
Antioch
Damascus
Tyre
Jerusalem
Alexandria
Memphis
Thebes
Elephantine
Dedan
Jerusalem

400 mi
200
0

600 km
400
200
0

50 mi
0

80 km
0

Copyright © 2007 by Barbour Publishing, Inc.

N

54

HOSEA

INTRODUCTION TO HOSEA

In our present age, fixed truths, moral absolutes, divine imperatives, sure hope, and life-transforming power often seem to be overshadowed by uncertainty, insecurity, and subjectivism. Yet in the story of Hosea, we are confronted with the truth about God's persistent and unlikely love for an unfaithful people, the Israelites, even as we marvel at the tragic and remarkable beauty of one prophet's unconditional love for his faithless wife that exemplifies the love story between God and humanity.

AUTHOR

Hosea's prophecy may have existed first simply in spoken form, then later it may have been gathered together in written form by disciples or scribes. Still, this work is tradition-ally attributed to Hosea, the son of Beeri (1:1). We don't know much about the prophet's life except for the little that we learn from chapters 1 and 3.

PURPOSE

The purpose of the book of Hosea is to remind God's people of their unfaithfulness and of the judgment that will come because of that unfaithfulness. Hosea teaches that, in spite of their unfaithfulness, it is impossible to escape the love of God, who is ultimately their only hope of salvation from themselves.

OCCASION

When Hosea is called to serve as God's prophet, the nation of Israel is in a state of rebellion. Based on the kings reigning during his prophecy (1:1), we know that the nation of Israel has been split by civil war (1 Kings 12) and that Hosea is sent to the northern kingdom of Israel, which is characterized by corrupt kings, crime, and compromised mo-rality (Hosea 4:1–2).

THEMES

Both themes of love and judgment run through Hosea's prophecy. God's saving love is faithful even in the face of unfaithfulness. Yet, the consequence of that unfaithfulness will be faced. Hosea's ministry is meant to awaken the Israelites to their own unfaithful-ness to God and to call their adulterous hearts back to Him.

HISTORICAL CONTEXT

God called Hosea to the northern kingdom, or Israel, at a time when the nation was in a position of strength and wealth, probably during the later years of Jeroboam II's reign. Hosea was a contemporary of other Old Testament prophets: Amos, Isaiah, Jonah, and Micah. Already on the horizon was the Assyrian menace, and within thirty years, Israel had fallen in defeat.

HOSEA 1:1–2:1

AN UNUSUAL CALLING

Setting Up the Section

God calls Hosea to an unlikely method of ministry: Hosea becomes an example of God's message to a rebellious and unfaithful people.

📖 1:1

CALLED BY GOD

The book of Hosea provides its reader with some important facts that ground the story in its historical context. God calls Hosea during the reigns of Uzziah, Jotham, Ahaz, and Hezekiah, kings of Judah, and during the reign of Jeroboam II, king of Israel. Israel has split from civil war (2 Kings 13:12–13), and the people are pursuing nearly everything except God. Even their kings are often quite corrupt. Hosea is a contemporary of Amos, Isaiah, Jonah, and Micah—other Old Testament prophets charged with declaring God's love and faithfulness in the face of Israel's wayward rebellion. Yet Hosea is given a unique charge (as we will see).

📖 1:2–2:1

HOSEA'S FAMILY

What the Lord requires of Hosea is shocking indeed: to forsake the natural hopes he may have for a happy marriage and instead consign himself to endure the emotional anguish and dishonor of a wife who will be persistently unfaithful. Hosea fulfills God's calling in his marriage to Gomer (1:2–3).

The names that the Lord requires Hosea and Gomer to give to their children express the Lord's intention in the most decisive and unmistakable way. The name *Jezreel* declares God's intention to punish Israel for her unfaithfulness to Him. *Lo-ruhamah* means "not loved," as the Lord is prepared to not love Israel anymore because she has broken His covenant. *Lo-ammi* means "not my people." This harsh denial of their place as God's nation is ultimately what the Lord is warning this generation of Israelites about: Their fate is based on their unfaithfulness (1:4–9).

Critical Observation

The Lord's instruction to Hosea has been widely taken to mean that the Lord commands Hosea to marry a woman of ill repute, perhaps a prostitute. Some scholars maintain that the whole account of Hosea and Gomer is only a parable and not a description of what actually happened. It is a story to make a point. Another view suggests that perhaps Gomer is not a prostitute, but instead the term *adulterous wife* is used metaphorically, as *prostitution* is used metaphorically to refer to Israel's spiritual adultery. Since the most natural reading is to take the story literally, that is how it is approached here.

God uses revelation by action throughout the Bible—most obviously in the ultimate revelation of His love in the incarnate person of Jesus Christ. Jeremiah remains a bachelor his entire life, against all social expectations and his own desire, as an enacted prophecy against the people of God (Jeremiah 16:2). The death of Ezekiel's wife and the odd behavior God commands His prophet to display in connection with it are made symbolic of God's purpose and plan for His people (Ezekiel 24:15–27). Abraham was asked to sacrifice his son, Isaac (Genesis 22:1–18), as a demonstration of his faith and also to picture the future sacrifice God makes by sending His own Son to die on the cross for the salvation of all His children.

Ultimately, after God has judged and punished this generation of His people, He will return to them and restore them to Himself and renew His covenant with them. God's promise to restore His people unto relationship with Himself is fulfilled, at least in large part, in the gathering of the Gentiles into the church after Pentecost (Romans 9:22–26). It is this promise of restoration that is prophetically enacted in Hosea's relationship with Gomer (Hosea 1:10–2:1).

Take It Home

Throughout all generations, God's people are called to examine themselves and their faith—to make their calling and election sure, to strive to be certain that they belong to the people of God, not only in an outward way, but essentially and eternally.

HOSEA 2:2-23

PUNISHMENT AND RESTORATION

Setting Up the Section

Hosea describes God's coming punishment of Israel for her sin, telling of God's wrath and anger and, ultimately, His saving love that brings about the restoration of His people.

📖 2:2-13

HOSEA'S ANGRY GOD

The Old Testament prophets devote an immense amount of their preaching to what the modern church has neglected almost altogether: the judgment and the wrath of God. The centerpiece of the prophetical preaching is God's divine wrath against sin and the impending doom of those who betray His covenant and do not believe His Word. Hosea describes the punishment that God intends to put upon Israel in stark uncompromising terms: God will make Israel like a desert, blocking her path with thorn bushes; strip her naked; slay her with thirst; and ruin her vines and fig trees (2:2–13).

God wants His people to know the reality of His judgment and wrath and to attend to many false prophets in their thinking and living. The prophets of the Old Testament, like Christians today, had to contend with many whose messages were all sweet and lighthearted (Micah 2:11). Recognizing the reality of God's wrath toward sin helps make sense of a broken world, and accepting it spurs God's children to take their own lives more soberly. The suffering we experience in this world is the curse of God upon humanity because of rebellion against Him. The curses Hosea describes are the very curses God promised to visit upon His people if they betray His covenant with Israel in the days of Moses (Leviticus 26; Deuteronomy 28).

📖 2:14-23

THE PROMISE OF RESTORATION

God promises a new and tender courtship of Israel and holds forth the possibility of bringing new life in their relationship through a return to the wilderness—a place where Israel had previously experienced both judgment and cleansing. This is intended to give hope that the coming punishment is not intended to ultimately hurt the nation but instead help them and restore them to a right relationship with God (2:14–15).

Like other prophets, Hosea foretells that the eventual consequence of God's wrath will be a restoration in which a new covenant will be written on the hearts of wayward Israel (Jeremiah 31:31–34; Ezekiel 36:26–27). The Valley of Achor (or Valley of Trouble) points back to Achan's sin of taking riches God had said were off-limits when the Israelites first took the promised land (Joshua 7:26). The Israel of Hosea's day has chased after the "gifts" of her lovers. But the grace of God will reverse the curse so that what was once a marker for sin becomes a door of hope (Hosea 2:15).

Israel's hope is found in what God is going to do in their hearts. They will forever banish the name Baal from their religious life. The term *Baal* literally means "master," and it was the term used for the false gods that the Canaanites worshiped. The Israelites' acceptance of this name for God began the process of compromise and the nation's fall.

What comes out of one's mouth is a representation of what is in the heart (Proverbs 13:3; 16:23). Thus by calling God *Baal*, they are in essence showing that they have given their hearts to false worship. Yet God will cleanse them, and they will address God in terms of a deep love relationship rather then abandoning Him in false worship. Israel will call God *husband*—a term of endearment and relationship. Thus the restoration will be great (Hosea 2:16–17).

Instead of the wilderness being a place where the wild animals are a threat and a danger to mankind, it now becomes a place where the animals themselves are brought into covenant relation with the redeemed people. What Hosea describes is a restoration of the creation order in which God is going to make all things new again (2:18). It is a vision of the new heavens and the new earth (Isaiah 11:6–7; Revelations 21:1).

Despite Israel's unfaithfulness, God is going to pursue her again, and this time the marriage covenant will be stronger—one that will bring an eternal relationship. This new covenant will be one in which love will rule. It is the beginning of an unprecedented relationship of love between God and His people. It is a new covenant.

God gives righteousness, justice, love, and compassion as the means by which He obtains His bride (2:19). It is God's righteousness and justice, not Israel's, that redeems her. God is the One who pays the price to make us His own. Faithfulness becomes the summary of the other four qualities in a single word (2:20). The unfailing goodness of God is the basis for Israel's salvation.

The goal of God's wooing of the people is that they will know Him. To know God implies the deepest relationship with Him. To know God is to love Him, to be one of His people, to abandon all other gods, and to be eternally committed to Him. What God is promising here is that Israel will be bound in an unbreakable covenant, and all the people from least to greatest will know Him.

God promises to reverse the famine of 2:9 by making what has become a wilderness a land that meets the needs of His people. God is going to respond to the people's call for help by providing for them. Jezreel, the name of Hosea's firstborn, had been a warning of brokenness for Israel (1:4–5), but now it implies salvation and prosperity. The name *Jezreel* literally means "God sows" (2:21–23).

Hosea concludes this promise with a final reversal: the reversal of the names Lo-ruhamah and Lo-ammi. God will have compassion on those who have not had compassion, and He will call those who are not His people to be His. The people's response ("You are my God") fulfills the prophecy of 2:20, that they will know the Lord, and reverses the rejection described in 1:9 ("I am not your God"). God will resolve all of the self-inflicted consequences for our sins. Rather than eternally punishing mankind, God has offered a way of salvation (2:23).

Take It Home

We are reminded by passages such as Hosea's that the stakes are high—heaven or hell (the love and favor of God or His wrath and curse; eternal life or everlasting doom). An understanding of the immensity of the issues of life or death should drive each of us to live a serious and self-examined life. In the end, our hope is in the Lord, who will renew our faith even in the midst of our own unfaithfulness.

HOSEA 3:1–5

RECONCILIATION

Love Covers a Multitude of Sins   3:1–5

Setting Up the Section

Hosea is called to reconcile with his wife despite her adultery. God draws a parallel between the story of Hosea's love for his wife and God's love for unfaithful Israel.

📖 3:1–5

LOVE COVERS A MULTITUDE OF SINS

God requires Hosea to reclaim his wife, Gomer, though she is an adulteress (3:1). This command is extraordinary considering how seriously God takes faithfulness, but He gives Hosea a model in His own love for the unfaithful Israelites. The general view of this passage is that Hosea must purchase his wife, who is on sale as a slave, perhaps for debt. God describes how the Israelites were unfaithful to Him by loving sacred raisin cakes, which were used in the worship of false deities (Jeremiah 7:18). The Lord's love cannot be extinguished even by the people's outright apostasy (Hosea 3:1).

Hosea purchases Gomer with an assortment of items—fifteen shekels of silver and five bushels of barley—which demonstrates how he had to tap all of his resources to recover his unfaithful bride. Hosea initiates a period of discipline during which his wife will live with him for many days before the resumption of full marital relations (3:3). This interim is meant to signify the exile Israel has to undergo before the restoration in the last days (3:5). The word *return* is used repeatedly throughout Hosea's prophecy—a total of twenty-two times—and is a significant theme of the message. Like Gomer's return to Hosea, Israel's return to the Lord does not come without a cost and a period of purification and exile. Israel, like Hosea's wife, is ultimately restored to her true happiness with her rightful God through a miracle of God's grace.

THE CASE AGAINST ISRAEL

Setting Up the Section

Hosea lays out God's charges against Israel, describing the people's sinfulness and God's holiness.

📖 **4:1-3**

THE WORD OF THE LORD

In this passage, Hosea is laying out a prophet lawsuit—a charge from the Lord that comes with evidence and judgment (4:1).

The charges are fairly straightforward and damning. "There is no faithfulness, no kindness, no knowledge of God in your land" (4:1 NLT; see Proverbs 24:2). There is instead plenty of transgression—cursing, lying, murder, stealing, adultery—that is already bringing about negative consequences for the people and even the land (Isaiah 33:9; Jeremiah 4:28). The land mourning is likely a reference to a drought (Hosea 4:3), and the death of the animals is mentioned in other Old Testament prophecies (see Jeremiah 4:25; 9:10).

📖 **4:4-19**

THE PRIESTS' CULPABILITY

As it had been in 2:2, God's main point in this lawsuit against Israel is that the priests have forsaken their true calling and responsibility, and they are responsible for the spiritual defection of the people and the debacle that God is about to bring upon them for their breech of the covenant (4:4).

So far as it is possible to assign particular blame for Israel's apostasy, Hosea is willing to say it is the ministers' fault that the people will perish under God's judgment. The priests have led them astray, kept them from a true knowledge of God and His covenant, and have encouraged unbelief and disobedience. But God, in His holy vengeance, now intends to bring justice.

Hosea explicitly says that the priests have perverted the law of God. In fact, under their false teaching, Israel is perishing for lack of knowledge. No doubt that teaching included a great deal of paganism (drawn from the surrounding culture), a radical undermining of the authority of God's law, and a relaxing take on the standards of holiness God requires (4:5-6).

Hosea blames the priests because they bore the greatest responsibility for the spiritual life of the people of God. Their ministry of the Word and worship, or lack thereof, had a far greater influence upon the people—for good or for ill—than the ministry of any other. Sin multiplied under and among these false teachers (4:7-8).

Demystifying Hosea

Malachi provides what may be the Old Testament's most succinct description of the calling of a priest or a minister in the Lord's reminiscence of the priestly ministry of Aaron: "True instruction was in his mouth and nothing false was found on his lips. He walked with me in peace and uprightness, and turned many from sin" (Malachi 2:6 NIV). The priests of the northern kingdom in Hosea's day are the perfect antithesis of that description and therefore are the subject of God's stern rebuke and judgment.

This greater responsibility and consequent accountability does not absolve the rest of the Israelites. God will punish both the priests and the people for their wickedness (4:9). Like Gomer, the Israelites will give themselves over to prostitution. This part of the prophecy describes how God will punish the Israelites for their persistent unfaithfulness—through depriving them of prosperity and joy and by launching a full-scale attack on the Baal cult (4:10–14).

Hosea warns Judah (Israel's southern sister) not to follow Israel in the path to destruction (4:15–19). The use of the name *Ephraim*—in reference to Israel—signifies that because of their lack of allegiance to David, the northern kingdom does not even deserve to be called Israel (4:17). Themes of drunkenness and prostitution continue as Hosea presents God's case against His people (4:18).

Take It Home

Hosea teaches us that the spiritual health of the priests and ministers of God's message is a matter of great importance and bears directly on the spiritual health and well-being of the larger community. As a body of believers, we must support, encourage, and hold our leadership accountable to the Word of God. We must pray for our leaders, knowing that our spiritual journeys are intertwined, just as Moses prayed for Levi (Deuteronomy 33:11).

THE JUDGMENT

The Point of No Return   5:1–15

Setting Up the Section

One of the solemn messages Hosea and other Old Testament prophets are called to deliver is the terrible seriousness of rebellion against God. Not only will God's people someday have to give an account for their unfaithfulness, but there will also be immediate consequences for their rebellion.

📄 **5:1–15**

THE POINT OF NO RETURN

Hosea calls again to get the people to listen—there is judgment against them, and God wants their full attention. These opening verses renew the fact that God is making a direct charge against Israel's leaders, the priests, and even the royal family (5:1–2). Tabor and Mizpah are places associated with worship of Baal. Legal imagery continues as well in the use of words like *judgment* and *testifies* (5:1, 5).

God sees everything and declares that Israel is corrupt, or unclean. This image points back to Hosea's unclean wife, whom God calls Hosea to love in spite of her unfaithfulness. The speaker in this verse can either be Hosea or Yahweh (5:3). Israel's sin is so tremendous that it prevents them from returning to God even if they want to, a concept that resurfaces in the New Testament (5:4; see Mark 3:29; 1 John 5:16).

God has even withdrawn from receiving the people's sacrifices. This is another of the curses that God long ago promised to visit upon those unfaithful to His covenant (Deuteronomy 31:18). The New Moon festivals that will devour the people and their fields (Hosea 5:7) likely refers to pagan rituals that are mentioned elsewhere (Isaiah 1:14).

Ephraim is reduced to waste, and Judah acquires a territory of Benjamin by military force (5:8–9). This action violates the sacred tribal land allotments which God's covenant had fixed and is what Hosea is probably talking about when he says Judah's leaders move boundary markers (5:10). These actions of violation provoke God's wrath (Proverbs 22:28).

God identifies Himself as the real threat to a sinful people floundering about in unfaithfulness (5:14). Not even their allegiances with Assyria will cause them as much oppression as their allegiance to idols (5:11). God is their judge and the only One who can save them from themselves (5:12–13). The consequences of the people's rebellion do not stop with destruction and despair. God withdraws Himself until they are able to repent of their sins (5:14–15).

Take It Home

The sins of Israel take hold because they are permitted to take hold. It becomes so much the habit of life as to make these people beyond the reach of even prophecies about their own destruction. These words call each of us to seriously examine our lives, to deal with sin as soon as we recognize it, and remember not to underestimate how far-reaching its affects can be. The psalmist reminds God's children: "We are the people he watches over, the flock under his care. If only you would listen to his voice today!" (Psalm 95:7 NLT).

HOSEA 6:1–11

ISRAEL REFUSES TO REPENT

Setting Up the Section

Most of Hosea's prophecy focuses on proving how Israel betrayed the Lord and His covenant and enumerating the curses which God is about to visit upon His people for their faithlessness and apostasy. Hosea also proclaims that after God is finished with His judgment, He will return to bless a future generation of His chosen people.

📖 6:1–3

THE LORD PROMISES FORGIVENESS

Finally, in the midst of the despair of God withdrawing His life-giving presence from His people, there is a glimmer of hope and forgiveness. God will return to bless His people. Hosea has been hammering away at Israel with his message of doom and the grim promise that she is about to fall under God's unrelenting judgment. And now, in the next breath, Hosea proclaims the compassion and mercy of God and His willingness to forgive His people in defiance of the wrongs they have committed against Him.

Hosea does not contemplate that his contemporaries will dodge God's wrath—they will be judged. But at some point in the future, God will return to His people with grace. The *us* (6:1–3) refers not to Hosea's contemporaries but to people in a distant time in the future. Similarly, when God said to Israel in the wilderness in Deuteronomy 4 that He will send them into exile, He isn't referring to that very group of people but to people in a distant time.

God is a God of great mercy, and He will forgive and restore human beings to fellowship with Himself, even when they are guilty of every manner of sin against Him—if they will repent (6:1). Even when they have defied His grace, spurned His commandments, and abused His gifts, His grace reaches the heights and the depths. Just as Christ was raised on the third day, so the image of Israel's revival and restoration to live in God's presence is described (6:2). If there is anything that Israel can hope in—even in the midst of God's judgment—it is God's own merciful return (6:3).

Take It Home

In the midst of judgment, God's love shines like a beacon of hope. As great as Israel's sins are—and as great as our own—the mercy of the Almighty God will sweep them away like the coming of dawn if only they repent. God is a holy God who demands justice but who also delights in mercy and freely offers grace to His people. "Who is a God like you, who pardons sin and forgives the transgression of the remnant of his inheritance? You do not stay angry forever but delight to show mercy" (Micah 7:18 NIV). "May your unfailing love rest upon us, O LORD, even as we put our hope in you" (Psalm 33:22 NIV).

📄 6:4–11

WORSHIP GONE WRONG

The tone shifts noticeably in verse 4 as Hosea returns to the main idea at hand for the Israelites—God's sorrow at their sin. God is suspicious of the people's love and desire to return to Him—their love is as ephemeral as the morning mist (6:4). God reminds them of what He has proclaimed through earlier prophets—that He requires more than empty promises and He desires acknowledgement of Himself (6:6). The word *mercy* in 6:6 is the same word rendered *love* in 6:4. In reference to God, this word translates to "grace" and "loving-kindness." But with reference to Israel, it refers to that love and loyalty that is their part of the covenant with God. Hosea's great point is that Israel has been disloyal to God and the covenant; she has failed to do her part.

Israel has come to think about her God, the living and true God who created all things and knows the hearts of His people, in the same way that the pagans around her think of their false gods and idols. The Israelites had come to believe that by offering sacrifices and performing rituals, they could ingratiate themselves with God and get Him to do good things for them, allowing them to live however they please. To worship God as Hosea's contemporaries worshiped God, with outward rituals but no inward devotion, is to be false to God. God is not interested in that kind of worship at all (6:6).

Just as God judged and banished Adam from the garden for breaking the covenant, God is banishing His people from the benefits of the covenant they have broken (6:7; see Joshua 23:16). Hosea provides a powerful image of a city "stained with footprints of blood" (6:8 NIV).

Israel has lost a sense of what worship is intended to be. Her worship had first become a true hypocrisy before it became naked paganism. Israel does not love God and does not care about what pleases Him. They leave their worship of God, do exactly as they please, commit whatever sins they desire to commit, and live between their trips to offer sacrifices a life of unrelieved disobedience and rebellion against God (6:9–10).

Take It Home

Worship is the true test of where a church, or any churchgoer, really stands before God. Worship is the test. Israel's worship had clearly gone far wrong (4:12–14). God demands more from us in our worship than just lip service. Israel's sin is the same one the Pharisees committed in Matthew 9:13. Outward rituals and religious formalities do not please God unless one's heart and life are aligned to His will.

HOSEA 7:1–16

ISRAEL'S GREAT CHALLENGE

Setting Up the Section

Hosea dwells on Israel's complete, final, and irreversible failure of faith. The people continue to be religious and call upon the Lord, but all the while they do not really put their trust completely in Him. God longs to redeem His people, but they persist in their sin. The great challenge for Israel is to admit that she has lost her faith and to return to God's truth.

7:1–8

LIVING BY SIGHT

Israel, on account of her disobedience and disloyalty to the Lord, is teetering on the brink of extinction. God's desire to "restore the fortunes" is a reference to the same healing and restoration of the covenant relationship described in 6:1 (6:11–7:2). It is the recovery anticipated in the New Year festival. Israel's real hope lies in the Sovereign God who knows how to deliver His people, as He has so often in the past. But instead of trusting in this, the people are putting faith in the sort of diplomatic maneuvering that never brings true success (7:1–2).

Israel's failure, Hosea says, is a failure of faith, and all of her terrible disobedience is evidence of the fact that she does not really believe in the Lord or trust in Him. Because their faith is weak, the Israelites continue to regularly and instinctively count more upon that which they can see and hear and touch than upon an unseen God. This faithlessness leads to a time of tumultuous political uncertainty (7:3–7).

BLIND TO THE TRUTH

Israel has for so long beckoned to the world of sight and ignored the unseen realities of the life of faith and of God's covenant, that she now has become totally blind and deaf to those realities. Her faith is so feeble that she is completely cut off from understanding what faith in God alone gives. No amount of evidence can make Israel realize what total folly she has chosen for herself (7:9–10).

Critical Observation

Israel persists in making terrible decisions that only further her destruction. Hosea pictures Ephraim in her clumsy waywardness like a dove flapping every which way (7:11). The context for what Hosea is referencing is the foreign policy decisions that Israel made to play off Egypt and Assyria (2 Kings 15:19–20; 17:3–6). Israel thinks she can find a way out of her mess, but God will see to it that all her plans are frustrated and that she gets what she deserves. He will not be mocked! Israel had hoped that Assyria or Egypt would be her savior, but lurching between the one and the other, she became hateful to both of them. Assyria will become her conqueror, and Egypt will make sport of her when she is destroyed.

The simple evidence is that Israel continues to maintain the pretence of faith in God without actually being sincere. The people do not think they are faithless—they pray and worship God. Yet Hosea says these actions are meaningless because of the intentions of their hearts to continue harboring sin. Everything we do is abundantly clear to God; He is not deceived by our calculations to look good. Just as God said to Samuel when He was anointing David king, "The LORD doesn't see things the way you see them. People judge by outward appearance, but the LORD looks at the heart" (1 Samuel 16:7 NLT).

God's revelation through Hosea concludes with another warning of final disaster and an implication that the nation will return to Egypt and God will no longer choose them to be His people (7:13–16). God is tired of the way He has been misrepresented—through lies, turning away, and evil plots (7:13–15). The wailing is a reference to the worship of Baal (see 1 Kings 18:28), and God calls them out on the duplicity of their cry for help, implying that the people are actually calling for Baal (7:14–15). Israel's arrogance and failure to call on the one true God makes them a laughingstock even among their enemies in Egypt (7:16).

Take It Home

Israel has become interested in pleasing people more than drawing near to the One who actually, and finally, holds their fortunes in His hands. They know that God is the only true deliverer, and yet they fail to practice daily on this knowledge. Their faith is so weak that they are more inclined to trust themselves and others than God. Like the Israelites of Hosea's day, our faith is weak. The greatest way for us to grow in grace is to seek God by practicing, nurturing, and exercising our faith in community, Bible study, and prayer.

HOSEA 8:1–14
REAP THE WHIRLWIND

Inevitable Judgment   8:1–14

Setting Up the Section

Hosea's prophecy continues to describe how Israel is about to reap the whirlwind of God's judgment for their unfaithfulness. His manner is serious and somber and sets the tone for the punishment to come in the chapters ahead.

📄 8:1–14

INEVITABLE JUDGMENT

The theme of this chapter is to prepare Israel for the punishment that she is about to receive. The trumpet signals the approaching danger. The eagle is more accurately translated as a *griffon vulture*, which signifies that death is already settling over Israel and the birds of scavenging are taking their places (8:1). Israel's cries of acknowledgment in the midst of her unfaithfulness only serve to further arouse and inflame God's anger and judgment. The people refuse to turn to God; they have "rejected what is good" (8:2–3).

God reviews Israel's rebellious ways. She has set up kings and princes He does not approve of (8:4) and uses the treasures of the land to fashion idols of gold and silver that violate the covenant and bring destruction (8:5). Jeroboam I, the first king God had not appointed or anointed, also initiated the idolatrous cult. This example is a reality that both Hosea and the people know. The reference to the monarchy also signifies Israel's attempt to do without God.

The calf-idol of Samaria refers to the two calves at Bethel and Dan (1 Kings 12:28–30), and these man-made imposters will be destroyed just as they have brought about the destruction of Israel (8:5–6). The next set of verses is a return to Israel's political misdeeds, particularly their alliances with foreigners. Hosea quotes two proverbs—"sow the wind and reap the whirlwind" and "the stalk has no head, it will produce no flour" (8:7 NIV). These proverbs seem to underscore the inevitable judgment that Hosea is prophesying—events have been set in motion by Israel's disobedience (8:7).

Hosea continues to hammer home the punishment that awaits Israel for her unfaithfulness. She will be "swallowed up" by those she believes to be potential allies, and she is now considered worthless, for she has failed in her divine purpose (8:8). The image of Israel as a wild donkey underscores her aimlessness and isolation. The reference to selling herself to her lovers returns to the themes of prostitution from Hosea's early prophecy and further illuminates how desperate she has become (8:9). The result of Israel's unfaithfulness and sin is no longer something she can deny or avoid—she is no longer a nation and certainly not a nation worthy of being claimed as God's people. She has lost herself (8:10).

In the conclusion of this chapter, Hosea returns to enumerating Israel's religious misdeeds by describing how she has turned to other gods. Altars that were intended to cleanse the people from sin became, ironically, places where their sin increased as they misused them for Baal (8:11). Even God's guidebook to the people became indecipherable to their sinful hearts—seeming like a foreign thing (8:12). God gave His law to the people, but they came to think of it as strange and far removed from the real interests and issues of their lives. Israel has lost all true regard for the law of God and all true interest in keeping God's commandments. She has made a life's work of rebelling against that law and defying it at every turn.

Hosea promises doom to Israel for her disobedience, though all along she has claimed to believe in God. No one can ever save themselves by keeping the commandments of God; but it is just as true that everyone who is truly saved by the grace of God will practice obedience to His commandments. Jesus saves us in order to sanctify us, to make us holy—being obedient to God's law. He saves us to make us zealous for good works, and by *good works* He means all that we do in obedience to His commandments.

Hosea puts it bluntly: Israel has chosen for herself the path of disobedience to God's law, and God is now preparing her doom (8:13). Throughout the Bible, it is proclaimed from the rooftops that those who are truly the people of God will love and obey His law. Those who do not, whatever they may protest to the contrary—and Israel does protest her faith in God to the bitter end—will not be numbered among God's children and will not be spared His wrath in the Day of Judgment.

Again and again, Hosea says this: Israel calls upon the Lord to save her, but she will have God only on her own terms. She has no intention of living according to the commandments of God. She wants His forgiveness and His help, but she does not want to be ruled by Him and by His law. The name *Maker* for God refers to His election of Israel from among the nations, not their physical creation (8:14; see Psalm 100:3; Malachi 2:10).

God will not listen to the prayers nor will He accept the sacrifices of people who will not do what He says. He instead promises to send fire to consume their fortresses. God's judgment will include both Judah and Israel (8:14–15).

Take It Home

One idea that sometimes gets lost in Hosea's sobering prophecy of inevitable judgment is the truth that Israel has forgotten—that obedience to God leads to blessings in this life and the life to come. Hosea is full of this simple and happy truth. Hosea is here to remind the transgressors of what their choices are really reaping and also to remind them that the way of the Lord leads to great reward. God gives us His commandments because He loves us and knows what is best for us. The only absolutely reliable plan for the achievement of happiness and self-fulfillment is the plan for living by the law of God.

HOSEA 9:1–10:15

PUNISHMENT TO ARRIVE

Setting Up the Section

Israel tried to be like other nations by seeking to become wealthy by the same means that the nations used: the fertility cult. But Israel isn't like the other nations; Israelites are God's children, and God will not bless them to operate with this level of harlotry. When Israel embraces these pagan religious practices, they are acting in a way that is inconsistent with their own identity and calling.

9:1–17

NO REASON TO REJOICE

Israel's harvest has failed, and God commands them to stop rejoicing. Their harvest has failed because of their prostitution against God. When Hosea refers to "the wages of a prostitute at every threshing floor" (NIV), he is talking about the immoral acts that often accompany the party atmosphere at harvest in which sexual license is considered to encourage agricultural prosperity (9:1). The harvest they seek from this harlotry will not produce prosperity for the nation. In fact, their produce will not sustain them at all. God will keep the product of their harlotry from feeding the nation (9:2).

Not only is God going to prevent the harvest from sustaining the nation, but He will also drive Israel from the land. Because they have defiled themselves, they will be unfit for residence in the holy land and will instead eat defiled food in a foreign land (9:3).

They have no offerings to give that are suitable for use in worship. Because of their harlotry and the consequence that is coming, there is no sacrifice that will be acceptable to God (9:4). The "bread of mourners" refers to the fact that those who are in mourning, and who must deal with the burial of a dead body, contaminate the food they touch. Therefore, such bread is unfit for offering to God (see Deuteronomy 26:12–14).

Israel has embraced false worship and rejected God. Though they have maintained a form of ceremonial worship, they have nothing to recommend themselves to God. No matter how much they adhere to the proper forms, it is not a worship that brings glory to God (9:5). The people are suffering from the plight of famine—the food is unfit to offer to God because of its poor quality and because it comes from an environment where death and contact with the dead are common. The people, devastated, will go down to Egypt, just as Abraham did, to find relief. The famine-ravaged Israelites will seek deliverance in Egypt and will not find it (9:6).

Critical Observation

Memphis (9:6) is the Greek name for the Egyptian Mamphta, which is the capital of Egypt at this time (Isaiah 19:13; Jeremiah 2:16; 44:1; 46:14; Ezekiel 30:13). Its name means "the dwelling of Phta," the Greek Vulcan. In it is the well-known court of Apis. There, in the home of the idol to whom the rebellious Israelites look for refuge, they will be gathered to be buried. This place is a favorite burial place of the Egyptians. Hence the place of their refuge is the place of their destruction.

The false prophets had continually deceived the people, promising them that days of destruction will never come. They have escaped this day of judgment for only so long, but now it is upon them. In God's purpose, the days of judgment are inevitable. Hosea gives to the false prophets the title which they claim for themselves: "the prophet" and "the man of the spirit" (ESV). Yet, these prophets are not God's men, and they do not have the Spirit of God in them. They are mad and crazy prophets who speak destructive lies to the people. They lead the people astray (9:7-8).

The reference to Gibeah brings us back to Judges 19-21, in which a Levite's concubine is raped and murdered at Gibeah. The Levite, to obtain vengeance, cuts her body into twelve pieces and sends the pieces to the tribes of Israel to provoke their outrage. This begins a civil war and a series of grotesque atrocities. Hosea declares that the people of his day have fallen to the level of this most corrupt generation of Israel's history. They are just as judged by God (9:9).

One does not expect to find edible grapes in the desert, and such a discovery would make a real feast for a traveler. Similarly, the firstfruits of a fig tree in spring would be especially delicious to people in the ancient world. The point of both metaphors is that Israel in her youth was a special source of delight to God, yet something happened. The people went to Baal Peor and consecrated themselves to shame. Just like fruit going bad, the people, upon arrival in Israel, gave themselves over to Baal and became a stench to the One who loves them (9:10).

Demystifying Hosea

Baal Peor was the location of a shrine to Baal in the plains of Moab, some twelve miles north-east of the Dead Sea (Numbers 25:1–9). After Balaam failed to bring a curse down on Israel, the Israelites brought one down on themselves by yielding to the temptation to have sexual relations with Moabite women. A plague began in Israel, and the plague did not come to a stop until the priest Phinehas took a spear and ran it through the bodies of an Israelite man and a Moabite woman. By calling the attention of Israel to this, the people will see that their apostasy to Baal began before they entered the promised land.

Ephraim's glory will depart. As a sign of judgment, they will not be able to have children. Since children are a sign of God's blessing, God will remove the ability to be fertile. Instead of the blessing of children, Israel will bear the consequence of their sin (9:11–12).

God formed this nation to be strong and glorious, planted in a great meadow. Yet, instead of growing and becoming strong, they are leading their children out to slaughter. Rather than growing, they are acting like those who worship Baal and thus killing their children. Just as those who worship Baal sacrifice their children to him, Israel is now doing the same (9:13).

Israel had attributed their fertility to Baal, and now barrenness is the only appropriate judgment. Since they turned to Baal for life, the only logical consequence is for God to give them over to death. Thus, God will remove the fertility of the land (9:14).

Gilgal is the prototypical city of Israel—it contains every evil that the book of Hosea condemns. Gilgal is the city that prompts Yahweh to declare Israel His enemy. Gilgal is described as a cult center in 4:15 and 12:11. The rebellion that is here is so hated by God that He is going to drive the people out of the land and punish all the leaders who have led Israel into such apostasy (9:15).

Israel is so cursed that life will not be given to them. God will show them how cursed they are as a nation. They will be wanderers among the nations—exiled and forced to live as aliens and strangers in the world. They will lose their blessing, their home, and their fertility. In short, they will live cursed because they have rejected God and turned to Baal (9:16–17).

📖 10:1–15

THE CONSEQUENCES OF SIN

Israel and her reach are compared to a spreading vine (10:1), a metaphor that Jesus Himself used when describing the life of God's children. The message from Hosea is that in the midst of their prosperity, Israel grew unfaithful to her God and thus "must bear their guilt" (10:2). Hosea predicts the destruction of both the kings and the cults that have failed Israel so miserably (10:3–7). And Israel will be so distraught and desperate that, in the absence of both their false saviors, they will cry out to the mountains to cover them up and for the earth itself to consume them (10:8).

God is in control and will give Israel what she deserves—divine judgment. It is not what

God wants to do, but it is what Israel has sown with her wicked ways. The Bible is full of conditional statements like the ones here in 10:12–13. The prophet says that if Israel will trust and obey the Lord, the nation will prosper; but because she has disobeyed Him and His covenant, she is suffering and faces destruction.

Long before, when God made His covenant with Israel during the days of Moses, He had promised them that if they fully obey Him, they will be set high above all the nations and all manner of blessing will be poured out upon them. But, at the same time, the Lord promised Israel that if she betrays His covenant and proves disloyal to Him, then He will curse her and deprive her of all of those blessings (10:10–13).

The Bible is full of declarations having to do with sowing and reaping (10:12). The book of Proverbs is devoted to the theme that godly living brings blessing and prosperity and that sinful living brings ruin. In this chapter, Hosea is reminding Israel that her suffering is a result of her disobedience to God.

Critical Observation

Hosea does not say, nor does the rest of the Bible, that all of these consequences are to be visited upon the Israelites immediately. God brings the fruits of faith or unbelief to light in His own timing. Hosea's own ministry stretched over twenty or thirty years, and when he began to preach Israel's doom, she remained for some time a nation at peace and enjoyed an almost unprecedented prosperity. Only slowly, during the course of Hosea's life and work, did the judgment he prophesied begin to appear. And, of course, Israel had been in deep rebellion against the Lord for two centuries prior to Hosea's ministry.

Scripture measures blessedness and punishment in different ways than mankind is accustomed to measuring these things. To be holy and near to God, and to have one's life blessed by salvation, are the markers of true life (1 Timothy 6:19). And these joys are so strong and so great that they can lift even a much-afflicted life right out of the sorrows and pains of this world.

Hosea prophesies doom for Israel on account of her betrayal of the covenant, but the doom she suffers at the hands of Assyrian armies is but a foretaste of the judgment that awaits. The blessing that God promises to lavish on those who love and serve Him, though rich beyond words in this world, is rich beyond thought in the world to come. You will never take the measure of what faith brings or what unbelief brings until you see the full issue of each in the next world (10:14–15).

Take It Home

Does God really mean that if we are faithful we will prosper and if we are not we will suffer? If it is for the nation of Israel, is it true for all of God's children? We must trust that the ways of the Lord bring blessing (Psalm 1). Yet we also know that in this life we will encounter trials of many kinds, just as Jesus Christ did (James 1:1–3), and we should not assume that trials or suffering are consequences of our own sin (consider Job; Psalm 73; Matthew 5). Even in the midst of a suffering world and our own suffering, the joy of the Lord and His banner of love over His children preserve and protect in this world and in the world to come (Revelation 22:1–7). This is the reason for the hope that is within us (1 Peter 3:15).

HOSEA 11:1–12

GOD'S DISPLEASURE

Setting Up the Section

This chapter draws heavily on two components of Israel's history: the Exodus and the destruction of Sodom and Gomorrah.

▣ **11:1–5**

REVISITING THE EXODUS

Hosea warns that God will undo Israel's exodus and send His people to a new Egypt (Assyria) and into servitude to a new pharaoh (the Assyrian king). The childhood of Israel refers to the occasion when Israel was first in Egypt (11:1; see Exodus 4:22). The metaphor of Israel as God's son is distinct from the earlier terminology (Hosea 1:10) that describes the people as God's children and the corporate nation as God's adulterous wife (1:2). By calling Israel a son, God is making the point that He trained them and gave them what they needed to serve Him and do His work. This description highlights the rebellion of Israel. Another reason the reference works is because this text is used to refer to Jesus' move from Egypt back to Israel (Matthew 2:15). The uniqueness of referring to Israel as a son here is God's way of doing two things in this text: highlighting Israel's sin and foreshadowing a picture of the Messiah.

Many scholars have observed that Jesus' fulfillment of Hosea 11:1 corresponds to the typology that one finds throughout Matthew, in which Jesus recapitulates the story of Israel in the way that He lived His life. Jesus spends forty days in the wilderness, just as Israel is there forty years. Jesus gives His law on a mountain, just as God gives the law at Mount Sinai. Jesus miraculously feeds His followers in the wilderness, just as Moses gives the people manna. Jesus has to walk in the path of Israel without sin so that He can be proven worthy to take the penalty for mankind.

If you look at the history of Israel, you see how through the centuries the people disregarded the prophets' messages. The more God spoke, the more they rebelled. The more God revealed Himself, the more they ran from Him. From the moment they left Egypt, they were fighting against the will and plan of God, seeking to do things their own way. The text continues to reflect upon what God did for Israel to care for the people. God cared for the needs of the nation—describing Israel as His child and His animal. Yahweh fed Israel throughout the Exodus (11:2–4). Hosea warns that the Exodus will be undone and Israel will return to its former condition of slavery. Yet this time the captivity will not be in Egypt but in Assyria (11:5).

📖 **11:6–12**

LESSONS FROM THE PAST

Hosea turns to another example from Israel's past—one of judgment and not redemption: the story of God's destruction of Sodom and Gomorrah. Under Assyrian domination, Israel will become like the cities that were eternally annihilated because of their rebellion against God. The image of the sword slashing through the bars probably means that when the Assyrians come, they will put an end to the boasting of the Israelites and destroy all of their vain attempts at securing their own future. All the things that they once trusted in, and all their self-focused wisdom, do nothing for them. They cannot protect themselves from what is coming (11:6).

The Israelites are deepening their rebellion against God. The reality is that the more they deepen their rebellion, the more they depend upon false religious practices to get them through. Therefore, there will not be the type of deliverance that God had provided in the past. They will feel the sting of this rebellion (11:7).

The mood of the text changes abruptly when God reveals His heart. Like a father who is facing the rebellion of a strong-willed child, God puts on the table the conflicting feelings of His love and His anger. In verse 8, He is seeking to resolve His compassion for Israel and the punishment demanded by their sin. This text is metaphorical, as God shows His love in terms that human minds can understand. God has very real feelings about the horrendous nature of sin. Zeboiim and Admah, together with Bela, are the other cities of the plain in the same region as Sodom and Gomorrah (Genesis 14:2). These cities represent the depravity that God destroyed (Genesis 19; Deuteronomy 29:23). God mentions them as a way to get the attention of the Israelites.

Hosea presents Israel as a city in danger of repeating the history of Sodom, Gomorrah, and the cities of the plain. When God says He will not unleash His anger, it does not mean that Ephraim is going to escape punishment. Rather, it means that God will not give full vent to His fury, as He did in the case of Sodom. In other words, Israel will not suffer the total, irreversible annihilation that Sodom experienced (11:9).

Hosea uses an intense image to talk of the restoration of Israel—he describes God as a lion with a mighty roar. Yet, this roar will not be to destroy Israel but to restore it. The image, like many in the prophets, is disorienting: A lion roars and the birds come to it rather than flee (11:10–11; see Numbers 24:8–9). Hosea's point here is that there is to be a new exodus in which God will again play the part of the lion and deliver His people from their enemies and into a new land. This call will bring them back. Israel will no longer be a silly dove wandering to and fro (7:11). This foretells of the day when the people will return not only from Egypt and Assyria but also from the west, the regions around the Mediterranean (11:10–11).

HOSEA 12:1–13:16

LESSONS FROM HISTORY

Setting Up the Section

Hosea continues his meditation on the history of Israel's relationship to God—tracing the nation's sin and how it has provoked God's judgment.

📖 12:1–14

ISRAEL'S SIN

Hosea persists in employing legal language to describe God's case against Israel—laying out God's charge against Israel (12:2). Hosea brings up examples from Israel's past, as well as Judah's, in which Jacob rebelled and wrestled to get his way (12:3–5). Hosea returns again to his crucial themes of love, justice, and patience, commanding Israel to return to the Lord in repentance as Jacob did (12:6).

The Lord unmasks Israel's pride through Hosea and warns His children never to imitate Israel in her fundamental and tragic blasphemy. God shows through Israel what pride can do and, by recording it in scripture, warns His children to stand against it. Israel's spiritual pride is plain dishonesty. It is the big lie of Israel's life. Pride is false security. Ephraim has boasted and taken credit for her economic prosperity, luxurious lifestyle, and success, when in fact it is God's favor she has enjoyed (12:8).

God shifts the focus of His complaints from the Exodus and pre-exodus to the message of the prophets. Hosea will pick up this shift in the opening of his next complaint (12:12–13). Once again, God declares that He will undo the Exodus and return Israel to the status of no longer being a nation. God speaks of a return to wilderness rather than a return to slavery. God asserts His sovereignty over them. The feast referred to in this text is the Feast of Tabernacles, or Booths (Leviticus 23:33–44). This verse looks ahead to the time when Israel's people will be scattered from their homeland (Hosea 12:9).

God's complaint has shifted to how Israel is presently ignoring His warnings—even the ones His prophet Hosea is speaking. God is warning the people, albeit sometimes in puzzling forms (visions and parables), but they are too rebellious to listen to the warnings (12:10). The obvious answer to God's rhetorical question (12:11) is that there is nothing besides sin in Gilead. *Gilead* represents all the country east of the Jordan, and *Gilgal* represents the land west of the Jordan. They both have sinned and sacrificed to Baal. And in both, God has shown forth His mercies.

Critical Observation

Hosea returns to the story of Jacob by citing incidents from Jacob's life in order to make a comparison between the patriarch and his descendants. Hosea compares Jacob's experience to the Exodus and to the ministry of the prophets. First, both Haran and Egypt are foreign lands that serve as places of refuge. Second, Jacob works like a slave for a ruthless master. In the same way, the Israelites are enslaved by Pharaoh. Just as God creates a situation in which Laban is eager to have Jacob leave (Genesis 31:1–14), God delivers Israel from the Egyptians, who are also ready to be rid of Israel after God afflicts Egypt with plagues. In both cases, the Israelites depart with the wealth of their hosts. The prophet who brings Israel out of Egypt and guards them through the wilderness is no doubt Moses (Hosea 12:12–13).

Yet, Ephraim has continually rebelled against the Lord. Hosea asserts that Ephraim has *provoked* God, a term that implies exasperating God through worshiping idols and placing one's heart away from God. These crimes are worthy of capital punishment. They will have to pay the penalty for this rebellion. Idol worship is the worst offense to God. God wants to be worshiped solely. Anything less is a provocation toward Him (12:14).

📖 13:1–16

GOD'S ANGER AGAINST ISRAEL

God continues to describe His people's unfaithfulness in terms of their idolatry. He recognizes that despite the consequences of their sin, they persist in it by making even more idols. He compares them to the morning mist, suggesting that rather than preserving them and making them a great nation as He promised to Abraham, they will surely pass away (13:1–3).

Israel is too proud to be saved, and the wrath of God is surely coming upon them. This is the culmination of Hosea's message of doom—and it describes the destruction of Israel in no uncertain and seemingly final terms. God recounts the many ways that He has been faithful in providing for and working out the Israelites' salvation—bringing them out of Egypt, caring for them in the desert, and feeding them (13:4–5).

Yet the Israelites grow proud and forget God. This is their deadly sin. Israel's chief problem is not idolatry—that is only an aftereffect. The people worship idols because they make no room for a God who deserves their loyalty and devotion. But the God of Abraham, Isaac, and Jacob demands that Israel acknowledge no one (not even Israel herself) but Him. For the nation to worship God, she would have to stop worshiping herself, and this she could not do (13:6).

God will not be mocked. The Lord had warned Israel that this would happen if she broke the covenant (Deuteronomy 6:10–12; 8:17–18). If we forget to be grateful to God for the blessings of our lives, He will take what He has given us "like a bear robbed of her cubs" (13:7–8).

The Lord solemnly makes the point and swears that Israel's boasting will be overturned, her cities in ruins, and her security gone. This is the tragedy of pride (13:9–16).

The God who gives can take away, and the God who gives and is not properly acknowledged promises to take away as part of His judgment upon dishonesty and ingratitude. This, then, is the Lord's warning through Hosea, His prophet: Pride is a hopeless illusion that will certainly be shattered (13:10–13).

Scholars disagree over the precise meaning of the ransom described by God. Some suggest that it points ahead to Christ paying the ransom for His people (13:14; see 1 Corinthians 15:55). However, in Hosea's context, those factors are in the future. Ultimately the Lord decides against paying the ransom, declaring that He will have no compassion. The images in the final verses of Hosea are truly ghastly—the people will bear their guilt, and even little ones and pregnant women will be subject to the violence (13:16).

HOSEA 14:1–9

BLESSING FROM REPENTANCE

Return to God	14:1–3
God's Response	14:4–9

Setting Up the Section

Following the total disaster and judgment described in the previous chapter, Hosea ends with the blessing and hope that his own story—of loving restoration of his unfaithful wife Gomer—parallels. Hosea's vision of Israel's restoration is partial.

📖 14:1–3

RETURN TO GOD

Hosea is still desperate to have Israel hear God's plea to return to Him. He reiterates the theme of the book—that their sins have been their downfall—and encourages them to turn to God in repentance (14:1–2). Hosea's last chapter is a reprise of a main theme of his preaching from the very beginning of the book: It is a call to repentance, an invitation to Israel to repent of her sins (14:2–3).

As Hosea has already declared, God demands sincerity of heart. Repentance is not merely the recognition of one's own sin. It will not be enough for Israel to recognize that she has disobeyed the Lord and betrayed His covenant. Even Pharaoh confessed that he had sinned in not letting Israel go from Egypt after the plague of hail. But he did not really repent. Repentance, as God requires it, is not merely sorrow and remorse for sin. Judas was so overcome by sorrow when the enormity of his betrayal of the Lord Jesus came home to him that he committed suicide, but he had no repentance.

Critical Observation

Repentance begins with a change of mind and heart about sin. Sin becomes not a thing to be loved but a thing to be abominated. In Psalm 51, David expresses the mind of every man or woman whom the Spirit of God has brought to a true repentance. Repentance wants nothing so much as to be right with God and to walk with God. Repentance is a turning away from sin to God for pardon and forgiveness. True repentance is always the fruit of a genuine faith in Christ, and it is called into being by the wonderful discovery that there is forgiveness with God. Indeed, there is no real repentance ever in the heart of a person who does not think that his sin can be removed and forgiven. Israel must believe that nothing besides God can save her (14:3). Repentance is a change of will and behavior—just as Israel denounces her sin, she also draws near to God, in whom the fatherless find compassion.

📖 **14:4–9**

GOD'S RESPONSE

Hosea declares that repentance is just the beginning of a great new adventure with God. God will heal Israel's waywardness and love them freely, and Israel will blossom like a flower (14:4–5). It is a beautiful picture to end a serious and solemn prophecy (14:6–8).

The final verse of Hosea is an editorial note, reminding the reader to take careful heed of the message of the book and repeating that message succinctly (14:9). The Lord Himself echoes Hosea's last word in John 15:5 when He says "Those who remain in me, and I in them, will produce much fruit" (NLT).

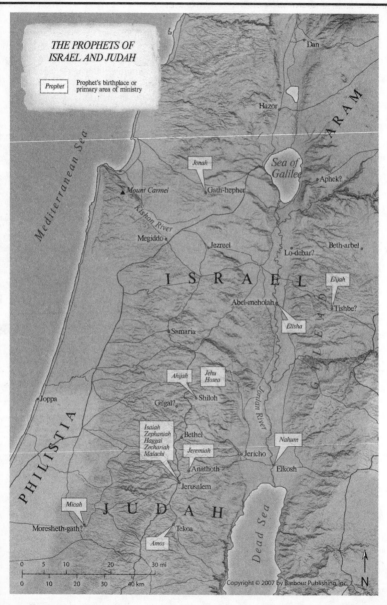

THE PROPHETS OF
ISRAEL AND JUDAH

Prophet — Prophet's birthplace or primary area of ministry

Dan

Hazor

Mediterranean Sea

Jonah

Gath-hepher

Sea of Galilee

Aphek?

ARAM

Mount Carmel

Kishon River

Megiddo

Jezreel

Lo-debar?

Beth-arbel

I S R A E L

Elijah

Abel-meholah

Elisha

Tishbe?

G I L E A D

Samaria

Ahijah

Jehu
Hosea

Gilgal?

Shiloh

Jordan River

Joppa

Isaiah
Zephaniah
Haggai
Zechariah
Malachi

Bethel

Jeremiah

Nahum

Anathoth

Jericho

Elkosh

P H I L I S T I A

Jerusalem

Micah

J U D A H

Dead Sea

Moresheth-gath?

Tekoa

Amos

| 0 | 5 | 10 | 20 | 30 mi |
| 0 | 10 | 20 | 30 | 40 km |

N

Copyright © 2007 by Barbour Publishing, Inc.

JOEL

INTRODUCTION TO JOEL

The book of Joel is an intriguing book, beginning with the fact that we know little about the author, his historical time frame, or even whether he was writing to the northern kingdom of Israel or the southern kingdom of Judah. We are left, then, with the words themselves—the brute force of the message of the divine author.

We may be unaware of the specifics of Joel's personal information or the audience to whom he writes, yet he delivers the message of God with boldness and clarity.

AUTHOR

Joel (meaning "Jehovah is God") is a popular name in the Old Testament, with a dozen other men bearing the same name. However, little is known about the prophet Joel.

PURPOSE

Joel writes in response to a devastating attack by locusts. But the destructive insects are described as an invading army, symbolizing the potentially greater destruction awaiting those who do not heed the words of the prophet and repent. Then, beyond the immediate situation in the land, Joel writes of the Day of the Lord, when judgment will come to the enemies of God's people and Israel will eventually be restored.

THEMES

The Day of the Lord—a time, known only to God, when He will exact judgment on the nations—is a key theme throughout Joel. The concept encompasses other related themes, including the need for repentance, the certainty of coming judgment, and eventual redemption and restoration for the people of God.

HISTORICAL CONTEXT

Without any references to specific events, it is difficult to put Joel's message into a specific historical context. Some people cite the enemies of Judah that are listed (Egypt, Edom, Philistia, and Phoenicia [3:4, 19]) and suggest an early, pre-exilic date for the book. But with no mention of the northern kingdom and a specific reference to Greece (3:6), others feel the book must have been written much later—and was perhaps the last of all the Old Testament prophetic books. So, proposed dates of writing can vary by as much as six or seven centuries.

CONTRIBUTION TO THE BIBLE

Perhaps the most well-known use of Joel's prophecies is on Peter's lips on the Day of Pentecost, when the Holy Spirit comes upon the church. Joel's insight into the fresh manner in which God's Spirit will interact with human beings is a tremendous contribution to scripture (2:28–32; Acts 2:14–21).

JOEL 1:1–2:11

DESTRUCTION: PRESENT AND FUTURE

The Present Destruction   1:1–12
The Future Destruction   1:13–2:11

Setting Up the Section

The terrible arrival of a swarm of locusts is the catalyst for Joel's writing. In his opening section, he responds to the great destruction, calling on the people to mourn. Such a sobering event should also remind them that an even worse time of suffering is in store for those who refuse to humble themselves before God.

📖 1:1–12

THE PRESENT DESTRUCTION

It may seem slightly disconcerting that the exact nature of the problem taking place in Joel is unclear, but the terrible situation is only going to get worse. Wave after wave of locusts have overrun the nation's crops (1:4), and that is in addition to a drought (1:10–12).

For a nation characterized as drunkards (1:5), the loss of the grape harvest is particularly disheartening. Along with the failure of all the other crops (wheat, barley, fig, pomegranate, apple, and so forth), the situation is indeed dire. A disaster of this magnitude had not been witnessed by recent generations (1:2–3). The locusts are described as a lion-like nation with such numbers that they cannot be counted, invading without mercy (1:6–7).

Demystifying Joel

It is rather common in scripture (as well as in other ancient literature) to read of invading armies described as swarms of locusts. In Joel's case, it appears he has reversed the imagery. He describes a literal invasion of locusts in terms of a human army attacking (1:6–7). As far as the effects on an agrarian society, locusts could be every bit as merciless and cruel as enemy soldiers.

Joel addresses the elders of the nation (1:2) because they should have borne a special responsibility to clothe themselves with humility before God and seek His mercy on behalf of the people. Yet they are the ones who have allowed the spiritual state of the nation to decline, so they probably feel the effects of the crisis just as much as anyone. All the priests can do is mourn; the daily grain and drink offerings have been suspended during the crop failure and drought (1:8–9). All previous sources of joy have withered away (1:12).

📖 **1:13–2:11**

THE FUTURE DESTRUCTION

Joel exhorts the priests to demonstrate appropriate behavior, considering the situation they are in. They are to dress for mourning—in dark, rough sackcloth rather than their usual clothing. Instead of offering their usual prayers, they are to wail (1:13). Then they are to prepare the people: Declare a fast and call an assembly. The nation as a whole is to cry out to God together (1:14). Joel will soon clarify that it isn't the actions being taken that will appease the wrath of God but rather the proper attitudes by the people (2:12–13).

He describes a future destruction that he identifies as "the day of the Lord" (1:15), which he says is approaching. Joel will use this phrase several times in his short book, as do numerous other prophets. It refers to a time, known only to God, when He will exact judgment on the nations. The event will trigger much great suffering, although the end result will be the deliverance and restoration of those who remain faithful. The precise timing of that day remains a mystery. But as the people begin to attempt to cope with the devastation resulting from the locusts, their fear and confusion should put them in a somber state to ponder the severity of the Day of the Lord.

Critical Observation

The Hebrew words for *almighty* and *destruction* sound quite similar, so Joel's statement in verse 15 has added impact. Specific historic events are associated with the Day of the Lord, including Israel's fall to Assyria and Babylon's subsequent conquest of Judah.

This is a time for the people of God to come before Him with the truth. It is a time to speak to Him about their trials and to acknowledge Him as the only One who can ever provide food, shelter, safety, and joy. Such an acknowledgment should occur *before* disaster strikes, but even in the depths of their despair, God's people can call on Him for help. No such help can be found from any other source (1:16–20).

When Joel writes of *fire* (1:19–20), it is probably used as a metaphor. Perhaps the locusts are portrayed as a fire that devours all the nation's crops. Or maybe he intends to acknowledge the accompanying drought. In the heat of the Middle East, when water is short, it doesn't take long for the land to dry out and become unable to sustain plant growth—essentially the same result as fire.

Scholars are divided as to what Joel really means when he warns about the Day of the Lord and the invading army. Some believe that he continues using the army metaphor to describe actual locusts. Others think that as he begins to say more about the Day of the Lord, he speaks of a conflict involving human armies. If that is the case, the shift is subtle as his description of insect devastation in chapter 1 sets up the image of an even worse catastrophe to follow.

Either way, the coming event is in relation to the Day of the Lord. It will be a day of darkness, gloom, clouds, and blackness, and it will involve the encroachment of the largest army ever seen. At first it will be the sheer size that is noticeable: The army will appear "like dawn spreading across the mountains" (2:1–2 NIV). Only later will people realize, as Joel reveals, that this is the Lord's army with forces "beyond number" (2:11 NIV).

Demystifying Joel

Even for those who want to understand this army as a continuation of Joel's description of literal locusts, it is fair to consider it the Lord's army. Just as other prophets explain that the Assyrian and Babylonian armies had acted to fulfill the will of God, so, too, will this army of locusts.

The analogy to locusts is a fitting one. The land will lie beautiful and plush, so much so that it is compared to the Garden of Eden, but by the time the army has passed through, all that will be left is a desert wasteland. Again, a comparison to fire is appropriate to describe utter loss (2:3).

The appearance of this army will stun those who see it. The noise and destruction will dishearten all observers. Nothing can be done to stop its progress. It is described as marching straight ahead, plunging through defenses, scaling walls, and even entering private homes. The impact of the aggression will shake the earth. In response, entire nations will be in anguish and become pale with fear (2:4–11).

In this sense, the Day of the Lord will indeed be "dreadful" (2:11 NIV). And Joel's question ("Who can endure it?") must have seemed unanswerable to those hearing his description of things to come. Thankfully, Joel doesn't stop here. He provides an answer in the following section.

JOEL 2:12–32

SURVIVING THE DESTRUCTION

Setting Up the Section

After a rather distressing section pertaining to a current plague of locusts and an even worse similar scourge to come, in this section Joel at last offers some hope to the readers and listeners. Yes, the coming Day of the Lord will be dreadful, but there are things the people can do to avoid its potentially terrifying consequences.

📖 **2:12–17**

A CALL TO RETURN TO THE LORD

When the Day of the Lord arrives, there is nothing people can do to stop God's judgment. However, it is never too late for *God* to act. Speaking through His prophet, God provides a note of hope for those remaining in a situation that appears completely hopeless. He invites the wayward people to return to Him "even now" (2:12). However, such a return will accomplish nothing if it is based on hypocrisy or empty ceremony. God knows the hearts of people and sees through insincerity.

The people are called to return to God with all their hearts—weeping, fasting, and mourning. However, God cares little for their outward expressions of sorrow, per se. He is more intent on seeing humbled hearts than torn clothing. And God reminds His people that He is gracious, compassionate, slow to anger, and abounding in love. He doesn't *want* to send calamity on those who claim to be His people. Perhaps He will put off their impending doom (2:12–14).

In addition, the people are told to gather in a sacred assembly that should take priority over everything else. Nursing children are to attend, as are newlyweds. The priests can then intercede for the people (as should have been their role all along). The people will be reminded that their prior refusal to act as if they belonged to God has left surrounding nations with the wrong impression. When God disciplines His people for their defiant behavior, outside observers will see the consequences and perceive the Lord's corrective judgment as His absence. They will doubt the power and the concern of Israel's God, and they will scoff at His people (2:15–17).

📖 **2:18–27**

THE SHORT-TERM RESULT

Joel calls the people to repent—young and old, priest and populace. In return, the Lord promises to respond dramatically and bountifully. He will hear their cries and take pity on His people who have no other recourse than His mercy. He will bless their land far beyond their expectations, including ample new grain, wine, and oil. He will protect them from foreign threats. Rather than Israel being an object of scorn, it will be the other nations who falter and fall (2:18–20).

Critical Observation

The locust invasion previously described by Joel gives more impact to what he writes here about the smell arising from a retreating army (2:20). Historic accounts tell of enormous locust swarms that flew out to sea, drowned, washed up on shore, and created a terrible stench.

God will replace His people's fear with gladness and rejoicing. He will send rain and make the ground fruitful again. He will restore what the locust horde had destroyed, promising that the people will eat plentifully and be satisfied. Here, as in other places throughout scripture, rain is perceived as the blessing of God (2:21–24).

As terrible as the losses had been that resulted from the locusts, the land will recover and the people will be able to eat their fill. In return, they will praise the Lord and have a greater awareness that only He is truly God (2:25–27).

In spite of the people's previous sins, God will temper His judgment with mercy and compassion. His people will not be destroyed. It is terrific news for those who appeared to be doomed. Yet even better news is promised for the future.

📖 2:28–32

THE LONG-RANGE RESULT

The date of these future events is left a mystery. God's promise of the future will come "afterward" (2:28). As it turns out, some of Joel's prophecy from this section will be remembered and applied in connection with the arrival of the Holy Spirit on Jesus' followers shortly after the Lord's death and resurrection (Acts 2:14–21).

God speaks through His prophet of a great day to come, when His Spirit will pour out—not just upon Israel but also on all faithful believers (Joel 2:28). The power of God will be felt by young and old, men and women. God's plan will be known through dreams, visions, and prophecies (2:28–29). When that day arrives, the effect will be so dramatic that onlookers will presume the recipients of God's Spirit are drunk (Acts 2:13).

Demystifying Joel

When Joel 2 is quoted by Peter (Acts 2:17–21) and Paul (Romans 10:13), it becomes clear that the ultimate fulfillment of the prophecy will be a *heavenly* Jerusalem and Mount Zion. And from the New Testament perspective, another important detail is drawn out of the shadows and brought into clear light: The Lord Jesus Christ is the Son of God who died on the cross for sinners and rose again. He is the Lord of the resurrection. It is His name people must own in order to receive the fullness of salvation that comes by the grace of their merciful God.

Yet that time will also include a sense of foreboding of the coming judgment. The Day of the Lord will include the greatest of blessings for some, but it will also involve an unspeakably frightening curse for others. It will be reminiscent of the destruction of Pharaoh and his armies during the time of the exodus of God's people from Egypt. Joel provides few specifics, yet he includes hints of blood, fire, and billows of smoke (2:30). The light of the sun and moon will be affected, perhaps from the great conflict to take place. The coming of the Day of the Lord will be great for some and dreadful for others (2:31).

Yet God will ensure that those who call on His name are delivered. It will be a terrible time, but there will certainly be survivors. God is both Judge and Savior, and His justice will prevail (2:32).

Take It Home

Joel looks ahead to the Day of the Lord. How do you feel as you contemplate a day that will involve dread and judgment for some? If you remained more aware of a coming day when God will deliver those who remain faithful to Him, how might it affect your day-to-day life?

JOEL 3:1–21

THE COMING JUDGMENT

Setting Up the Section

Up to this point, Joel has primarily dealt with God's message to His own people. In this section, after God has just promised redemption and restoration of Israel, the Lord turns His attention to the judgment of other nations that have treated His people badly throughout history. Their relentless cruelty has not been overlooked. Their judgment will be harsh indeed, and although Israel had been guilty of much wrongdoing in the past, they will experience God's great forgiveness.

📖 3:1–16

GATHERING THE NATIONS

Joel continues to peer into the future as he relates God's message. The still-to-come Day of the Lord looms ahead, and God continues to describe what will happen in those days (3:1). It will include a restoration of Judah, Jerusalem, and Israel (3:1–2), and the prophet will soon go into detail about what such a recovery will entail (3:17–21). But first God will address the offenses of other nations.

The nations are to be *gathered* in a sense that sounds much like a summons to appear in court. The charges against them are quite severe. For one thing, they have ransacked the wealth of Israel (3:5). They are also guilty of scattering God's people throughout the various lands of the time. And while it is true that they were acting under the auspices of God's control, they treated their captives horribly. The remaining specific charges that are included in the narrative are some of the worst imaginable offenses, with human trafficking and child prostitution among them (3:3).

The Valley of Jehoshaphat (3:2, 12) has never been identified as a specific geographic location, in the past or present. However, the precise location is not as important as the name itself. *Jehoshaphat* means "the Lord judges." It matters little where the judging is taking place; what matters is that the time has come for justice to be exacted against those who had long persecuted God's people.

Demystifying Joel

The specific nations and offenses listed (3:4–6) present some challenges to determining the time of Joel's writing. The Philistines are among the earlier enemies of Israel, yet the reference to scattering the people points some scholars to the Babylonian captivity (3:2, 4). At that time, the temple treasury was plundered (2 Kings 25:8–17), although neither the Philistines nor Phoenicians (Tyre and Sidon) were involved. Some believe that this is a case where perhaps a number of Israel's persistent enemies are listed to represent *all* of the persecutors of God's people throughout their history.

The various nations committed numerous offenses against Israel and Judah during times when God's people had forsaken the Lord and were vulnerable. Israel's enemies presume they have gotten away with their despicable behavior, but God continues to hold them responsible for what had been done. The insulting treatment of God's people is a transgression against God. It had been God's silver and gold that was stolen. It had been God's people who were sold for wine and thrust into prostitution (3:2–6).

It will appear for a time that Israel and Judah are no more, with their populations removed and deported to faraway countries. But God will then reverse the harm that had been done. He will recall His people from the various places to which they have been sold, and He will return on them what they had done to Israel and Judah. Judah's enemies will see how it feels to witness their children sold to distant lands (3:7–8). (This prophecy comes true soon thereafter, as the Greek Empire begins to spread and various countries find themselves subjugated and/or enslaved.)

Just as God had promised to rouse His people from among the nations, Joel tells the nations to rouse their warriors. If they are going to be foolish enough to oppose the Lord of Israel, they may as well prepare for it. Their tools for everyday living ("plowshares" and "pruning hooks") should be converted into weapons of war ("swords" and "spears"). They should join forces and assemble (3:9–11).

But they will be marching toward their judgment. The gathering place will be the Valley of Jehoshaphat, where God will sit and judge their great wickedness. They will come forth in all their pride and power, but they will be approaching their own destruction.

Those who defiantly oppose God will not long stand. They will meet utter defeat. The comparisons are made to swinging a sickle and trampling grapes—two common actions the people of that time are familiar with. Just as wheat falls before a reaper's scythe, so will the enemies of Israel fall. Just as grapes are trodden on to fill the winepress with juice, so will flow the blood of those hostile peoples (3:12–13).

Critical Observation

The apostle John uses similar imagery in his apocalyptic vision recorded in Revelation. There, too, God's judgment is compared to both reaping and trampling on grapes (Revelation 14:14–20).

God's judgment of the nations is connected with the Day of the Lord, and afterward the Valley of Jehoshaphat [God's judgment] will become the "valley of decision" (3:14). Again, this event is said to be accompanied by great signs in the skies—a darkening of the sun, moon, and stars (2:10; 3:15)—and a shaking of the earth (2:10; 3:16).

As terrible as the Day of the Lord will appear to those who oppose God, people who turn to Him will find surprising security. God will be a refuge and stronghold for those who remain faithful (3:16).

📄 3:17–21

JERUSALEM RESTORED

Numerous prophets had made it clear that because of the persistent sins of the people, God will allow Jerusalem to fall to the Babylonians. Yet here, even after the city had fallen and the people had been dispersed to various lands, God will still rule from Jerusalem and Zion. The earth is still the Lord's. Nothing has been ultimately lost (3:16–17).

Joel's closing description portrays such a positive outlook for Jerusalem that it must be a reference to a yet-future time. Certainly, Jerusalem has not yet experienced a period where it could be said that foreigners will never again invade her (3:17). But someday the city will truly be holy—set apart for the glory of God. Joel's description anticipates Revelation 21–22 and the description of the New Jerusalem.

The surrounding land will also undergo a wonderful transformation. In a lush contrast to the opening description of the territory in the wake of the locust infestation, Joel foresees a time when "mountains will drip with sweet wine, and the hills will flow with milk" (3:18 NLT). While other sources refer to Canaan as a land of milk and honey, Joel provides a distinctive descriptive pairing of wine and milk. Vineyards were frequently planted on hillsides, so the description is appropriate. The addition of milk suggests abundant herds, readily sustained by the water that will never again be in short supply (3:18). In fact, the water will be associated with the presence of God—a fountain flows out of the temple to water the land.

Critical Observation

Acacias (3:18) tend to grow in arid desert areas where not much else survives. The picture of their being well watered suggests a wilderness being refreshed and capable of sustaining new life.

In contrast, those who remain hostile toward God and His people (symbolized by Israel's persistent enemies, Egypt and Edom) will lack water and life. They who had shed innocent blood will be left a desolate, desert wasteland (3:19). But Judah will be forgiven of their past sins, and God's presence will be with His people forever (3:20–21).

When the Day of the Lord arrives, one age will end and another, eternal one will begin. The Lord's coming will overwhelm the current created order and, by the plan and power of God, there will be a new heaven and a new earth fit for a renewed population of resurrected bodies. For the new Israel, the age of discipline will finally yield to the age of perfect delight.

Take It Home

In the New Testament, Paul teaches that, "in [God] we live and move and exist" (Acts 17:28 NLT). People have spent centuries attempting to understand the biology, chemistry, astronomy, and physics of creation. Yet God is bigger than everything the scientists, astronomers, and cartographers can comprehend. When people complete their lives, they still have an existence in God. God's sovereignty is not limited by what people understand to be physical realities. As you reflect on Joel's prophecies, how do you respond to the fact that no matter how grave the judgment of God will be upon the sins of some, those who place their faith in Him can count on full pardon and eternal life?

AMOS

INTRODUCTION TO AMOS

The prophet Amos was a contemporary of Old Testament prophets Hosea and Isaiah. He stood for justice in an era of Israel's history in which the nation was politically strong but spiritually weak.

AUTHOR

The first verse of this book attributes the writing to a man named Amos. Though his prophecy is directed to Israel, the northern kingdom, Amos himself is from Tekoa, a town in Judah, five miles south of Bethlehem. His work as a shepherd and gardener implies he belongs to the working class until the Lord commissions him to be one of His prophets.

PURPOSE

Amos's prophecy condemns the powerful, self-satisfied, wealthy upper class that had developed in Samaria, the capital of Israel.

OCCASION

Amos's ministry falls in the first half of the eighth century BC, during the last half of the reign of Jeroboam II (793–753 BC). Israel is enjoying a measure of domestic affluence and international power that she has not known since the reign of Solomon. Israel and Judah have expanded to the point that they nearly encompass all the land that David and Solomon controlled two centuries before. It is a time of military conquest and economic prosperity. It is also a time of moral darkness.

THEMES

Themes in the prophecy of Amos include God's sovereign power, the covenant agreement between God and Israel, and the day of the Lord's judgment.

AMOS 1:1–2:3

THE COMING LION

Setting Up the Section

The opening section of Amos is a series of oracles of judgment pronounced against Israel's neighbors: Syria (Aram), Philistia, Tyre (a city in Phoenicia), and so on. In each case, these nations are condemned not for their false religion and worship but for their various crimes against humanity. They have violated principles of morality that are universally recognized by human beings. But Amos does not preach these oracles to these nations themselves. They are rather part of Amos's sermon against Israel—Israel being, as we learn in 1:1, the focus of Amos's preaching and prophecy. The point of these oracles of judgment is that if these foreign nations cannot escape God's wrath on account of their sins, Israel most assuredly will not escape it for her similar sins.

The six nations listed in the first two chapters are the principal nations bordering on Israel, and they are the world as Israel encountered it. Syria (Aram, see 1:3–5), Philistia (1:6–8), and Tyre (1:9–10) are simply Israel's neighbors; Edom (1:11–12), Ammon (1:13–15), and Moab (2:1–3) share ancestry with Israel; and Judah (2:4–5) was once one nation with Israel.

Demystifying Amos

Uzziah was king of Judah between 791 and 740 BC. Jeroboam II (not the first Jeroboam, who was the very first king of Israel after the division of the kingdom after the death of Solomon) was king of Israel from 793–753 BC. Jeroboam II is also known as Jeroboam the Great. Apparently what we have in the book of Amos is the preaching of the prophet over a comparatively short period of time, hence the "two years before the earthquake" (1:1). That earthquake must have been very powerful, for it left its mark on Israel's history. There is mention of it again hundreds of years later in Zechariah 14:5.

Amos 1:1 reveals that even though Israel is in a time of prosperity, God's prophet knows Jeroboam's kingdom is not far from total extinction after his death. Verse 2 mentions a roar thundering from Jerusalem. This roar from Jerusalem is probably of a lion about to pounce, ready to lunge at its victim, Israel. Israel has voluntarily cut herself off from the temple in Jerusalem and its worship, but that is where the Lord's presence is represented. Part of what the Lord holds against Samaria, the capital of Israel, is the sanctuaries they have built rather than attending the temple in Jerusalem.

The recurring phrase regarding not just three sins but four is a reminder of the Lord's mercy and patience. Punishment does not happen because of the first sin, or the second, or the third. There are multiple opportunities for repentance before judgment falls (1:3).

Notice that God condemns the nations not for their false worship or religious practices but for their violations of the obligations they owe to other human beings—in Syria's case, her barbarity and inhumanity in war.

Demystifying Amos

Gaza, mentioned in verse 6, is representative of Philistia. Gaza is one of Philistia's chief cities and is accused of brutality.

In verse 9, Tyre is accused of slave trading, but the sin for which she is to be destroyed is her violation of covenant she made with another nation, apparently Israel. This is significant because it reveals a second similarity with Edom, who is also condemned for violations of brotherhood (1:11).

Edom has already been implicated in slave trading (1:6, 9), but the fourth sin for which God is angry is like Tyre's: a violation of family bonds. Edom is indeed Israel's brother, descended from Esau as Israel is from Jacob, and Isaac is the grandfather of both. But Edom has long harbored animosity toward Israel. The cities of Edom (1:12)—Teman to the south and Bozrah to the north—are mentioned to make the point that the entire country will suffer God's wrath, from top to bottom.

The last two nations, Ammon and Moab, are condemned for atrocities committed against the most vulnerable, fragile, and helpless of human beings: pregnant women and their unborn children in the first case and dead bodies in the second. And the Ammonites did this for temporal advantage, to enlarge their borders. They stepped on the weak to advantage themselves (1:13–2:3). In verse 14, Rabbah, Ammon's only significant city, receives the threat of destruction at the hand of Assyria.

The first three verses of chapter 2 complete Amos's prophecy against the surrounding nations. Moab and Edom hate each other, and evidence of this is the disrespect for dead bodies described in 2:1. The idea may have been to prevent the king's body from being resurrected.

The harsh, brutal reality of human sin that results in these kinds of cruelty—slavery, war, desecration of bodies—lies at the base of Amos's charge against these nations and the threat of divine wrath.

AMOS 2:4-16

THE PATH TO APOSTASY

Setting Up the Section

The two oracles of judgment in chapter 2—against Judah and Israel—show the progress of apostasy. Things are not as bad in Judah during Amos's ministry as they are in Israel, but eventually Judah will be guilty of all the sins that Amos accuses Israel of in verses 6–12.

At best, relations between the divided kingdoms—Israel to the north and Judah to the south—took the form of a peaceful coexistence. But more often, the two kingdoms interacted with outright hostility and sometimes war. Amos's Israelite audience would have enjoyed his message thus far. They would have been glad to hear of the Lord's judgments to befall their surrounding enemies and glad to learn that Judah is going to suffer.

While the six nations in the first section are condemned for crimes against humanity, Judah is condemned for a failure to obey God's law as revealed by Moses and the prophets. The *law*, as it is used here, means much more than simply commandments or rules—it means instruction from God about the life He has called His people to live (2:4).

The remaining verses of chapter 2 describe Israel as guilty of the same crimes against humanity that the pagan nations around her have been accused of.

Israel has blatantly disobeyed the commandments of God's Word, involving herself in incestuous and promiscuous sexual relations, especially, no doubt, in regard to fertility rites at the temples and shrines. Amos represents Israel as deliberately throwing off the claims of the Lord.

In verse 8, the garments "taken in pledge" (or as collateral for a debt), according to God's law, are to be returned at night to the debtor (Exodus 22:26–27). According to this description, however, the Israelites do not return these garments but instead use them at altars, making their religious life the context for their disobedience. Moreover, fines are to be according to the Law of Moses, a vehicle for making restitution, not for enriching the wealthy, who are drinking them up in orgies at their sanctuaries.

The Amorites, mentioned in verse 9, are inhabitants of the region before it became known as Canaan.

In verses 10–12, Israel's sins are against God's goodness. He has done so much for them, and they are repaying Him with selfish indifference to His will. God has spoken to His people through His prophets and used the plight of Nazirites, who consecrated themselves only to God.

Verse 12 twists the oracle from what God has done for His people to the way in which they have repaid His goodness. That which God has provided, Israel has ignored or disobeyed. Nazirites vow not to drink wine, yet the Israelites force them to do it in an act of cruel blasphemy. Or perhaps, more likely, this statement is to be taken metaphorically to describe Israel's utter indifference to the spiritual challenge and example of such godly people.

Critical Observation

In both Judah and Israel, the mistreatment of God's revelation is the first cause of the disaster that is about to befall them both. Judah receives the truth from God but chooses instead the traditions of culture. And what is true to a degree in Judah is entirely true in Israel.

Verses 13–16 describe God's wrath as inescapable, regardless of anyone's earthly wealth, power, or talent. As before, with the other nations, God's judgment will come in the form of an attack by a stronger nation. This will prove to be Assyria, of course, just a few decades later. The Assyrian's theory of conquest is the complete devastation of a nation, the depopulation of its territory, and the terrorization of its remnants.

Take It Home

Amos's prophecy raises the issue of how much the people of God incorporate the practices of the culture around them. This issue is still relevant for the church today, with people of faith landing on both sides of the balance. How much is our faith affected by the cultural customs we incorporate?

AMOS 3:1–15

WITHIN BUT WITHOUT

Setting Up the Section

In this section, the indictment that Amos has drawn up against Israel in 2:6–16 is expanded, clarified, and proved. Israel believes she, as Yahweh's people, was delivered from bondage in Egypt on eagles' wings, but her rebellion, disobedience, and unbelief render her the object of God's wrath, not His care and protection.

The opening words of chapter 3 are repeated in 4:1, 5:1, and 8:4. Amos speaks to Israel as one nation, though the nation has long ago been divided and its people have been addressed separately already in this prophecy. The verses following will make it clear, however, that Israel, the northern kingdom, is chiefly in Amos's view.

In some translations of verse 2, God claims that Israel is the only nation He has *known*. In others, the word *chosen* is used. Either word points out the covenant relationship God has with these people.

The questions in verses 3–6 make a point. In verses 4–5, the coming of God's judgment is certain. Just as nature moves when it has purpose and need, so will God's justice move on His people. Verse 6 refers to the blowing of a trumpet, a ram's horn, which would have been familiar to the people of Amos's day. While the preceding questions rhetorically point to a "no" answer, the questions in verse 6 point to a "yes" answer. Perhaps the last question makes the main point—these people are not expecting disaster and do not see themselves in Amos's question.

With verse 7, Amos switches from rhetorical questions to direct statements. Yahweh not only does bring disaster upon the unrighteous, but He communicates His intention to do so through His prophets. Just as one pays attention when a lion roars, so the Lord's prophet cannot ignore or fail to deliver His Word (3:8).

The pagan nations around Israel, mentioned in chapter 1, are invited to observe Israel's life to see whether the sins of Samaria deserve God's judgment (3:9–10). The point here is that Israel's sins are so egregious that even the wicked nations around her will stand in judgment of her.

The picture painted in verse 11 is that Israel's strongholds and fortresses—the things she has trusted for protection—will prove little obstacle to the Assyrians. Neither will Israel's wealth be her protection. According to verse 12, the wealthy in Samaria, who indulge themselves on fine and comfortable furniture, will be swept away. Only a few will survive.

Demystifying Amos

Verse 13 introduces a new oracle. It is directed to Israel, referring to the nation as the *house of Jacob*. Jacob was the son of Isaac, grandson of Abraham. He had twelve sons, and the tribes of Israel were tracked according to each son. In referring to Israel this way, the heritage of the nation is brought to mind, including their covenant of obedience to God.

Verses 14–15 combine the image of Bethel, a name which means "house of God," with a variety of other houses. When the house of God falls, no house remains. Israel's great houses are monuments to her corruption and her ill-gotten wealth.

AMOS 4:1–13

THE POINT OF NO RETURN

Setting Up the Section

Chapter 4 begins a new indictment against Israel that opens with a call to the upper-class women.

Bashan was known for the size and quality of its livestock (Deuteronomy 32:14; Psalm 22:12). In Amos 4:1, the women are likened to animals fattening themselves on rich pasture. They live their lives for pleasure, yet the poor remain oppressed. They make demands of their husbands for the household service they should be providing.

There are a variety of opinions about the meaning of the hooks in verse 2. What is certain is that the reference is to the women of Israel being humiliated by their enemies.

We do not know the location of Harmon, mentioned in verse 3. Some have supposed it to be a dump where the women's bodies will be thrown after their deaths. Other translations simply refer to it as a fortress or palace. In either case, the breaks in the walls are an important element of the description. What should have protected these women becomes simply a portal through which they are undone.

In verse 4, Amos taunts the Israelites by saying that all they are accomplishing with their worship is the multiplying of their sins and the deepening of their judgment. He exaggerates their practices as if they are doing almost nothing but making pilgrimages to Bethel and Gilgal. The implicit question becomes: What good is all of this doing?

The description in verse 5 reveals the unbelief and self-absorption of these people. Their inappropriate worship—freewill offerings are to be private, yet they brag about them—makes matters worse, not better. This theme of inauthentic ritual is strong with Old Testament prophets.

Verse 6 begins a new section that continues through verse 11, marked by the first-person pronoun *I* and the refrain that the people have not returned to God even with all He has done to draw them back. There is a deliberate contrast between what Yahweh has done and what Israel is doing. Israel has been busy rebelling against the Lord; the Lord has been busy seeking to bring her to repentance.

All of the catastrophes listed in this section have been signs of God's wrath, and Israel has ignored them all. According to verses 12–13, the God whose justice and judgment Israel must now face is the sovereign Lord who controls nature. She cannot withstand the Lord when He comes against her in judgment.

Take It Home

Amos is particularly difficult for the modern reader. Like Israel in the eighth century BC, we are a prosperous people. Also, in our scientific age, we are much less likely to connect events in the world with the action of the Almighty. But every Bible reader, sooner or later, has to decide how to understand that God is both merciful and wrathful.

AMOS 5:1–27

REPENTANCE AND THE DAY OF THE LORD

Setting Up the Section

This book begins by condemning the nations that surround Israel for their sins and with a promise of God's judgment. If these other nations will not escape God's wrath, how much more judgment must Israel face, a nation who has sinned against God's grace? Chapter 5 is an eloquent plea addressed to the nation of Israel, in hopes that at least some of her people will hear it and respond.

The poetry of verses 1–3 follows the form of a Hebrew funeral dirge. At this time, Israel is at the height of her prosperity under Jeroboam II. Like the virgin mentioned in verse 2, it seems that Israel's best days are ahead. But verse 3 reveals that her military strength will be wrecked and her soldiers slaughtered in battle.

Instead of empty rituals, God wants His people to seek Him (5:4–5). Bethel, Gilgal, and Beersheba are important sites in Israel's history. Apparently all three cities held shrines to which Israelites made faithful pilgrimages—even Beersheba, which lay at the southern-most end of Judah. But the people had been commanded to go to Jerusalem to worship. Amos is once again pointing out the futility of Israel's religious practices. Her people worship, but instead of following God's guidelines, they make their own rules. They offer worship that offends the Lord rather than pleases Him.

The "house of Joseph," mentioned in verse 6, is a reference to the northern kingdom of Israel. Regions were often identified by their principal tribe. In this case, that tribe is Ephraim, made up of the descendants of one of Joseph's sons.

Verses 7–11 have a unique structure. Verse 7 characterizes Israelite life as unjust and unrighteous, something that Amos has already established. Verses 8–9 function as a kind of doxology. The verses describe God in terms of His power and majesty. He alone can save Israel from the disaster that looms. Then, the characterization that began in verse 7 continues in verses 10–11. By the middle of verse 11, the announcement of judgment begins.

Verses 12–13 reveal that, in essence, the religion of the Israelites does not touch their lifestyles; they are heedless of the claims of justice and God's law. Verses 14–15 state what the people need to do if they indeed want to be the people of God they claim to be. The last half of verse 14 reveals the state of mind of the Israelite people— they mistakenly believe God to be on their side, even while they are disconnected from their true spiritual state.

Take It Home

Amos 5:14–15 has great application for us in that it offers a clear account of what God requires of His people.

If the people do not turn back to their God, the destruction will be so great that farmers will have to be summoned to wail because there will not be enough professional mourners to go around (5:16). Yahweh will pass through Israel as her destroyer, reminiscent of the angel of death passing through Egypt long before (5:17).

Verses 18–20 include the earliest recorded use of the expression *Day of the Lord*. It will occur many more times in the prophets of the Old Testament and again in the New Testament. But clearly, it is already a familiar phrase by this time as a religious figure of speech. Because of their disconnection from God's view of their spiritual state, the Israelites think that the Day of the Lord will bring happiness and triumph to them when, in fact, it will bring disaster.

Amos has already said that the Lord won't accept Israel's sacrifices. However, in verses 21–24, he says the Lord won't accept Israel's praise, either. This continues the theme in Amos that God is looking for meaningful relationships with His people, not empty worship. Because the people have refused to hear this message, God indicates that it is time for His justice to flow as naturally, strongly, and completely as water flows down a mountain.

Verse 25 can be seen as a rhetorical question, in which case the assumed answer is no. We don't know if the people neglect to offer sacrifices on their journey because they are disobedient or because the rituals of sacrifice are not implemented yet.

The prophet continues making the point that Israel's sacrifices are disconnected from her faith relationship with God (5:25–26). The people of Israel seem to think that as long as they offer Yahweh sacrifices, all will be well, no matter their obedience in other areas of life. Amos is reminding them that their own history is the disproof of that idea.

Verse 27 refers to a place beyond Damascus, which is Assyria. Assyria does eventually defeat the northern kingdom of Israel.

AMOS 6:1–14

A HARD TRUTH

Setting Up the Section

Amos continues to focus on the northern kingdom in this section. The influential and the rich who live and work in the capital cities are the target of Amos's condemnation. Both their complacency and their coming judgment are described.

As he has done before, Amos, at the opening of chapter 6, presents Israel as serenely confident of God's approval without good reason to be so confident. Zion, a synonym for the capital city of Judah, seems to be a reference to the whole southern kingdom. Samaria, capital city of the northern kingdom, is used in the same way to represent the whole kingdom of Israel.

The cities mentioned in verse 2 may have fallen during Amos's lifetime or before. Either way, he lifts these cities up as a reality check to Israel, that trusting in her own supremacy may be a futile effort. Amos accuses his nation of bringing a "reign of terror" by its disobedience (6:3 NIV).

Verses 4–8 describe the affluence of the wealthy in Israel. The average Israelite may have eaten meat only three times a year, the poor even less. Only the rich can afford to spend time playing and listening to music. The reference to David suggests that the people think of themselves and live as if they are kings. And they drink so much wine that they don't bother to pour it first into cups; they take it straight from the bottle. The anointing of the body was common in the ancient Near East, especially after bathing. It soothed the skin and served as a protection against both heat and lice. The rich added expensive spices and perfumes to the oil. The wealthy who have prospered the most in their rebellion against the Lord will be the first to suffer the Assyrian wrath. That is always the conqueror's way, of course: Cut off the head, and the body will fall easily enough. What God wants His people to also notice, though, is how the body—the innocent and the poor—suffers the consequences of the head's actions and choices.

Israel's military self-confidence will be turned into a cruel joke. The picture in verses 9–10 is that of ten men who have survived the terrors of the siege so far and are found taking refuge together in a single home—probably a large home. This is a picture of the wealthy of Samaria, but even these will die, probably of disease, a feature of siege warfare, as suggested in verse 10. The few remaining survivors hope that Yahweh will consider the judgment sufficient and, if they keep a low profile, perhaps He will not bring upon them any further punishment. But according to verse 11, their defeat is certain.

Two supremely unnatural and absurd activities—running horses up cliffs or plowing the rocks (or the sea; either reading is possible) with oxen—serve as analogies to point out how preposterous and unreasonable Israel's behavior has been (6:12–13). Defying the Lord successfully is just that impossible. To deal with it, God sends brutal conquest by another power (6:14). At this moment, during Jeroboam's reign, the other nations of the region are relatively impotent, including Egypt and Assyria. In that vacuum, Israel's power seems impressive. All of that will change quickly. Lebo Hamath, mentioned in verse 14, is Israel's northernmost boundary and Arabah her southernmost. So the description is one of total defeat.

Take It Home

What honest Christian cannot find himself or herself in Amos's words? How many times have we found ceremony replacing godliness in our own lives? How many times have we caught ourselves going through motions in respect to our faith and the things of God?

AMOS 7:1-17

THE CONTEST FOR THE TRUTH IN THE CHURCH

Setting Up the Section

While the prophecy thus far has included accusations and condemnations, this chapter marks a change. Here, Amos begins to describe a series of visions. Much of the rest of his prophecy will follow this same form.

Each of Amos's visions opens in the same way—attributing his vision to the Lord. Locusts represent an unstoppable agricultural disaster in the ancient world. In this first vision, this swarm of locusts is to fall at a difficult time in harvest, destroying the fruit of the second planting (7:1). This is the part of the harvest that is reserved for the farmers themselves. Without it, neither they nor their livestock will have food to carry them over to the next harvest.

In verses 2–3, God is described as relenting. This is not the first time in scripture the picture is painted of God desisting from a planned course of events in response to human appeal. Moses interceded for Israel when Yahweh threatened to destroy His people (Exodus 32:9–14). Here Amos is the intercessor, and as a result of his intercession, there will be no swarm of locusts (Amos 7:2–3).

Critical Observation

Repeatedly throughout this section, Amos refers to the nation of Israel as *Jacob*. This is a common custom in the writings of the Old Testament. Nations are sometimes identified by the name of their ancestors. Jacob is the forebear of the twelve tribes of Israel.

The vision described in verses 4–6 is of fire sweeping over the land. Amos again appeals to the Lord, and the Lord, even in His wrath, again relents.

In the third vision, a plumb line illustrates the deviation of Israel from the true path (7:7–8). A plumb line is a string with a weight tied to one end. A person holds it upright vertically, and the weight drops the string straight down toward the ground. Anything that isn't straight will look crooked next to the plumb line. God will set a straight line beside Israel, and her crookedness will be evident to all. This time Amos is given no opportunity to intercede. The Lord has determined to punish Israel as Amos has described throughout this prophecy.

The objects of God's divine wrath are mentioned in verse 9—the false places of worship and the royal families who have abandoned God's covenant and forsaken their responsibilities to lead God's people in the ways of righteousness.

Amos's message in verse 9 is the last straw for the priest Amaziah. Amaziah not only wants to punish Amos, but he wants to discredit him and get rid of him (7:10). The quickest path to this goal is creating trouble for Amos with the current government. For Amaziah to say that the land cannot bear Amos's words is simply to say that these words should not be tolerated.

Demystifying Amos

Amaziah is the chief priest at the sanctuary at Bethel, one of the major sanctuaries set up in the northern kingdom in opposition to Jerusalem. Amaziah is not a descendant of Aaron, and therefore, under Mosaic Law, he should not have held that position. No doubt he takes personally Amos's condemnation of Israelite life and worship. The accusation that Amaziah brings against Amos is suited to provoke the maximum response from the king. Jeroboam had reigned for a long time, and almost certainly there was opposition to him abroad in the land. Upon Jeroboam's death a few years later, his son is assassinated, further suggesting that there had been political intrigue already during the later years of Jeroboam's reign, so he would have been alert to any threat to his throne. Amos is certainly no political conspirator. He has not spoken treasonously against the king, he has taken no action against the king himself, and he has not conspired with anyone else to do so. But the Lord's public condemnations of the king and of the nation through His prophet could easily be taken in that way, and so they provide Amaziah with a pretext for his charge.

In verse 11, Amaziah exaggerates, as do most people who wish to cast someone else in a bad light. Amos never predicts that Jeroboam will die by the sword (in fact, he died of natural causes), but Amos had said enough about the nation's sins and God's impending judgment by military conquest that it was only a small step to saying that Amos predicted Jeroboam's death.

The treatment that Amos receives reveals animosity and superiority on the part of Amaziah (7:12–13). The insinuation is that Amos is preaching in Israel because the money is better in the wealthy north. Amaziah is judging Amos by his own standards. He thinks of his own work as simply a job, and he imagines it to be the same for Amos. In verses 14–15, however, Amos clarifies the issue. He is not a prophet for hire; he is called by God. This sets him apart from Amaziah, a bureaucrat doing the king's bidding.

Demystifying Amos

The temple in Jerusalem is the only authorized center of Israel's worship. But to keep Israelites loyal to the northern kingdom and to prevent them from advertising Israel's illegitimacy by traveling to Jerusalem three times a year for worship, sanctuaries were set up at Bethel and elsewhere (1 Kings 12:25–33). Most of the old Mosaic ritual is still visible in Bethel, but the *yahweh* who is worshiped at Bethel is a god of Amaziah's devising, not the living God who revealed Himself to Israel at the Red Sea and gave His law to her at Mount Sinai.

While Amaziah wants Amos to stop prophesying against Israel, he receives not only a prophecy against Israel but also against his own family (7:16–17). Verse 17 is a ferocious judgment pronounced against Amaziah for his false ministry. His wife will become a prostitute to survive, his children will be killed, his property will be despoiled, and the nation to which he purported to provide spiritual leadership to will be destroyed. The last line of the curse is the explanation of the previous four: Israel will be conquered and its people sent into exile. The other punishments can all be explained as typical effects of military conquest and exile. In any case, events will prove which of the two men has been speaking the truth and is a servant of the true living God.

AMOS 8:1–14

TOO LATE

Setting Up the Section

Chapter 8 opens with a basket of ripe fruit. While Amos may be seeing a physical bowl of fruit, he is likely seeing a vision. Significant to this scene is that the fruit is ripe. In this way, the fruit is an image of Israel.

In describing the basket he sees, Amos says it includes ripe fruit. Typical fruit for Amos's region and era included figs, olives, and grapes.

Amos has already referred to music in Israel's temple worship (5:23), but when the Lord's judgment falls, the only music to be heard at Israel's sanctuaries will be wailing. Dead bodies will be scattered everywhere (8:3).

Verse 4 begins with a call to listen. This is the formula that Amos uses repeatedly to begin new sections of his prophecy (see 3:1; 4:1; 5:1).

We are again given a description of Israel as religiously scrupulous, at least outwardly—the people observe the Sabbath and the other festival days punctiliously—but they are morally bankrupt (8:5–6). They don't do business on the Sabbath, but they can't wait for it to be over so they can resume their acts of greed. They were able to buy off the poor, because the poor people were reduced to pennilessness after paying high prices for food and, in turn, became desperate for money.

Critical Observation

From the beginning of His covenant with Israel, Yahweh reminds His people that He will be a protector of the poor and will hold anyone accountable who misuses them. Twice before in Amos, we have heard the Lord use the word *swear*. In 4:2 He swears by His holiness, and in 6:8 He swears by Himself. Here, in 8:7, He swears by the "Pride of Jacob." Earlier in verse 6:8, God states that He abhors the pride of Jacob. In this earlier instance (noted in some translations by a lowercase *p* in pride), the reference is to the haughtiness of Israel trusting in her own strength. Here (noted by some translations by an uppercase *P* in Pride), it is a reference to God Himself.

The Nile River, mentioned in verse 8, rose and fell every year and often caused great damage by its flooding. It is a useful illustration of the convulsion to come in the land of Israel. An enemy will sweep over Israel like floodwaters and leave nothing but devastation behind. The same expression is used again in 9:5.

In verse 10 we read of the Israelites mourning, wearing sackcloth, and shaving their heads. Amos compares their mourning to that found at the funeral of an only son, which would have been understood by Amos's listeners to be an ultimate and bitter loss.

According to verse 12, the Israelites will stagger from one sea to another. This reference implies the Dead Sea to the Mediterranean, which is a way of saying that this will affect all of Israel. The famine will be so severe that it will consume not only the old and weak but also the young and strong (8:13).

In verse 14, Samaria's shame is a contrast to the mention of Jacob's pride in verse 7. It refers to the false gods who have been added to Yahweh's worship at Israel's shrines. To swear by a god is to commit themselves to the reality of those gods and their power to help them. Yahweh is saying, "You chose those gods over me, let them save you now." They can't! Israel's lack of true repentance shows that in that same day, they will still be found calling on other gods and looking to their idols as well as to Yahweh.

AMOS 9:1–15

FUTURE BLESSING

Setting Up the Section

The theme of this conclusion is that no one can escape God's wrath. God punishes unfaithfulness, and no person can get in His way.

Verses 1–4 contain the fifth and last of the visions that God gives Amos—this one of the destruction of the temple. (The first four visions are recorded in chapters 7–8.) The pillars of the temple support the roof, and the cut stone thresholds are at the bottom of the great doors. The picture here is of the complete collapse of the temple from top to bottom. One of Israel's sanctuaries is in view, probably the principal one at Bethel. The picture of the building collapsing on the worshipers indicates that Israelite worship is conducted in some significant measure inside the sanctuary, in the Canaanite fashion, not outside in the court in the orthodox fashion prescribed in the Law of Moses.

The structure of verse 2 is a common biblical figure of speech that uses two extreme parts together. In this case, heaven and hell are extremes that communicate that all of God's creation is included. There is nowhere to hide. The mountain mentioned in verse 3, Mount Carmel, was known for its thickly wooded mountainside honeycombed with caves. For Amos's contemporaries, this image would serve to reinforce the pervasiveness of God's judgment, as would the reference to *exile* (or *captivity*) in verse 4. Even an enemy nation will not be powerful enough to keep God's judgment at bay.

The Nile's rising and falling is used as an image of destruction in 8:8. Here, in 9:5, the Nile serves as another image of the totality of the Lord's judgment—like a flood that covers the land before it recedes, it leaves nothing but destruction behind.

Verses 5–6 have a hymnlike quality in their mention of God's power and their images of water and the heavens.

With verse 7, the Lord begins to speak in the first person, asking two rhetorical questions that place Israel, spiritually speaking, on equal ground with all others. First, Israel is no more exempt from God's judgment than the people of Cush, a reference to Ethiopia. Israel, by her lack of faith and her betrayal of God's covenant, has become just like these other people instead of the people of God she was called to be. Since the Philistines and the Arameans (NIV) (or Syrians, KJV) were hated enemies of Israel, the comparison would have been particularly galling to Amos's audience.

There is a hopeful element to verses 8–10. The kernels of grain that fall through the sieve to the ground represent the believing remnant of Israel. The pebbles—those who don't believe—will be caught in the sieve and thrown out. They will die by the sword— Amos's last reminder that the Lord's wrath will come upon Israel in the form of military conquest.

In verse 11, Amos first sees David's kingdom (his "tent" NIV) as destroyed but then as renewed and rebuilt. The restoration of David's dynasty is another way of speaking about the Messiah and His kingdom, as the Messiah is, in all biblical prophecy, the future of David's dynasty and the hope of his kingdom.

Edom was a particularly bitter enemy of Israel. Here it represents the nations of the world that, in the last days, will be subject to the kingdom of God (9:12). David was the only king of Israel who not only conquered Edom but held it. So Edom makes a particularly good representative for the nations of the world that will become subject to David's descendant, the Messiah.

Verses 13–14 describe a time of unprecedented bounty. The picture is of fields so fertile and harvests so large that the reapers will still be gathering the grain as the soil is being turned over for the next planting. And the image of wine flowing downward from the hills where the grapes are grown is, again, a picture of unimaginable plenty.

Critical Observation

We have this picture very often in the prophets and as early as Jacob's blessing of Judah in Genesis 49:10–12: The Messiah will restore the world to its pure state, as it was in Eden before the fall. Additionally, there will be peace, enabling the people of God to pursue their life's work without fear.

Amos closes with a promise that when the people of God are restored and resettled in the promised land to enjoy the blessings and benefits of God's favor, they will never be judged again. The judgment of the nation is upon them. This has been Amos's primary theme from the beginning of the book, but when the Day of Judgment is passed and Israel is restored, it will be for good.

Take It Home

Amos's prophecy concerns all the people of God, Jews and Gentiles alike. The living, faithful church—whether Jewish or Gentile—is the true Israel of God, as we are often told in the New Testament. Also, the promise here is primarily a promise of eternal salvation, of the life of heaven, and of the complete fulfillment of human life as it will be experienced at the consummation of all things. Amos's description of the future here is simply another version of that description of heaven that John gives us at the end of the book of Revelation. Amos ends with a promise of a wonderful day, a day of fulfillment, joy, and perfect satisfaction for every human being who is numbered among the true people of God when history comes to its close.

OBADIAH

INTRODUCTION TO OBADIAH

The book of Obadiah is the shortest of the Old Testament, yet its brief message has numerous applications far beyond its relevance to Edom. Obadiah provides a warning to anyone who mistakenly believes that sin will go unnoticed (and unpunished), but he also offers confidence that for those who continue to seek God, the Lord is able to both forgive and deliver.

AUTHOR

Personal facts are scarce concerning the prophet Obadiah. He provides no family references or pertinent locations that enlighten the reader as to his biography. Even his name (meaning "worshiper of the Lord") was a common one in his day. At least a dozen Old Testament men are named Obadiah.

PURPOSE

Obadiah has a single purpose in writing: to bring God's message of judgment to the people of Edom. The nation's deeply rooted sense of pride will result in its certain downfall.

THEMES

Obadiah highlights the problems that arise from unbridled arrogance and self-centeredness. Edom (the descendants of Esau) has family ties to Israel (the descendants of Jacob), so Edom's sadistic glee in response to the previous troubles of the Israelites does not go unnoticed; they will be judged for their actions.

HISTORICAL CONTEXT

With so few clues provided, it is difficult to determine a precise date for the writing of Obadiah. But the conflict between Edom and Israel was ongoing and had existed throughout their entire histories. If the event referred to in verses 11–14 is the Babylonian destruction of Jerusalem (586 BC), then Obadiah was most likely written during the exile.

CONTRIBUTION TO THE BIBLE

Obadiah is a seldom-quoted book. Even the New Testament writers, who cited many of the Old Testament prophetic writings, are silent in regard to Obadiah. Yet the message of this short writing has practical applications that make it a significant contribution to scripture.

BOOK OF OBADIAH

THE PROBLEM WITH TAKING JOY
IN THE SUFFERING OF ONE'S ENEMIES

Judgment in Store for Edom   1–14
Deliverance in Store for Jacob   15–21

Setting Up the Section

The concise writing of Obadiah is a pointed accusation against the nation of Edom, whose people had survived while they saw Judah fall to powerful enemies. More than that, Edom had taken perverse pleasure in seeing their enemies suffer and had even acted aggressively against Judah during a vulnerable time. What Edom didn't realize, however, was that Judah's fall was a result of God's judgment on His people. Obadiah now reveals that God will certainly judge Edom as well and that judgment will be severe.

📖 1–14

JUDGMENT IN STORE FOR EDOM

Israel and Edom had a long and interwoven history. Sometimes they had joined as allies against a common enemy. More often, however, the original rivalry between Jacob (Israel's forefather) and Esau (Edom's forefather) created ongoing conflicts between the two nations.

The timing of Obadiah's writing is debated, but it is clear that Judah has experienced a bitter defeat at the hands of enemies (verse 11). The Edomites foolishly believe they are exempt from a similar outcome. Edom was located along a span of wilderness that stretched from the southern tip of the Dead Sea to the northern portion of the Red Sea. It was mountainous territory where the inhabitants lived among rocky cliffs, confident of their security and the impenetrability of their cities. It is as if they feel untouchable, high among the stars (verses 3–4).

But from their heights of arrogance, they are about to fall and become small among the nations (verse 2). They may dwell above much of the world, but God is higher still and will bring them down (verse 4).

Demystifying Obadiah

Israel had requested permission to travel through Edom during their exodus from Egypt, but the Edomites had marched out with a large and powerful army to deny them passage (Numbers 20:14–21). Later, when Israel was an established nation of its own, the Edomites waited until other people attacked Israel and then invaded and took prisoners (2 Chronicles 28:16–21). And when Jerusalem eventually fell to the Babylonians, the Edomites cheered and celebrated (Psalm 137:7–8).

During a typical theft, the robber(s) will leave behind some of the person's belongings, but Edom's loss will be total. Even worse, those whom Edom considers their close friends and allies will prove deceitful. The very people whom they trust enough to sit around the table and share a meal with will destroy them with alarming treachery. The wisdom and power of the most accomplished descendants of Esau will not be adequate to anticipate this trouble nor deliver their countrymen from a horrifying slaughter (verses 5–9).

God disciplines those He loves, which is a difficult concept for outsiders to understand. When nonbelievers observe God's people undergoing a period of corrective discipline, they tend to presume that God has no abiding love for those who worship Him. Some even take a perverse pleasure in celebrating the suffering of God's people, but it is never wise to gloat over those whom the Lord has called His special possession. He will stand up for them in the day when He comes to judge and will bring upon the heads of their enemies the very vengeance those people had sought for them. Edom will learn this lesson too late, as they find themselves covered with shame and destroyed (verses 10–14).

📄 15–21

DELIVERANCE IN STORE FOR JACOB

Jesus will later teach that, "So in everything, do to others what you would have them do to you," saying that this so-called Golden Rule "sums up the Law and the Prophets" (Matthew 7:12 NIV). The prophet Obadiah records how the Edomites have treated God's people despicably, and God's pronouncement of their judgment is, "As you have done to Israel, so it will be done to you" (Obadiah 15 NLT).

After contributing to the (temporary) defeat of Jerusalem, the Edomites had apparently celebrated with strong drink. But the cup of God's wrath (see Isaiah 51:17) is in store for them to drink. Edom represents all the nations who have opposed God—they all will one day completely disappear from existence, while Jerusalem is restored. The house of Esau will have no survivors (Obadiah 16–18).

Critical Observation

While Obadiah's prophecy focuses on Edom, other Old Testament prophetic books include prophecies against these people (Jeremiah 49:7–39; Ezekiel 35:1–15; Malachi 1:1–4).

Mount Zion (Jerusalem) will be delivered, once again holy and home to the house of Jacob (Israel). Surrounding land that had been ceded to other nations will be reclaimed and restored. People will be called out of exile to resettle in their homelands. Deliverers will be assigned to help govern, but the kingdom will be the Lord's (verses 19–21).

The short book of Obadiah confirms what many other prophets teach in greater detail. The Day of the Lord will one day bring judgment on all who persistently defy God and live in disobedience, while bringing deliverance and restoration to those who repent and seek God's mercy. What appears to be injustice is only temporary. God is aware of every deed and attitude of every person, and He will punish or reward accordingly.

Take It Home

Obadiah's message to Edom is a relevant lesson for many people today. Even though Edom and Israel were ongoing enemies, it becomes clear that God was displeased for one side to take delight in the suffering and downfall of the other. Can you think of times when you have taken pleasure in seeing someone "get what was coming to him or her"? The command to "love your enemies" (Matthew 5:44) begins by being more sensitive to others' pains and problems. What can you do in the weeks to come to develop a stronger empathy with those you don't normally get along with?

JONAH

INTRODUCTION TO JONAH

Jonah is the only prophet who is recorded as having run away from God. In this way, Jonah is not known for his piety but for his prodigality. Jonah, in his rebellion, disobedience, and hardness of heart, is a man who typifies the rebellion of Israel as described by other prophets. Ironically, the name *Jonah* means "dove," a bird often associated with peace.

AUTHOR

Very little is said of the prophet Jonah outside of the book of Jonah itself. It does seem safe to conclude that the Jonah in 2 Kings 14:25 is the same person who is the subject of the book of Jonah, especially since both are identified as the son of Amittai.

The book of Jonah does not name its author. While it is about Jonah, there is no specific claim as to whether Jonah actually wrote it.

PURPOSE

The book stood to reveal to Israel the possibility of repentance, even for those whom Israel would have considered the most wicked. The point was, if repentance is a possibility for the most wicked, then repentance is a real possibility for Israel herself as well.

OCCASION

Jonah is a prophet in the northern kingdom of Israel during the first half of the eighth century BC. His predecessors are Elijah and Elisha. The ministries of Hosea and Amos immediately follow that of Jonah.

THEMES

Throughout the book of Jonah runs the theme of second chances, worked out through opportunities for repentance, some taken and some wasted. Hand in hand runs the theme of those who choose to obey God and those who don't.

HISTORICAL CONTEXT

Jonah is associated in 2 Kings 14:25 with the reign of King Jeroboam, a time of prosperity for Israel. Assyria, whose capital city is Jonah's target of Nineveh, has already begun to exercise her dominance in the Near East, but for a time her control will wane, allowing Israel to expand her borders. Israel's empowerment at this time may have been a factor in her lack of repentance. This makes the story of Jonah all the more pointed, in that a nation Israel considered to be wicked repents before God when His own people won't.

CONTRIBUTION TO THE BIBLE

In the New Testament, Jesus mentions Jonah (Matthew 12:39–41; 16:4; Luke 11:29–32). When asked for a sign, Jesus refers the religious leaders to the sign of Jonah that already exists. He points out the parallel of Jonah's three days in the fish and the Son of man's three days in the heart of the earth.

OUTLINE OF JONAH

JONAH 1:1–17

JONAH AND THE SAILORS

Setting Up the Section

At the opening of Jonah's story, he is given a divine commission to go to the great city of Nineveh, capital city of Assyria and a potential threat to Israel (see Genesis 10:8–11).

📖 1:1–3

RUNNING FROM GOD

The description of Nineveh as *great* in verse 2 probably refers to its size and its influence, but its sins were great as well. Its wickedness has come to God's attention, and Jonah is to be God's messenger. But instead of doing what God instructs him to do, Jonah catches a ship heading in the opposite direction (1:1–3).

The city of Nineveh is located on the Tigris River, more than five hundred miles to the northeast of Israel. But Jonah goes west toward Tarshish, which seems to have been located on the western coast of Spain. Jonah flees from God's presence, a truth repeated twice in verse 3. Jonah is not trying to flee the literal presence of God, but he is attempting to avoid his role as a prophet.

📖 1:4–11

A POWERFUL STORM

But God does not let Jonah flee. He hurls a storm in Jonah's path—a storm so great that it terrifies veteran sailors and threatens the ship (1:4–5). The sailors begin casting the cargo overboard in an effort to save the ship and their own lives. At the same time, each sailor is praying to his gods for deliverance. These pagan sailors would have worshiped gods they thought influenced the seas on which they traveled.

As the sailors gather the cargo to throw overboard, they find Jonah deep in sleep (1:5). The ship's captain is irritated to find Jonah sleeping while the rest of the crew members work to stay alive during the storm. He doesn't ask Jonah to help cast the cargo overboard, but he does command Jonah to pray to his God (1:6). The text does not reveal if Jonah obeys the captain's orders.

The captain and the sailors understand the storm to be a religious matter. When praying doesn't stop the storm, they try another religious technique: casting lots to find the person whose sin has caused the problem (1:7). The lots land on Jonah and identify him as the culprit.

The sailors are in fear for their lives, but in spite of the imminent danger, and the likely urge to throw him overboard, they interrogate Jonah, asking about his origin, purpose, and heritage (1:8). In his answer, Jonah separates himself religiously from the sailors but apparently reveals insight into his mission. From his responses, the sailors immediately know that Jonah has indeed caused the storm and that his sin has endangered the entire ship's crew (1:9–10).

The response of the sailors—appalled at Jonah's disobedience—shows that even the pagans are shocked at how this man has chosen to defy God. They, too, are experiencing the consequences of Jonah's actions, so they ask Jonah what to do to appease the wrath of his God (1:11).

📖 1:12–17

GOD'S PROVISION

Jonah tells the sailors to throw him overboard and the sea will calm (1:12). Given the intensity of the storm, this request would have made his death seem a certainty. Some believe this shows repentance on Jonah's part, but others feel that Jonah wants to die to avoid God's command to confront Nineveh. The sailors could have responded quickly to Jonah's instructions, yet because they are reluctant to cause his death, they make one more risky attempt to save him by rowing for the rocky shore (1:13). When they conclude that Jonah's solution is their only alternative, they pray once more before casting him into the sea (1:14). Many scholars agree that at this point the sailors are praying to Jonah's God. Having prayed, they pick up the prophet and cast him into the sea (1:15).

As Jonah sinks beneath the waves, the winds cease and the sea calms down. This confirms for the sailors that Jonah's God is the only true God. Thus, at the end of the chapter, we see the sailors worshiping by sacrificing and declaring their faith in God (1:16). In trying to avoid preaching to the Ninevites, Jonah has unwillingly preached to the sailors, and they have come to faith in his God.

The fish that God provides for Jonah has become the focus of this story, yet it is simply a provision of the Lord (1:17). The miracle is not the fish itself or in the details of how the fish swallows Jonah; the miracle is God's grace toward Jonah, saving him from almost certain death in order that Jonah may receive all that God's call on his life has to offer.

Critical Observation

Jesus refers back to Jonah's plight in the belly of the fish in Matthew 12:39–41, comparing Jonah's three days and nights to the three days and nights the Son of man spends in the earth. This is called the sign of the prophet Jonah.

JONAH 2:1–10

JONAH AND HIS PSALM

Jonah's Petition   2:1–9
Jonah's Deliverance   2:10

Setting Up the Section

Jonah 2:1 picks up the story from under the sea. Verses 2–9 present Jonah's prayer in psalm format.

📖 2:1–9

JONAH'S PETITION

Jonah's descriptions of what is happening to him in the water affirm that he knows God is in control and responsible (2:2–3). The word *Sheol* typically means "grave" but sometimes has connotations of the underworld. Nevertheless, Jonah's words reveal that he acknowledges death as an imminent threat.

Jonah mentions seeing the temple, most likely the temple in Jerusalem (2:4).

In verses 5–7, Jonah describes his situation with graphic detail. He acknowledges God's rescue. In verses 8–9, he appears to contrast Gentile pagans with his own belief in God. This sense of separateness, and even at times superiority, speaks to the core of Jonah's dilemma. God called him to preach to a wicked place, to those who were enemies to his own people. His unwillingness reveals his inability to see how much God values even those who have not yet come to know Him.

🖹 2:10

JONAH'S DELIVERANCE

There is little emphasis on the actual fish itself here, perhaps because the fish is obedient to his commission. Jonah's prayer is answered, and he is not only expelled from the fish but also returns to dry land (2:10).

Take It Home

In chapters 1 and 2, the pagan sailors are the ones who seem to act with pure hearts, acknowledging the true God and worshiping with sacrifices and declarations of faith. Jonah, on the other hand, acts rebelliously by disobeying God, and in doing so he endangers many people. It is easy for those of us who consider ourselves to be on God's side to assume that our attitudes will be right. We must always be vigilant, however, that we are acting as servants of the Lord.

JONAH 3:1–10

JONAH AND THE CITY

Setting Up the Section

In chapters 1 and 2, Jonah's sin is apparent yet still somewhat subtle and passive. But this changes in chapters 3 and 4, for Jonah's preaching and the repentance of Nineveh reveal his sinfulness in its ugliest dimensions. In the following chapters, all appearances of piety vanish in the account of the prodigal prophet.

🖹 3:1–3

A SECOND CHANCE

God commands Jonah for the second time to deliver His message to the Ninevites (3:1–2). It is almost a repetition of the command given to him in 1:2. This time Jonah obeys the Lord. Verse 3 describes Nineveh, perhaps including its suburbs, as large; the mention of a three-day journey refers to how long it will take to walk around it.

🖹 3:4–10

NINEVEH'S REPENTANCE

Jonah's message is simple, to the point, and frightening: In forty days, Nineveh will fall (3:4). Just like the sailors in chapter one, the people of Nineveh take Jonah's words of imminent divine judgment seriously—they believe. The faith of the Ninevites is not simply a fear of judgment. They call a fast and put on sackcloth—a sign of helplessness and despair (3:5). The text specifies that the belief and repentance starts with the common people and rises upward to Nineveh's leadership (3:6).

Because the king also believes Jonah's warning, he makes every effort to assure total compliance to the citywide repentance. He begins by personally repenting. The king then makes a proclamation which requires all of Nineveh to fast and to abstain from drinking water (3:6-7). Both men and animals are to be covered with sackcloth, and all the people are to call upon God and stop their wicked ways and violence (3:8).

The wicked ways of the Ninevites are not detailed, except for use of the word *violence* (3:8). Nineveh's motivation is that God may change His mind (3:9). God had instructed Jonah to deliver not a promise of things to come but a warning. The Ninevites understand God's message correctly. God takes note of Nineveh's repentance because it involves more than mere words or token gestures. The Ninevites have changed more than outward appearances; they have changed their evil ways (3:10).

Critical Observation

Jesus' reference to the repentance of the Ninevites is particularly informative (Matthew 12:38–41). If the Ninevites can repent with so little evidence, then surely the problem with the Jewish leaders, scribes, and Pharisees was not a lack of evidence. Like Jonah, the Jewish leaders, scribes, and Pharisees did have evidence but refused to believe that God would act in a way unexpected by them—and thus no evidence was enough to change their willful rejection.

JONAH 4:1-11

JONAH AND THE SHADE

Jonah's Anger Against God   4:1–3
The Plant and the Prodigal   4:4–11

Setting Up the Section

Had Jonah been any other prophet in the history of Israel, he would have been overjoyed with the results of his ministry—the repentance of the great city of Nineveh. In chapter 4, Jonah blurts out his reasons for rebelling against the command of the Lord. The events in this chapter reveal Jonah's sin.

📖 4:1-3

JONAH'S ANGER AGAINST GOD

In spite of the repentance of Nineveh, Jonah is angry with God (4:1). Jonah is not hesitant to explain, and he protests to the Lord in prayer (4:2). Jonah is angry with God because He shows grace toward the Ninevites, who are enemies of Israel. Instead of learning this lesson about God's loving and merciful character, he complains that he would rather die than live (4:3).

📖 4:4–11

THE PLANT AND THE PRODIGAL

God acknowledges Jonah's anger toward Him (4:4) and presses on with another experience: the giving and the taking away of a plant.

Jonah goes outside the city, where he makes a shady booth from which he can watch the spectacle of the destruction of Nineveh (4:5). God causes a plant to grow, and for the first time in the narrative, Jonah is described as being happy (4:6). With the advent of the worm that eats the plant, and with the arrival of the scorching wind, Jonah loses his comfort and his happiness (4:7–8). Jonah could have chosen to walk away from his suffering and join the Ninevites in their worship of God, but he allows his anger to keep him in discomfort and isolation. He once again begs God to let him die.

For the second time in this chapter, God offers the opportunity for Jonah to examine his anger; and again, Jonah chooses anger over any other emotion (4:9). He is so adamant about his anger that he insists upon keeping it and wishes to die.

God has the final word in the book of Jonah, and His last words press to the heart of the matter. He wants Jonah to see that just as Jonah had compassion on the plant, God had compassion on the people (4:10). God wants Jonah to examine his feelings for the plant—they were strong, even though Jonah had nothing to do with the plant's growth or existence.

The book of Jonah does not end nicely and neatly. We are left somewhat suspended by God's final words of rebuke. We are never told if Jonah repents.

Take It Home

Jonah had rejected the principle of grace. Resisting and rejecting the grace of God is just as great and just as common a sin today as it was in Jonah's time. God's grace takes unexpected forms. He was gracious to Jonah, saving him by means of the great fish. God is gracious to His children by using even pain and adversity in their lives. May we today embrace God's grace however it is bestowed upon us.

MICAH

INTRODUCTION TO MICAH

Sometimes called the prophet of the poor, Micah is a contemporary of Isaiah and speaks a similar message, though, as recorded in the Bible, shorter. King Hezekiah initiates sweeping spiritual and moral reforms in Judah in response to the preaching of Micah and Isaiah, but unfortunately these reforms are short-lived.

AUTHOR

The first verse of this book ascribes the authorship to Micah, a prophet about whom we know very little outside of what is revealed through this prophecy. The prophet is mentioned in only one other place in the Bible, in Jeremiah 26:17–19. In this account, Micah is described as a prophet during the reign of King Hezekiah. When Micah prophesied a bad end for Jerusalem, the king repented, saving Jerusalem from the destruction Micah had prophesied.

PURPOSE

Micah prophesies to stir his readers to action. His writing takes the form of three oracles of judgment. This judgment falls on his countrymen, who act as oppressors, as well as on his society in general, which is filled with corruption. Micah also reminds his people of God's restoration (as do other Old Testament prophets), which awaits them in the future.

OCCASION

The first verse of this prophecy identifies the monarchies under which Micah prophesies—Jotham, Ahaz, and Hezekiah. This places Micah in the eighth century BC. The prophecy references the destruction of Samaria and the invasion of Sennacherib in 701 BC, which would agree with that chronology.

THEMES

While Micah's prophecy is not a theological treatise, running through it are the themes of God's sovereignty, His consistency of nature, and the destiny of the remnant of the faithful.

MICAH 1:1–16

THE JUDGMENT TO COME

Setting Up the Section

Micah begins with the announcement of judgment because of sins against God and unfaithfulness to God's covenant. This is a major theme of the prophets, leading up to the destruction of the northern kingdom in 722 BC and the devastation and exile of the southern kingdom some 150 years later. This lesson also reveals the nature of God's divine justice, the ferocity of divine wrath, and the final and conclusive judgment of all people at the end of the world.

The kings listed in 1:1 reign from 742 BC to 686 BC. It is widely thought that Micah mentions only the southern kings—though he mentions the northern kingdom (Samaria) as well as the southern (Jerusalem)—because he did not regard the northern kings as legitimate and did not want to dignify them by mentioning them by name.

The call goes out to the entire earth, even though the message concerns Samaria primarily and Jerusalem to a lesser degree. They are all being summoned to a trial to face the Judge of all the earth (1:2). In verse 3, the Lord appears from heaven as an avenging judge.

The specific sins will be enumerated in chapters 2 and 3 and again in chapter 6. But here the case is put generally as rebellion (1:5). The capital cities are mentioned both to represent the entire nation and because it is where the living embodiment of the corruption that has destroyed the nation originated. The punishment on Samaria and Jerusalem foreshadows punishment for all people who worship idols (1:6–7). The meaning of the second half of verse 7 could be that, because idols are bought with the revenues of the cult prostitutes, the conquerors whom God will use to punish Israel will break them up not only for their precious metals but also for spending the money earned from them on the same prostitutes.

The description in verse 8 of the prophet stripped of clothes is not a picture of penitence but of exile. Exiles, barefoot and naked, tramp miserably away from home in long lines under the supervision of enemy soldiers. The same idea is expressed with the howling of the jackal. Jackals howl in the waste places, in the wilderness, and that is what Judah will be reduced to. The gate is the place in the community where announcements are publicly made (1:9).

The following verses (1:10–16) mention several Judean towns, all of them within fourteen kilometers of Micah's hometown of Moresheth. All of the names are omens—they are given some special significance by means of a play on the name, either on the meaning or the associations of the name, or on its sound.

The first name, Gath, is significant because the city does not exist at this time, having been destroyed by Sargon (1:10). The idea, as any Israelite would immediately realize, is that the house of David is now falling, just as the house of Saul had done before. Dust is a symbol of abject humiliation and defeat (1:10; see Genesis 3:14). Verse 11 continues the name-play. The idea in verses 11–12 is that the towns of Judah are hoping for help from the capital, but it is under siege. Lachish is apparently the place where idolatry got its foothold in Judah, spreading outward from there (1:13). With the loss of Lachish, which is a key defensive point and, in fact, holds out longer in 701 BC than the other towns and villages of Judah, the nation must expect to pay tribute. The idea of verse 14 is that towns that belong to Judah and contribute to her must now be paid for instead, as they are in enemy hands. Again in the name-play of the verses above, the allusion in verse 15 is literary, not literal. As David had to flee from Saul to the cave of Adullam (see 1 Samuel 22:1), so the sons of David—the kings and the nobles (the glory of Israel)—will be driven out.

Micah sees the future destruction of Judah on account of her sins, and he considers that the appropriate response is to mourn with true sincerity (1:16). But in this culture, there were professional mourners, so it wasn't always done with as great a depth of feeling. An official mourner does not grieve the loss of a husband as a loving wife does, or of a child as her parents do.

MICAH 2:1–13
FROM OPPRESSION TO HOPE

Setting Up the Section

This next oracle is a pronouncement of judgment against the leadership of Judah. But it goes beyond simply promising judgment against the northern kingdom (1:6–7) and the southern kingdom (1:8–16). This oracle specifically identifies one of the sins for which Israel will be judged.

The reference to the light of morning alludes to the time of day when the courts meet (2:1). The indication here is that the people in power are controlling the courts, which should be a place of justice for all, not just the powerful. But the first part of verse 2 explains how the powerful are taking others' physical property and taking advantage of the people. In this culture, if you take away a person's land, you take away that person's livelihood. Consequences include becoming a day laborer at best and potentially a slave.

Those in power are gaining possession of people's fields by lending money to the landowners and then foreclosing. The result of this is the evacuation of the middle class—most people in prosperous Israel are in the middle class in these days—and the creation of a large poor class serving a smaller, but much wealthier, ruling class. The violation here is in coveting others' property instead of recognizing their ownership and ignoring the fact that, regardless of what one might own and what others might own, all things belong to God and are to be used in His service and for the accomplishment of His will.

The people mentioned in verse 3 indicate a group acting with corporate solidarity. The people who are being ruined by these wealthy land barons are not completely innocent themselves, though. The entire social and religious fabric is rotten, not just the leaders and people in power. Because of this, the Assyrians will come and take the land itself, the very possession the Lord had promised to Israel (2:4). The sacred land of Israel will be distributed to infidels, people who had curried the favor of the Assyrians. This section clearly indicates that this takeover will be done with the help of God.

Critical Observation

God's judgment, as described in chapter 1, is an example of "an eye for an eye and a tooth for a tooth." While this kind of judgment can sound brutal, at the heart of it is the principle that a punishment should fit the specific crime. An eye for an eye is harsh. But it is more equitable than a life for an eye. Here are other examples of punishments that specifically fit the transgressions: Esther 7:9–10; Psalm 7:15–16; Ezekiel 36:6–7; Matthew 26:52.

Micah 2:6 launches an oracle against the false prophets and against the leadership of the people who favor these prophets and approve of their teaching. In its original writing, the imperative not to prophesy is directed to more than one person. This suggests that Micah is not the only one preaching against the sins of the day. We know that Isaiah and Hosea were contemporaries of Micah. There is also a remnant of faithful people who would have repeated the teaching of these faithful men.

The first half of verse 7 shows what the false prophets are teaching, and the second half reveals Micah's response to that teaching. The message of the false prophets amounts to an assurance that because God is love, Israel has nothing to fear. But Micah explains that while God is gracious, He is also a God of judgment to those who do not believe in or obey Him. And because Micah's generation is such an unbelieving and disobedient people, He is going to be a God of judgment to them, not a God of grace and mercy. He will reach out to them if they cry out to Him for mercy and forsake their evil ways, but they will not.

Micah includes some specifics. When men return from battle, as in verse 8, they are confident, assured, at peace, and not expecting trouble. But the leadership pillages them.

In other words, the leadership treats the people just like the enemy does. Women are being evicted from their homes, and the descriptions of those homes indicate the people of Judah are, at this time, prosperous and comfortable (2:9). The listeners are instructed to leave, to flee what is coming as a result of sin (2:10). Unfortunately, that means they must go away into exile.

Micah mocks the message preached by the false teachers as simply another version of what people want to hear (2:11). He is being properly cynical of the base motives of the false teachers.

Historically there have been two different interpretations of verses 12–13. Some see the verses as a further prophecy of woe and judgment. Most, though, take the verses to be a message of hope and consolation, a promise of at least a temporary deliverance—a direct prophecy of the deliverance of Jerusalem from Sennacherib's invading army in 701 BC. The sheep pen, or fold, is Jerusalem (2:12). The Shepherd of Israel is gathering His flock to protect it from marauders.

Demystifying Micah

The force of verse 13 lies in the description of the Lord as breaking open the way. Micah's contemporary listeners would have noticed a similarity to David's reference to the Lord breaking out against His enemies (the Philistines) in 2 Samuel 5:20, 24. In other areas of scripture, God is the One who breaks open a way to save His people. The second half of verse 13 is a spiritual picture of this procession out of the city; the Lord at the head of His people (eventually not the human king, but the King Shepherd of Israel, the Christ).

MICAH 3:1–12

JUDGMENT ON THE LEADERSHIP

Setting Up the Section

Chapter 3 contains three oracles of judgment of equal length and identical in form, with the same theme in every case—corrupt leadership.

Micah is the person speaking in verse 1. He uses imagery to show that the leaders are, in effect, consuming people for their own gain (3:2–3). (We've seen already in chapter 2 how they steal people's houses and render them destitute.) There is a startling new development in this oracle—the fact that the Lord will punish these false teachers in keeping with their crimes (3:4). The oppressed cry out to these leaders, and they do not answer or help them. So, when the leaders cry out to God for help, He will not answer them. This indicates a point of no return.

In verse 5, the prophet speaks for the Lord rather than on his own behalf, with the following verses addressing the false prophets. Verse 6 specifically mentions divination, or fortune-telling, something that is forbidden to people of God (Deuteronomy 18:10). It is

considered a betrayal of the sufficiency of God's revelation and a serious mistaking of the way to live a life pleasing to God.

In Micah's day, these false prophets held equal status with God's prophets, if not higher because of the popularity of their message. Yet, one hundred years later, these same false prophets will be walking through the ruins of Jerusalem like unclean lepers (3:7). But Micah is filled with God's Spirit and with the power to speak on His behalf to the people (3:8).

Verses 9–12 make up the third oracle against the corrupt leadership of the people. This last oracle speaks to the leadership in general, adding the priests, by name, to the leaders and false prophets.

Micah continues railing against the leaders for their unjust ways (3:9–10). Both the civic leaders and the religious leaders are accused of taking bribes instead of following God for justice (3:11). Verse 12 is the only verse in the Old Testament that is cited word for word somewhere else in the Old Testament (Jeremiah 26:18), some one hundred years later. The Lord relents because of Hezekiah's faithfulness, and this prophecy does not come to pass.

MICAH 4:1–13

ZION'S FUTURE

Setting Up the Section

While Jerusalem is still being addressed in chapter 4, the mood of the message changes. Micah 4–5 contains the first of the oracles of salvation. These are oracles of an eventual deliverance, unlike the apparent near-terms deliverance described in 2:12–13. These oracles describe a new epoch that lies beyond the judgment that Micah is prophesying for Israel and Judah in the near future.

The prediction that opens chapter 4 is similar to other instances in the Old Testament prophets such as Isaiah 2:2–4 and Hosea 3:5. The opening mention of the last days is used in the New Testament also to refer to the future when God will bring all prophecies to fruition (1 Timothy 4:1; 2 Timothy 3:1; 1 Peter 1:5; Jude 18). There is debate about whether these days refer to a time before Christ comes again or the time after Christ actually has returned.

In the opening verses of this fourth chapter, Micah overhears the nations and reflects on what he has seen and heard and what will come of it: The law of God will be embraced by the nations and the result will be peace, to the point that weapons will be retooled for growing food. This is a refreshing contrast to the forms of justice Micah has just condemned. The final verse of this segment has been described as a liturgical response on the part of the righteous: Until this vision is a reality, God's people will participate by faith.

Demystifying Micah

Almost every ancient Near Eastern religion and deity had a mountain dedicated to it, and most often a temple stood on that mountain (or hill, as the case may be). In this era, the mountain symbolizes God's bringing of order over chaos, access to heaven, and His presence on earth. All of this is the context for Micah's prophecy in verses 1–5: The Lord's mountain rising above the others means that Yahweh will reign supreme as the nations come to recognize and honor Him as the true God.

The opening phrase of verse 6—*in that day*—refers to the events of 4:1–5. The prophet is anticipating the reality of the exile that has already been prophesied. God's remnant will be made up of the weakest ones of society, and He will use those people to rebuild His strong nation (4:6–7). This can be seen as a foreshadowing image of what God will do through Christ—born in a stable yet God in human flesh. In fact, in the next verse, God directly addresses Jerusalem as He will later address Bethlehem (5:2). Eventually, the depleted people of God will become the nucleus of something far greater, stronger, and more permanent in the future. Judgment will come first; deliverance, salvation, and triumph later. Indeed, much later—far beyond the horizon of the people to whom Micah is preaching this message.

Take It Home

The response of the faithful in verse 5 reminds Christians of all eras that we are to bear witness to Micah's vision of the peace that comes from God's sovereignty. We can participate in it in advance, by living according to this same law in our lives today. We can whet our appetite—and that of the culture around us—for what is to come by living by faith in the reality we believe for the future.

Verses 9–13 contain two parallel sections: Each refers to *now* (4:9, 11), moving from the present distress of God's people to a future deliverance; each has a command (4:10, 13); each has a promise that is the rationale for obedience (4:10, 13); and each takes a similar view of present circumstances as being the outworking of a plan that people do not understand.

The suffering of the people in the coming captivity is foreshadowed in verses 9–10. Some Bible translations interpret *king* and *counselor* as a reference to human figures and thus interpret the question in verse 9 as sarcasm. But if verse 9 parallels verse 11, it suggests that these words are a reference to God. In this understanding, the question is rhetorical. Has God perished? Of course not.

There is a twist in verses 11–13. While these nations think they are destroying Israel on their own, in reality God is using them to punish and purify His people. While their actions are being used by Him at this time, eventually He will punish these nations for both their actions and their intentions.

God's plan and purpose is to bring eventual salvation out of the present distress and judgment. He will eventually order Israel to take action instead of simply writhing in agony (4:9, 13). But for now, Israel must pass through judgment until these nations—which, in their hubris, seek to destroy God's people and God Himself—will be destroyed. The commands of verses 10 and 13 are a summons that, in the meantime, those who belong to the faithful remnant are to step out in faith and endure the judgments of the Lord, knowing that vindication is in His hands.

MICAH 5:1–15

THE COMING CHAMPION

Setting Up the Section

The first verse of chapter 5 actually completes the closing thought from chapter 4. With verse 2, then, Micah begins a hopeful oracle regarding a champion who will come from Bethlehem. Verses 2–4 discuss the rule and triumph of the Messiah Himself, and verses 5–6 describe those who rule in His name. The ideal king of the ancient Near East is a shepherd king, one who provides for and cares for his people. The Messiah will be such a king.

The idea in verse 1 of Israel's leader being stricken on the cheek is an image of Hezekiah's total humiliation. He is so defenseless that he cannot even protect his face. He cannot defend his people—it's as if they have no king at all. It is in this context of Israel's humiliation and the demonstration of her powerlessness against a mighty foreign army that the great messianic prophecy is given. Once again, Micah is moving from the present distress of Israel—in this case, the Assyrian invasion of 701 BC—to a future deliverance.

Demystifying Micah

The Assyrian invasion in 701 BC is the context of this oracle. This is demonstrated by several things: 1) In verses 5–6, Nimrod, that is Babylon, is an inferior power, so this must be when Babylon is subject to Assyria, not later when it rules over the former Assyrian Empire; 2) in the verses following verse 5, Assyria is used as the representative of the forces of hostility to the kingdom of God, which makes sense if it is the great enemy of the people of God in the day of this prophecy; and 3) the term *leaders,* or *principle men,* at the end of verse 5 is rarely used, but it is one the Assyrian king Sargon used for his leaders.

Beginning with verse 2, Micah addresses the city of Bethlehem. With the advantage of hindsight, we know that Micah is about to share words related to the coming of Christ. The mention of old or ancient times seems to be a reference to the Messiah's bloodline—the ancestry of Jesse and David. It will be a new start from the original root.

The idea of verse 3 is that Israel's distress will continue until the Messiah comes. The *remnant*, or the *rest*, is the same idea as in Isaiah 11:11–12 and Zechariah 10:10, the gathering of those who have been dispersed because of exile or defeat.

In verse 4, the Messiah is called a shepherd, and this shepherd will protect His people from the *Assyrian*, as if describing an individual (5:5–6), but the name represents the enemies of the kingdom of God. The use of the number seven is a depiction of the idea of perfection (5:5). Then, the number eight offers the idea of even more than perfect. The Messiah's kingdom will have all the necessary leaders and the very best of them; the enemy will be no match for them. The golden age will be a messianic age. The consummation of the kingdom of God in the world will be brought to pass by the rule of this coming king.

The previous oracle links the earlier prophecies with the coming of the Messiah. In the oracle beginning in verse 7, the Messiah will expand His kingdom through the nations of the world by means of the remnant.

Dew is life-giving water that comes from God—humans are powerless to create or control it (5:7). This water comes from the Lord to and for people, and when it comes, it covers everything. This sets up the promise that comes next. As before in Micah, a parallel structure appears in verses 7–8. Each verse has as its subject the remnant among the nations, and each has a description in simile form of what the remnant will be—like dew and like showers in the first case; like a lion and like a young lion in the second. Each concludes with an explanation of the descriptions—in the first case, an image of salvation; and in the second, judgment and destruction.

The promise for the remnant includes a new strength for the group (5:9). But this eventual blessing can come only when God punishes His own people in order to purify them (5:10–14). The destruction in Micah's own day comes by means of the Assyrian invasion, and it will continue with the exile to Babylon (which has already been foretold by Micah). The specific details of the destruction highlight God's anger at Israel's worship of false gods. The word translated *destroy* or *demolish* in verse 14 is the same word used in Leviticus concerning the punishment of sin in the camp in order to maintain a holy people (Leviticus 17:10; 20:3).

MICAH 6:1–16
MORE ACCUSATIONS

Setting Up the Section

The first oracle in chapter 6 is a kind of lawsuit God brings against the people. Then the chapter closes with a pronouncement of Israel's sentence.

The opening phrase of the chapter highlights that these are the Lord's words spoken through Micah. The following case or lawsuit against the people is a common theme in the Prophets. The Lord is the plaintiff, witnesses are called, the evidence is presented, and a judgment is rendered.

The mountains in verse 2 are personalized and called upon as witnesses for several reasons: First, they are the original witnesses of the covenant God made with His people when they entered the promised land (Deuteronomy 27:12–13). Also, Micah indicates that they are enduring and unchanging, outlasting a thousand generations of God's people, and can therefore bear witness to the everlasting validity of God's covenant with His people.

God defends Himself against the complaint of His people, as they essentially blame Him instead of themselves for the present calamity (6:3). This extends the metaphor of God trying His people before a court, and here He is making His case. In the next two verses (6:6–7), Israel replies, saying it will perform rituals and sacrifices. But as seen often in the Prophets, God responds strongly, saying He doesn't want such things. Instead, we read one of the most well-known verses in Christian history, because it succinctly states God's desires for His people (6:8). It is a magnificent account of what true covenantal life involves and requires, and what God's gracious salvation must and will bring to pass in the lives of those who trust in Him. This idea expressed in verse 8 represents one of Micah's chief emphases. The failure of Israel's faith is demonstrated in the people's indifference to justice and mercy toward others, especially toward those who are poorer or weaker than themselves.

Critical Observation

In the Old Testament, a call to remember carries the idea of participation (6:5). In remembering, the people are reliving and reclaiming events of the past. This is very much the same thing that is involved, or is to be involved, in the Lord's Supper when we are told to "do this in memory of the Lord." We are to bring what He did into our present experience.

Verse 9 is a summons to the city to listen to what the Lord has decided. In the legal analogy, this is the sentencing phase of the oracle. The rod mentioned in this verse is a picture of the Assyrians, who will attack and who will function as God's chastisement of His people.

Demystifying Micah

An *ephah* (6:10) equals twenty-two liters or about a half-bushel. Lack of technological expertise made the manufacture of precise weights and measures impossible. All you needed to make an unfair profit was an ephah that actually held less than it should, so then you would get the price for a full ephah while giving less than an ephah to your customer. There was little a customer could do in the day before weights and measures inspectors. Besides, as Micah says in chapter 2, the authorities were in the pocket of the cheating merchants.

Verses 10-13 catalog Israel's sins, beginning with cheating in business practices. The wealthy who are called out in verse 12 are the royal family, the land barons, and the military elite. We have already heard of their unjust treatment of the middle class in 2:2, 8-9 and 3:11. What comes next is the righteous sentence of the Judge they have ignored (6:13). The actions to avoid God's punishment will be futile; verses 14-15 show how normal activities for sustenance and comfort will no longer suffice.

In the final verse of this chapter, we see the only mention of kings by name in a prophetic message. It suggests that the sins of Omri and Ahab, more than a century before Micah's time, had by this time served as a paradigm for falling away from faith and engaging in injustice (6:16; see 1 Kings 16:23-30).

The judgments pronounced in verses 13-16 are the very curses that God long before (all the way back to Deuteronomy and Leviticus) promised to visit upon His people if they proved unfaithful to His covenant with them.

MICAH 7:1-20

EVENTUAL HOPE

Setting Up the Section

While Micah's prophecy is full of solemn accusations and bleak acknowledgments, it ends with a sense of triumph. It is Micah's statement of faith.

Chapter 7 opens with an image that anyone in Micah's agricultural society would understand—a vinedresser and orchard manager who, after long and patient labor, finds his vineyard stripped by vandals. God feels the same way when He comes to delight in His people and finds, instead, so much sin. The last part of verse 2 can sound like a manhunt, but it is actually a reference to the way in which fellow countrymen are mistreating each other (7:1-2).

Micah again specifically calls out the leaders and judges for their sins (7:3). In verse 4, he calls the best of them a briar, and a group of them like a hedge of briars, again an agricultural reality for the original audience. Briars only keep people or animals from harvesting ripe fruit—they leave painful digs and scratches on those who try. In this case, the briars are obstructing justice.

The watchmen in verse 4 won't help protect anyone, and this repeats the idea that one should not trust in his own protection, because God is the only source of protection, safety, and peace. Further, even the most intimate human relations snap under the strain of the terror of enemies, and each one looks out for oneself, as is happening to these people (7:6). This is a fitting sentence for a nation that preys upon its brothers (7:5-6).

Micah watches in hope for the Lord and waits for God his Savior (7:7). The appropriate response to such a moral and spiritual catastrophe is just so: to wait upon the Lord.

Take It Home

The instruction to wait on the Lord is found in a great many other such passages: Psalms 37:7; 38:15; Lamentations 3:26; and many more. People must humbly submit and wait upon the Lord's outcome. It is not ours to worry or fret, or to take matters in our own hands by doing what the Lord forbids. We must simply wait upon the moving of God. In the meantime, a proper spiritual posture for the believer is to always look to God to redress wickedness and, in the meantime, serve Him faithfully. Micah watches in hope for the Lord, and he waits for God his Savior. This is the most appropriate response in the midst of a moral and spiritual catastrophe.

The next section of verses (7:8–13) opens almost like a psalm, with Jerusalem telling her enemy not to gloat. She is being punished justly for her sins; but precisely because the Lord always does what is right, the remnant within Israel who acknowledges their sin and repents will once again enjoy the Lord's favor. Though she sits in darkness now, she will again sit in the light. And, then, those who were the instrument of her downfall will reap their just punishment.

In verse 11, the prophet speaks to Jerusalem, but the idea of walls here is not to imply defensive fortifications. These walls are more like the wall that surrounds a vineyard. Their mention speaks to Jerusalem's prosperity, not her self-defense.

Verse 12 indicates the universal reach of Yahweh's salvation—not just to one people, but all people. This is the fulfillment of God's ancient promise to Abram (Genesis 15:18) in a new and still more glorious form—the promise extends not just to the area but to the people in that area. God's justice will see to it that nations that leave Israel desolate will suffer a compensatory desolation (Micah 7:13). This last judgment is described in highly figurative language, just as it is everywhere else in the Bible.

With verse 14, the prophet turns from representing the Lord to Jerusalem and begins to represent the people in prayer to God. Addressing God as Shepherd is appropriate in several ways. In the ancient Near East, a king's role was to resemble that of a shepherd, caring for and protecting his people.

Bashan and Gilead are both known for their rich pastures, and thus they build upon the image of a shepherd (7:14). They are places fit for a king's sheep to graze. Israel doesn't possess these places anymore; they have been lost to her because of her infidelity to God. But Micah is asking that Israel be restored. It is not a presumptuous request, because God has already promised that Israel's former dominion will be restored to her (4:8). Micah's prayer is that God's Word, His promise, will come true.

The Lord interrupts and speaks in verse 15, promising to show His people in the future wonders of His grace and power such as He showed Israel when He brought them out of Egypt and through the wilderness. The stories of the Exodus are faith affirming for the people of Israel. They remember God's mighty acts as He freed His people and miraculously led them toward the land He had promised them.

After the brief interlude in which God speaks, Micah takes over again in verses 16–17. In these verses, the images of nations with deaf ears and hands on mouths represent a sense of awe and even a sense of being put in one's place. In fact, all the images in these verses are of people who recognize the greatness of Israel's God.

The final three verses of Micah's prophecy include three terms for sin (*sin, transgression*, and *iniquities*) and six descriptions of God's character: His pardons, His forgiveness, His ability to let go of anger, His delight in showing mercy, His compassion, and His faithfulness. These terms are reminiscent of the Exodus account in which God identifies Himself to Moses (Exodus 34:6). Micah sings the praises of the true God while educating his listeners and readers about the character of God.

Take It Home

An unworthy, undeserving, but repentant people can hope in a glorious future precisely because of God's unchanging mercy and because of His fidelity to His promise. Micah's prophecy reminds us all that while we will experience God's chastisement, there is hope for every heart that has the ability and the willingness to repent.

NAHUM

INTRODUCTION TO NAHUM

Nahum is a book that calls into reckoning Judah's enemy, Nineveh. A careful reading of this book reveals that the author has a high view of God and His Word; he preaches against idolatry, immorality, injustice, and all manner of sin.

AUTHOR

We don't know many facts about Nahum, but there is no reason to doubt he is the primary author of the material that bears his name. From his writing style we can assume he was born into a family with enough means to provide him literary training.

OCCASION

Nahum witnessed the reduction of his nation to vassalage during the early campaigns of Assyria. These events, a prelude and a means to the judgment of both Judah and Nineveh, are part of the process that accomplishes the restoration of God's people.

PURPOSE

Nahum writes his short prophecy (1) to announce the doom of Nineveh and the demise of the mighty Assyrian Empire and (2) to bring a message of consolation to an oppressed Judah.

THEMES

The most basic theological perspective of Nahum is that of God's sovereignty. God is seen as supreme over nature and nations. He moves in just judgment against His foes but with saving concern for those who put their trust in Him. God is shown to be jealous and to abhor sin, but He is also long-suffering and has distinct purposes for His redeemed people.

HISTORICAL CONTEXT

The origin and setting of Nahum's prophecy can be deduced from the earliest and latest events mentioned: the fall of Thebes (663 BC) in Nahum 3:8 and the fall of Nineveh (612 BC), an event that is predicted throughout the book. The book of Nahum is intimately bound up with this period of dramatic change.

NAHUM 1:1–15

THE DOOM OF NINEVEH DECLARED

A Hymn to the Sovereign God   1:1–10
God's Justice for Nineveh and Judah   1:11–15

Setting Up the Section

Nahum begins his prophecy with a notice of its central focus—Nineveh (1:1)—and then turns his attention to a description of Nineveh's certain doom (1:2–15). Throughout the book, Nahum's prophecies deal with Nineveh's doom, its eventual defeat, and its destruction. In the opening section, doom is declared to be certain, because it has been decreed by the sovereign and just Judge of the world, who deals equitably with all.

📖 1:1–10

A HYMN TO THE SOVEREIGN GOD

    Nahum begins his prophecy with a two-part hymn that sets forth the theme of the section and depicts selected key elements of God's nature. The hymn emphasizes that God is a God of justice, who will punish the wicked and avenge His own (1:2). Further, He is a sovereign and mighty God who, although He is long-suffering, will defeat His guilty foes (1:3–6) and, though He is beneficent, will destroy those who plot against Him (1:7–10). The rehearsal of these general truths concerning the character and work of God provides a foundation for their application to the world situation of Nahum's day.

Nineveh, having plotted against God's people and afflicted God's people, will experience His judgment, while a previously punished Judah will know relief from affliction and be restored to peace and joy (1:12–15).

In the majestic hymn to Yahweh in verses 2–10, critical scholars have recognized the skeleton of an acrostic based on the Hebrew alphabet. The acrostic is difficult to trace in that the prescribed letter of the alphabet may occur within the line rather than as the first letter. However, the hymnic nature of verses 2–10 is undeniable.

By calling his prophecy a vision, Nahum underscores the fact that what he says is not of his own invention but is that which God has specially revealed to him. At the outset, then, Nahum makes clear that his words are not his own insights based upon his observations of the events of his time. Rather, they are nothing less than the message given to him by the sovereign God, whose word he must deliver however difficult it might be.

Nahum's prophecy is directed at Nineveh, as is made clear at the start. It begins with an indication of its theme: God is a God of justice who will punish the wicked and avenge His own (1:2).

Critical Observation

Nahum's employment of the idea of jealousy is in harmony with the familiar scriptural motif of the husband and the wife. This motif is often applied in the Bible to God's relationship to Israel. Israel had been the object of God's eternal love. She had been brought into the family of God in the exodus from Egypt. He had cared for her and nourished her in the testing of the wilderness and had brought her safely into the land of inheritance.

Thus vengeance becomes a key to understanding Nahum's prophecy. Because God is holy, He cannot let sin go unpunished. Because only God is perfectly holy, just, and wise, only He can exact the proper punishment (see Psalm 94). The last line of Nahum 1:2 is important for understanding the process of God's vengeance: It is not always immediate. At times He holds in reserve His wrath against His foes until the proper occasion.

Having drawn the reader's attention to a sovereign and just God who deals in judgment with the ungodly (1:2), Nahum further develops this theme as his hymn to Yahweh continues. The first part of the hymn (1:2–6) is drawn largely from traditional Exodus themes underscoring God's wrath against an unbelieving enemy. The second part (1:7–10) comes from a wider spectrum of praises to God for His defense of His own while defeating the enemy.

In all this, Nahum gives a graphic picture of the limitless and invincible power of God. Having painted such a poignant portrait, Nahum returns to the subject of the destruction of God's foes (1:8–10). God, in His judicial wrath, will come against them like a victorious commander pursuing his foes to the farthest recesses of the earth. Indeed, God's enemies will come to understand that He will overturn their insolent plotting against Him so thoroughly that, like men entangled in thorns or overcome with their own drunkenness, they will be easily overthrown. God's fiery wrath will consume them like fire. They will not devise their devious plot a second time.

The ruins of Nineveh show abundant evidence of the intensity of the conflagration that consumed the fallen city. Whatever application these verses have to God's enemies in general, it is obvious that Nahum's prophetic pronouncements have a particular relevance for Nineveh.

GOD'S JUSTICE FOR NINEVEH AND JUDAH

With the completion of the hymn, Nahum turns to the two nations and their capitals that are the subject of his prophecies. The latter half of his hymn has been directed against those who plot against God. Keying in on that term, Nahum turns to the supreme example of such activity: Assyria and its capital city of Nineveh. In four short verses, Nahum brings God's charges against Nineveh—it will be judged regardless of its seemingly limitless strength (1:11–12, 14). This judgment will result in a respite for Judah in its affliction (1:12–13). The section closes with a stirring message of good news: Because wicked Nineveh has been judged, a repentant Judah may once again worship God in peace (1:15).

This short section is distinct from the previous hymn in 1:2–10. In a dramatic structural shift from hymnic to narrative style, Nahum turns to Nineveh in application of the teaching of his hymn. Nineveh/Assyria is identified as a plotter, an identification that seems obvious in the light of the military exploits of its most prominent kings. The word translated in verse 11 as *wickedness* (NIV) is often translated *worthlessness*. It speaks of a character of life so totally reprobate that the term came ultimately to apply to Satan himself (2 Corinthians 6:14–15).

The initial phase of Nahum's messages against Nineveh follows in Nahum 1:12–14. For Nineveh, there is the solemn affirmation that her long night of cruel domination is soon to end. Nahum's use of the word *name* is particularly appropriate, as it here connotes *existence* (1:14). Nineveh/Assyria is to be destroyed and left without descendant.

So hopeless is Nineveh's case and so devastating will be her demise that she will not even have a memorial left to her greatness, nor will anyone erect a monument to her memory. Because of her debased activity, she has gained such contempt for herself that her demise will bring to the lips of the observers of her fall a sigh of relief and a song of rejoicing (1:15).

With the pronouncement of the irreversible decision of divine judgment, there is a good word for Judah (1:13). Nahum's prophecy is a near-historical realization of Isaiah's. Isaiah foresees the day when an oppressed Israel will be freed at last from oppressors and invaders, and its people will not only hear the message of the Lord's salvation but also experience the everlasting serenity that comes with His presence in royal power in their midst (Isaiah 52:1–10).

Critical Observation

The emphasis of Isaiah and Nahum on God's good news becomes an important motif for the New Testament revelation. Jesus' birth is announced as an occasion of glad tidings (Luke 2:10), and Christ announces that His ministry is in initial fulfillment of the message of salvation and joy that Isaiah prophesied (compare Luke 4:16–21 with Isaiah 61:1–2). Peter makes clear to Jew and Gentile alike that Christ has effected their full salvation, with the result that God's full peace can be enjoyed by all (Acts 10:34–43), a message of good news that Paul likewise affirms (Ephesians 2:14–18). It is no wonder, then, that Paul later builds on the theme of the message of good news and peace that Christ has provided both as scriptural evidence for the Jew and as a challenge to all believers to bear the gospel to a needy mankind (Romans 10:9–15; see Isaiah 52:7; Nahum 1:15).

NAHUM 2:1–13

THE DOOM OF NINEVEH DESCRIBED

Setting Up the Section

Having declared Nineveh's certain doom and Judah's sure relief, Nahum turns to the chief consideration of his prophecy: the fall of Nineveh. The whole section is filled with the book's basic thesis: God will punish wicked Nineveh and restore His own people. This theme is developed with regard to Nineveh by means of a long narrative section (2:3–10) and a woe oracle (3:1–7).

📖 **2:1–2**

GOD WILL PUNISH WICKED NINEVEH AND RESTORE HIS OWN

The fate of Nineveh is carried forward in the announcement of the arrival of its attacker. In the light of the critical announcement, Nahum issues a fourfold command. Each of the imperatives in verse 1 produces a staccato effect and lends urgency and dramatic appeal to the scene. Nahum's admonitions are probably to be understood as irony, perhaps with a touch of sarcasm. Because Nineveh's doom has already been announced (chapter 1), all such efforts are obviously destined for failure as God restores His own (2:2).

FIRST DESCRIPTION OF NINEVEH'S DEMISE

Nahum now turns from his introductory theme to the first of two descriptions of Nineveh's certain destruction. The section contains two parts: (1) a description of the attackers (2:3–6) and (2) the consequences of the attack (2:7–10). It is marked by several distinctive literary features by which the poet makes skillful plays on words.

Nahum's description of the attack against Nineveh begins with a consideration of its attackers (2:3–6). In these verses, there is a clear pattern describing the siege: the enemy's assembling of his forces (2:3), the initial advance (2:4), the all-out attack (2:5–6), and its aftermath (2:7–10). The scene progresses from one of preparation and advance to one of conflict.

As the account unfolds, the attackers have gained entrance to the city, for the Assyrians are seen as being captured and led away into exile, while the women, pleading for mercy and bewailing their fate, are led away moaning.

The inevitable consequences that follow the city's capture are then detailed in verses 8–10. The fate of the fallen city is in view. Conquered Nineveh is said to be like a pool of water. The simile is effective and appropriate. Mighty Nineveh lay in a favorable location that has blessed her with an adequate water supply. But now the blessing has turned into a curse at the hands of the enemy, whose siege has left Nineveh a "leaking water reservoir" (2:8 NLT). The panicked masses flee from the waters and the crumbling city.

Demystifying Nahum

In remarkable agreement with Nahum's prophecy that there is no end to Nineveh's treasures is the factual account in the Babylonian Chronicle that the spoil taken at Nineveh's capture is "a quantity beyond counting." The city is completely sacked.

THE DISCREDITED CITY

Contemplating the demise of arrogant Nineveh, Nahum utilizes a taunt song, a literary form common in the ancient Near East. Using an extended metaphor (or allegory), Nineveh is ironically compared to a lion's den, now no longer the lair of an invincible predator or a den of refuge for its cubs but reduced to ashes. Nineveh will be judged for its selfishness, rapacity, and cruelty.

Nahum can now ask, "Where?" The mighty lion of the nations (Assyria) used to proceed at will from its impenetrable lair (Nineveh) to return its prey to its pride (the citizens of Nineveh). Where is all of that now?

Like Nahum's first oracle (chapter 1), this section ends with a pronouncement of judgment for Nineveh/Assyria, but it includes a message of hope for Judah (2:12–13). Nahum's second oracle is not yet through, however, and before he adds a further note of good news (3:19), he will again consider the defeat and demise of Nineveh, detailing the reasons for the divine sentence (3:1–7).

NAHUM 3:1–19

THE DOOM OF NINEVEH DETAILED

Setting Up the Section

With the completion of the first description of Nineveh's doom, capped by a taunt song castigating the discredited city (2:3–13), the demise of Nineveh is rehearsed again, this time underlining the reasons for the devastation (3:1–7). Nahum will build upon that description with another taunt song, which will occupy the greater portion of the third chapter (3:8–19).

3:1–7

SECOND DESCRIPTION OF NINEVEH'S DEMISE

Nahum writes his second description of Nineveh's certain doom in the form of a woe oracle. The initial *woe* is a word drawn from a lamentation liturgy for the dead. As utilized by the prophet, while containing a prophetic declaration and description of the coming judgment, it also constitutes a formal denunciation of the doomed city. Woe oracles normally contain three elements: invective (3:1, 7), threat (3:2–3, 5–6), criticism (3:4).

In verses 2–3, Nahum moves to a vivid description of the coming battle. Whether reporting what he has seen in a vision or merely envisioning the future scene, his portrayal is done with picturesque brevity using vivid images.

This nation who had brought havoc and ruin to so much of the ancient Near East will now face death and destruction. Here again a notable crux occurs. Does the statement relative to Nineveh's harlotry (3:4) explain the death and destruction described in the previous verses, or does it initiate the following declaration of God's judgment against the city?

Further, Nineveh will be pelted with filth (3:6). The word translated *filth* denotes that which is detested. A strong word, it is usually reserved for contexts dealing with aberrations connected with pagan worship. The word carries with it the idea of the loathing that all such detestable practices produce; the thought is that despoiled Nineveh will be treated as a detested and abominable thing.

The woe reaches its climax with a sarcastic appraisal of Nineveh's hopeless plight: Nineveh is destroyed, destitute, and devoid of mourners (3:7).

A COMPARISON OF NINEVEH AND THEBES

Before Ashurbanipal's victory, Thebes seemed unconquerable. As described in verse 8, Thebes was surrounded by a strong defensive wall and a water system that included lakes, moats, canals, and the Nile. Thebes had been able to boast of the help of not only all Egypt but also its seventh-century allies: Sudanese Cush, Put (perhaps the fabled land of Punt in coastal Somaliland), and Libya. None of these, however, supplied strength and protection for Thebes at all.

Verses 12–13 depict the hopelessness of Nineveh's defensive measures. Nahum says the city's massive fortifications will crumble as readily before the eager attackers as first-ripe figs fall into the mouths of those who shake the trees. Further, its famed defenders will prove to be no more successful in protecting the city than untrained and weak women.

A CONCLUDING CONDEMNATION OF NINEVEH

With verse 14, Nahum approaches the end of his prophecy. The verses that follow form the second portion of an extended taunt song that functions as satire. This short section contains two short commands given in irony—verse 14 through the first part of verse 15, then the last part of verse 15 through verse 17. Verses 18–19 are a final gibe that forms both a concluding denunciation and a doleful dirge.

Nahum's sarcasm is evident throughout. He prophesies that Nineveh will know the besieger's fiery torch and sword as the enemy sweeps through the city like a horde of devouring locusts. Nineveh's merchants and officials flee and leave her alone, leaderless, and ill-equipped to meet the advance of the army that is about to surround her.

As Nahum approaches the end of his prophecy, Nineveh's leaders are compared to shepherds who have nodded off to sleep and allowed the sheep (the Ninevites) to be scattered (in flight or in exile) and subjected to harm. Even worse, no one comes to gather them. The choice of this motif as the final one for the book may suggest, as many commentators have observed, that the "sleep" of the shepherds/officials is death (3:18).

Critical Observation

Nahum's words have been dramatically precise in their fulfillment. They find corroboration in the findings of archaeologists who note the hasty strengthening of the walls at strategic defensive positions.

The fall of the city due to water (1:8; 2:8) has been attested both by archaeologists and ancient historians. Unusually heavy rains were known to have given difficulty to Nineveh, which was served by three rivers: the Tigris, the Khosr, and the Tebiltu. A high-water season and a sudden storm, accompanied by the swelling of any or all three rivers, would account for the fulfillment of Nahum's prophecy.

Nahum also predicts the burning of the city (1:10; 2:13; 3:15), a fact confirmed by archaeological excavation. Nahum's emphasis on the destruction of Nineveh's temples (1:14) is also confirmed by the excavations at Nineveh. Minute details concerning the events of the final days before Nineveh's fall—such as the drunkenness (1:10; 3:11), cowardice, degeneracy (3:4), and the desertion (2:8; 3:17) of the city by its leadership—are also abundantly recorded in the ancient traditions. Nahum's prophecies concerning the final slaughter of Nineveh's citizens (3:3) and the looting of the city (2:9–10), its utter destruction (2:10; 3:7), and the virtual disappearance of its people (3:17–19) are facts confirmed in the ancient records.

Nahum once more utilizes a rhetorical question to conclude the section, here with sobering effect. Had anyone escaped Nineveh's cruelty? The implied negative answer guarantees the universal rejoicing over Nineveh's demise. This last use of a rhetorical question (a double one, in the light of verse 18) is one of five such instances that have been woven into the book's fabric. Twice, rhetorical questions introduce the poet's satirical taunt song (2:11; 3:8). Three times a rhetorical question closes a unit with striking effect: underscoring God's irresistible judgment of sin (1:6) and emphasizing Nineveh's much-deserved destruction (3:7, 19).

Take It Home

Israel no doubt joined in the exultation and took comfort in the good news (3:19). Her dreaded enemy has faced God's judgment, a reminder of God's promise concerning His judgment of all Israel's foes. May Nahum's words, as well as those of God's prophets, teach all God's people to trust fully in Him, the Shepherd and overseer of souls.

HABAKKUK

INTRODUCTION TO HABAKKUK

Like Nahum, Habakkuk begins by referring to his message as an *oracle*, or a message placed upon his heart by God. Like Nahum, Habakkuk assures his readers that what he is about to relate is not from his own ingenuity but is from God. Unlike Nahum, however, Habakkuk does not state that his message is specifically directed at any one individual or group of people, though he will devote a great deal of space to a denunciation of the Chaldeans, which is a representation of the Babylonians.

AUTHOR

We don't know anything more about Habakkuk than what can be gleaned from this book. We do know, however, that his authorship of this message was accepted from very early on.

PURPOSE

The book of Habakkuk is less of a prophet preaching to his people and more of a prophet speaking to his God. Habakkuk asks probing questions which lead from the current state of Judah to the eventual future of the kingdom.

OCCASION

While Habakkuk may differ from the other prophets in terms of whom he addresses in his message, he is similar in that he is troubled by the disobedience of his people. In Habakkuk's case, however, rather than pleading with God for more time or with the people for more attention, he questions why God's judgment hasn't already fallen on his nation.

THEMES

While judgment and the eventual vindication of Israel is a part of Habakkuk's message, as with other Old Testament prophets, he also addresses themes such as faith in God's sovereignty.

HABAKKUK 1:1–17

THE PROPHET'S PERPLEXITIES

Setting Up the Section

Habakkuk plunges into a rehearsal of his spiritual wrestling with God. In so doing, he tells his readers of his perplexities as to the divine working and of God's answers to his questions (1:2–2:20). This chapter will consider Habakkuk's superscription, his two questions, and God's answer to the first.

🖹 1:1–4

HOW CAN GOD DISREGARD JUDAH'S SIN?

Immediately after the notice of the source of his prophecy (1:1), Habakkuk at once plunges into a dramatic rehearsal of a time when the impact of Judah's unchecked sin overwhelmed him. His questioning of God forms the backdrop for the examination of the relation of God's holy standards to the operation of the divine providence that follows later.

The nature of Habakkuk's complaint to God, begun in the invocation (1:2) and elaborated in the statement of the problem (1:3–4), can be better appreciated when one examines the words he uses to describe his perception of Judahite society. They depict a society characterized by the general spiritual and ethical havoc that exists where such sin abounds.

Habakkuk is disturbed by God's silence with regard to his country's injustice and his own cries for help and intervention. His questions and doubts have an extra emotional and spiritual dimension. He is an unhappy, perplexed, and frustrated prophet.

📖 **1:5–11**

GOD WILL JUDGE JUDAH

To the emotional and dramatic cry of the prophet, God gives a dramatic, amazing answer—God is already at work on the problem. He will send the Chaldeans (Babylonians) to chastise Judah (1:5–6). God then supplies some additional details as to the martial abilities of the violent Chaldeans (1:7–11).

Critical Observation

The term *Chaldea* is used in reference to the tribes that lived in southernmost Mesopotamia. They made up the biggest part of Babylonia. By at least 705 BC, Chaldean king Merodach-Baladan took the title "King of Babylon," with the result that the terms *Chaldean* and *Babylonian* became used interchangeably in the Old Testament.

God's reply mirrors the words Habakkuk had used. God tells Habakkuk to look at the nations (1:5). God is already at work in and behind the scenes of earth's history to set in motion events that will change the whole situation. And when Habakkuk learns what is to happen, he will be utterly amazed. In fact, he probably will not be able to believe it.

The reason for Habakkuk's astonishment becomes apparent in verse 6: God will raise up the Chaldeans. Verses 5–6, revealing Habakkuk's astonishment at God's sending the Chaldeans to judge His people, are crucial to understanding the setting of the book.

By telling Habakkuk of the Chaldeans' future prominence, the Lord reassures him of His sovereign control of the details of history. Since God's prophet will be surprised at the announcement about the Chaldeans, God goes on to supply a brief résumé of their character and potentially devastating power (1:6–11).

Contrary to Habakkuk's complaint, God assures His prophet that He sees all that comes to pass and hears the prayers and complaints of His people. Habakkuk's own word is sent back to him. Has Judah done violence? It shall in turn suffer violence at the hands of a violent nation whose well-trained and battle-seasoned army will move forward with such precision that the whole striking force will march as one to achieve its objectives, at the same time taking many captives (1:9).

Although the language is hyperbolic throughout verses 6–11, in light of the ancient records it is not inappropriate. Many texts could be cited concerning the Chaldeans' successful campaigning. The picture of Chaldean armed might is of one who holds all his foes in contempt and mocks them. Such a nation knows no god but strength (1:10).

Habakkuk is informed, however, that God's avenging host is not without responsibility. The Chaldeans will be held guilty for their actions. Had Habakkuk listened as carefully to the last line of God's answer as he did to the extended description of Judah's chastiser, he might have avoided the second perplexity that gripped his soul, the report of which is contained in the verses that follow (1:12–17).

📖 1:12–17

HOW CAN GOD EMPLOY THE WICKED?

God's answer and extended description of his agent of judgment against Judah puzzles His prophet. Habakkuk simply cannot reconcile God's use of the Chaldeans, a people more corrupt than those they are to judge, to punish His people. He begins his second perplexity with an invocation in which he expresses his consternation (1:12). Faced with the prospect of destructive judgment, perhaps even the death of the nation itself, Habakkuk cries out to Israel's God, the Holy One of her salvation, who alone is her refuge in such times.

The precise understanding of Habakkuk's impassioned words, "we will not die" (1:12), is difficult to grasp, but most see it as a statement of confidence in God.

Despite that confidence in God, Habakkuk has reservations concerning the situation. His reservations are detailed in verses 13–17. While he understands the necessity of Judah's judgment and the Chaldeans' role, he cannot comprehend why a holy God plans to use a nation more wicked than the nation He desires to punish. Not only does God's announcement seem out of character for a holy God, but also the use of the Chaldeans provokes another thought. Once this plan is put into operation, will not a helpless mankind always be at the mercy of these God-commissioned agents of chastisement (1:13–17)?

Adopting fishing imagery, Habakkuk portrays the scenario that God has set in motion as one of fishermen (Chaldeans) who use their powerful hooks and nets (military might and methods) to catch helpless fish and creatures of the sea (the various conquered peoples). The success of these fishermen will only cause them to rejoice and have their appetites whetted for still greater pleasures.

Habakkuk's fears are not unfounded, for the Chaldean war machine was effective enough to gain for them political dominance across the northern part of the Fertile Crescent and through the Levant to the borders of Egypt.

Critical Observation

Habakkuk takes his place beside many others—such as Job, the psalmist Asaph (Psalm 73), Jeremiah, and Malachi—who question God as to His fairness in handling the problems of evil and injustice. Like these other questioners, Habakkuk will be shown the necessity of fully trusting in God.

HABAKKUK 2:1–20
GOD'S SOVEREIGNTY

Instructions	2:1–4
The Chaldeans	2:5–20

Setting Up the Section

Habakkuk offers God's reply to his complaint, communicates an essential and time-less message about faith for all people, provides insight into the operations of divine government, and reveals the ultimate fate that will befall the wicked Chaldeans.

📖 **2:1–4**

INSTRUCTIONS

Habakkuk ends his complaint with a renewed statement of his confidence in God (2:1). He also reports his intention to assume the role of a watchman. As the city watchman mans his post atop the walls to look for the approach of danger or a messenger, or to keep watch over current events, Habakkuk will assume the role of a prophetic watchman, taking his post to watch for the Lord's reply.

Before God's specific points of reply are given to Habakkuk, He has preliminary instructions for His prophet. The Lord's commands are intended to prepare Habakkuk for the revelation of crucial issues relative to the operations of divine government that will introduce the discussion of the whole matter of Habakkuk's concern: the disposition of the voracious Chaldeans (2:5–20).

Critical Observation

The place of Habakkuk 2:4 in the history of biblical interpretation can hardly be overestimated. Its threefold citation in the New Testament (Romans 1:17; Galatians 3:11; Hebrews 10:38) attests to its basic importance to the Christian revelation.

Accordingly, verse 4 is best taken with what follows. Though it forms the essence of the divine revelation that is to be heralded to all, it is woven into the structure of verse 5, both verses thus serving as the basis for the woes that follow.

Habakkuk is told in verse 2 to write the issue of the divine reply upon tablets. He is to communicate a message of lasting importance. Everyone who reads or hears these words is to consider themselves a herald of a significant communication intended for all people everywhere. Probably the precise words are to be found in verse 4, the latter part of which is of crucial significance. The message is to be written plainly so those who pass by might be able to understand it and bear the news to others.

Habakkuk now is told the basic guiding principles upon which the operation of divine government unalterably proceeds until the coming of that final appointed time (2:3). The revelation of these truths will make clear the culpability of the Chaldeans (2:5), whose woe is pronounced in the rest of the chapter (2:6–20).

THE CHALDEANS

Beginning with verse 5, God's answer takes the form of a logical argument: If it is true that the arrogant have ungodly desires and never come to enjoy the blessings of God, how much more certain is it that the qualities accompanying such an attitude will ultimately betray them? The underlying implication is clear: The Chaldeans' selfishness and success will be their undoing.

The first woe: The plundering Chaldean will be despoiled (2:6–8).

Each of the five woes, beginning in verse 6, pertains to one or more of the Chaldeans' sins. The first woe centers on the Chaldeans' rapacity. The language recalls their multiplying of wealth at the expense of others. The depth of the Chaldeans' insensitivity toward others may be seen in that they add to their riches by extorting pledges from their debtors, something condemned in the Torah and a violation against all mankind. The charge, only an example of the Chaldeans' unjust activities, provides entrée into the following metaphor taken from the world of finance.

Verse 7 reveals that those who had been so oppressed will arise suddenly and send collectors who will press their claims for back payment with a force equal to that of the Chaldeans' former violence. The chief point is that the plundering Chaldean will eventually know the effects of plunder himself. He who has so misused others—conquering, looting, and enslaving many—will himself experience the conqueror's heel and learn the sorrow of those whose people and possessions have been carried off as booty.

The second woe: The plotting Chaldean will be denounced (2:9–11).

The second woe underscores the Chaldeans' capacity for cunning schemes against mankind. Building upon the imagery in the first woe, the Chaldean is portrayed as one who achieves wealth through violence and evil means. Verse 11, with its stone walls and beams, is a reference to the Chaldeans' building projects. In the end, the Chaldeans will have no lasting empire.

The third woe: The pillaging Chaldean will be destroyed (2:12–14).

The image of construction found in the second woe is continued in the third. The chief materials used in constructing the city are seen for what they are: bloodshed and injustice. Such conduct is an affront to a holy and righteous God. It marks the Chaldeans as those who, unlike the righteous who reflect God's standards, are arrogant and presumptuous.

Babylon (and all such wicked people) will be judged, not only for her unbridled arrogance, but also because God's purposes include a universal experiencing of His own glory. The words of verse 14 are adapted from Isaiah 11:9. Isaiah's prophecy looks ahead to the great messianic era in all its fullness and perfection; Habakkuk uses it to validate the pronouncement of the destruction of the Neo-Babylonian Empire.

The fourth woe: The perverting Chaldean will be disgraced (2:15–17).

The tie between the third and fourth woes is not as pronounced as between the first and second or the second and third. However, they do have in common a reference to a city or town (2:12, 17).

The fourth woe begins with an invective formed with a strong allegory. The Chaldean is a man who gives his neighbor a drink in seeming hospitality. The apparently innocent cup contains a draught of wrath, for it is designed to get its partaker drunk. The allegory depicts the giver of the drink as one who is forced to imbibe of his own drink and suffer the disgrace of exposure. Several familiar biblical motifs and expressions are contained in verses 15-16. The cup as a motif of judgment is well attested elsewhere. Particularly enlightening for the understanding of Habakkuk's fourth woe is Jeremiah's use of the cup to portray God's relation with Babylon (Jeremiah 51:6-8).

Habakkuk makes the same point, although the image is slightly different. The Chaldean now knows the shame he has brought on others. Therefore, he is given a sarcastic command: "Go on! Drink and expose yourself!" (2:16). The last imperative is graphic. It means to show oneself as uncircumcised. Not even in the marks of his body can the Chaldean claim covenant relationship with Yahweh.

The reason the Chaldean must drink the cup follows in verse 17. His will be a wanton disregard of the value of the natural world, the animal kingdom, and civilized humanity.

The scene shifts to the animal kingdom. It, too, will suffer violence at the hands of the Chaldeans. The natural and animal worlds are often made unwilling participants in mankind's sin and greed. It is a crime that has increasingly plagued human society. Such thoughtless conduct by the Chaldeans indicates again their godless arrogance and selfish presumption for which punishment must come.

The fourth woe is closed with a reiteration of the charge made against the Chaldean in the first. He will have a callous disregard even for the sanctity of human life. In his quest for power, he will destroy everything that stands in his way, be it lands, cities, or those who dwell in them.

The fifth woe: The polytheistic Chaldean will be deserted by his idols (2:18–20).

In drawing the woe oracles to a close, Habakkuk deliberately changes the order he has previously employed by beginning with the reason for the threatened judgment (2:18).

The religious orientation of the Chaldean is now examined and shown to be without foundation. His idolatrous polytheism is seen to be worthless. Since idols are only mankind's creation, to put one's trust in them is to trust one's own creation rather than the Creator.

Before going on to give the most crucial reason for the doom of the polytheistic Chaldean, Habakkuk delivers an invective and a threat (2:19).

The fifth woe ends with a pronouncement that displays the vast difference between Israel's God and the gods of Babylon. Unlike those gods, who have neither life nor word of guidance for their followers, Yahweh is a living God. The gods of Babylon (and their devotees) can only remain silent before Him.

The invective and threat against Babylon (2:19) thus have more than sufficient cause. Since the Chaldeans worship gods of their own creation (2:18) rather than the Creator, controller, and consummator of history, their condemnation is certain. This is their most besetting sin. The verdict is final. Habakkuk can be assured that the Chaldeans will be judged, for they will violate the standards of God.

Verse 20 has another application. Because the idolatry that leads to the neglect and rejection of God is a universal problem, all the earth is to be silent before the living God.

HABAKKUK 3:1–19

THE PROPHET'S PRAYER AND GOD'S EXALTATION

Setting Up the Section

A perplexed prophet had awaited and received God's instructions in chapter 2. In humble response, Habakkuk turns in prayer and praise to God.

📖 3:1–2

THE PROPHET'S PRAYER

Having heard and understood God's principles of judgment and their application, Habakkuk returns to the matter of Judah's judgment. What follows is his prayer psalm, a composition to be set to music for use in worship.

In verse 2, Habakkuk begins his prayer with a cry and a statement of praise that reflect his fear of God. The choice of the word *Lord* (Yahweh) rather than a more general term probably emphasizes the fact that Habakkuk addresses his words to Israel's covenant God. He has heard of Yahweh's past mighty deeds. Habakkuk has in mind the Exodus, the subject of verses 3–15.

In accordance with God's message of the near chastisement of Judah, Habakkuk prays for God's miraculous intervention. He asks that (as in the past) God will renew His deeds and thus again make known His work of redemption. With an aching heart, he urges God to be compassionate in the coming turmoil.

📖 3:3–15

THE REDEEMER

Habakkuk has prayed for God's mercy in the midst of judgment. He does so on the basis of his consideration of God's past redemptive acts for His people, some of which he now rehearses for all to contemplate. The prayer-psalm-poem consists of two distinct works (3:3–7 and 3:8–15). The first poem deals with Israel's movement up from the Sinai Peninsula, on the way to the Jordan River crossing.

In a graphic simile, the brilliance of God's glory is detailed. The association of the glory of the Lord with Sinai is unmistakable; the point here, however, may be that the same glory that was seen at Mount Sinai and traveled with the people on their journeys

(Exodus 40:34–38) now moves in surpassing brilliance ahead of them. This first poem closes with a consideration of God's initial strikes against the enemy (Habakkuk 3:6–7). The land of the Midianites is identified primarily with the southern part of Transjordan, and evidence now exists that Cushan was also located there.

The second poem is a victory ode that sings of the mighty strength of Israel's Redeemer. His power is displayed at the waters of testing (3:8–9), unleashed in the natural world (3:9–11), and viewed by the enemy (3:12–15). Whereas the first two sections deal in a general way with the entire Exodus event, the final section fixes its attention on the initial stage of the Exodus.

Addressing God personally, Habakkuk asks whether His actions against the waters are out of anger. All three words for wrath here characterize God's judicial activity against anything that opposes His will. Yahweh is portrayed metaphorically as Israel's mighty warrior who appears in His battle chariot, armed with bow, club, arrows, and spear (3:8–11). This is no cosmic battle between deities; Yahweh comes as Israel's champion against human opponents.

The reference to waters here probably refers to God's activities in the entire Exodus event. The theme of water is prominent not only in the triumph at the Red Sea (Exodus 14) but also in passing through the Jordan (Joshua 3–4).

The scene changes from preparation to engagement in battle. The predominant image in this description of nature's response is the agitation of cosmic waters. The description in verses 9–10 fits well with the details of the crossing of the Jordan. The drama of warfare continues in verse 11 with a hyperbolic description.

Habakkuk had begun his prophecy with a perplexity as to why God tolerates injustice (1:2–3). When he is informed of God's intention to use the godless Chaldeans to bring judgment to His people (1:5–11), the prophet is all the more perplexed (1:12–2:1). The words of the ancient epic poem that he now considers remind him of the just nature of God.

The poem closes with details that provide a follow-up to the previous scene (3:14–15). The enemy's warriors storm out against the people of God like brigands coming upon the helpless. If, as suggested above, verse 8 deals primarily with the events toward the end of the Exodus experience, verse 15 produces the basis for the whole chain of events: the great deliverance from Egypt. The double psalm thus ends on a note of redemption. Israel's God, who brought them through the waters of testing with a mighty power that left all nature in convulsion, and who led His people in triumph, is the One who has been with them since the deliverance out of Egypt.

THE PROPHET'S PLEDGE TO THE REDEEMER'S PURPOSES

Habakkuk ends his prophecy with affirmations of personal commitment and praise. Having been dramatically reminded of the past exploits of God against the wicked and His saving intervention on behalf of His people, the prophet is overwhelmed. Now that he understands who God is and the principles and methods of His activities, it is enough for Habakkuk. He will trust Him through the coming hour of judgment and rejoice no matter what may happen (3:16–18). The words for *rejoicing* here represent strong emotions; Habakkuk used them previously to express his anxiety over the unbridled avarice of the Chaldeans (1:14–15). Here he underscores his repentant heart and triumphant faith. Together these words express his resolve not merely to rest in the Lord's will through everything that will come to pass but to rejoice fully in his saving God.

Borrowing phraseology from the repertoire of ancient Hebrew poetry, he closes the account of his spiritual odyssey on a high note of praise (3:19). The order is significant. Whatever strength he has he owes to the One who is his strength; but basic to everything is the fact that Yahweh is his Lord and his Master, the center of his life.

Habakkuk 3:8–15 constitutes a victory song commemorating the conquest itself and points to the basis of that success in the Exodus event, particularly in the victory at the Red Sea. After Habakkuk pleads for mercy in the midst of wrath (3:2) and reviews God's past record (3:3–15), his reverential trust in God is renewed. Israel's great Redeemer is his also. He will trust in the Lord no matter what happens (3:16–19). He who had acted both in judgment and deliverance for Israel in the past can be counted on to do so once again, both for Israel and His prophet. Thus Habakkuk's final prayer of praise to Israel's Redeemer stands not only as a unified composition but also as the climax to the whole prophecy.

ZEPHANIAH

INTRODUCTION TO ZEPHANIAH

Zephaniah denounced the materialism and greed that exploited the poor. He was aware of world conditions and announced God's judgment on the nations for their sins. Above all, God's prophet had a deep concern for God's reputation and for the well-being of all who humbly trust in Him.

AUTHOR

Although some concern has been raised with regard to many passages in the book that bears his name, Zephaniah has generally been accepted as the author of most of this book. Zephaniah traces his patrilineage four generations to a certain Hezekiah. Jewish and Christian commentators alike have commonly identified this Hezekiah with the king by that name, though this is not conclusive.

PURPOSE

Zephaniah speaks out for God and against wickedness. He writes to inform and warn his people of God's coming judgment, not only against all the world, but also against Judah and Jerusalem. Zephaniah also writes to give the people details of the fearsome events of the Day of the Lord that must come because of sin and because of the Lord's undying concern for His people who have humble and contrite hearts.

OCCASION

The occasion for Zephaniah's prophecy lies in the deplorable spiritual and moral condition of Judah in the early days of Josiah's reign. Taking the throne as an eight-year-old, Josiah finds himself the head of an immoral society. As Zephaniah writes, he is cognizant of the conditions that will surely spell the end of Judah itself (2 Kings 23:26–27).

THEMES

Zephaniah is best remembered for his presentation of God as the sovereign and just judge of all. It is He who punishes the wickedness of people and nations, particularly those who have opposed His people.

HISTORICAL CONTEXT

Few scholars have failed to accept that this book's author, as the first verse states, prophesied during the reign of Josiah (640–609 BC). Most discussions about the setting of the book of Zephaniah concern which period of Josiah's reign provides the backdrop, though many favor Josiah's early reign, because many of the problems that Zephaniah describes in his nation would have been corrected in Josiah's reforms.

OUTLINE

ZEPHANIAH 1:1–18

THE ANNOUNCEMENT OF THE DAY OF THE LORD

Setting Up the Section

Zephaniah begins his prophecy with notices of his reception of the word of the Lord, his ancestry, and the time of his ministry (1:1). He then announces the coming of God's worldwide judgment and supplies important details concerning the devastation of that coming Day of the Lord (1:14–18).

📖 1:1–6

PRONOUNCEMENTS OF JUDGMENT

God's prophet warns of a universal judgment that will one day descend upon the earth and all that is on it. The pronouncement is solemn; its phraseology is at first reminiscent of the flood (Genesis 6:17; 7:21–23). The disaster envisioned here, however, is more cataclysmic, for every living thing that dwells on the land, air, and sea dies. Man's sin is weighty, involving not only himself but his total environment (1:2–3).

Zephaniah alludes also to the Creation. His catalog of death is arranged in inverse order to God's creative work: mankind, beast, the creatures of the air, and those of the sea (see Genesis 1:20–27). The coming destruction will begin with humanity, who has denied the Creator and involved in his sin all that is under his domain (1:6). Because of their idolatry and apostasy, Judah and Jerusalem will find God's hand of chastisement stretched out against them (1:4–6).

Demystifying Zephaniah

Baal is a god associated with the storm and fertility; his veneration, together with licentious worship rites, is a constant source of temptation to Israel. Fascination with Baal had been a prime reason for the fall of the northern kingdom and will prove to be so for Judah as well. Although Zephaniah's denunciation of those who worship the hosts of heaven on the rooftops is a further indication of the turn that the worship of Baal often took, the adoration of Baal and the stars was a besetting sin in Judah when Josiah came to the throne.

📖 1:7–13

EXHORTATIONS BASED ON JUDGMENT

In the light of the pronouncements of judgment, Zephaniah issues exhortations to Judah. Since the coming of judgment is certain, it is time for them to examine their spiritual condition. The unit is made up of two sections, each introduced by an imperative (1:7, 11) followed by additional details (1:8–9, 12–13). Accordingly, verse 10 is a hinge verse that proceeds on the basis of the time framework of verses 8–9 and predicts the lamentation of the merchants upon which the call for wailing is issued (1:11).

In view of the certainty and severity of coming judgment, Zephaniah advises silence and submission, fear and consecration. The motive for his call for silence follows in verse 7—the Day of the Lord. Although Zephaniah delays his description of the terrors of the Day of the Lord until the next section (1:14–18), the seriousness of that time is underscored in a dramatic metaphor of a sacrificial banquet. The sacrifice itself is Judah and Jerusalem.

Critical Observation

The metaphor of the sacrificial banquet provides a ray of hope in the clouds of doom. Although judgment is coming, there is still time. By acknowledging God as their Master and by responding in fear to the prospect of judgment in repentance from sin and repudiation of idolatry, God's people can join a believing remnant in coming to the feast as guests acceptable to Him. There is hope after all.

But there is also caution. Guests who remain unrepentant, and hence unclean, will be disqualified and will discover that they are not only invited guests but also victims. God has summoned others (the Chaldeans or Babylonians) who will destroy Judah, Jerusalem, and the unrepentant people who inhabit them (1:8–13).

In verse 8, Zephaniah gives a further message with regard to that coming day. Israel's leadership has adopted a foreign lifestyle, including its dress. There could be a veiled threat here. Do they prefer foreign attire? They will soon see the specter of foreign uniforms throughout the land. The threat is literally carried out (for examples, see 2 Kings 23:31–35; 24:10–16; 25:1–21).

Additional charges follow in verse 9, this time leveled against all the citizens of Judah and Jerusalem who have adopted pagan customs in their worship. In this case, the custom involves avoiding contact with the threshold of the temple by leaping over it. The practice had originated among the priests of the god Dagon, during the incident of the collapse of his statue before the ark of the Lord (1 Samuel 5:1–4). The verse goes on to report that the citizenry had perpetrated deeds of violence and deceit against the less fortunate in order to achieve their ambitions.

Further information concerning the sacrifice on the Day of the Lord is in Zephaniah 1:10. Although lamentation will come from all parts of the city, Jerusalem's greedy merchants will particularly be affected. From the Fish Gate through areas of commercial activity will come a great cry. Zephaniah tells the merchants to wail over their lost wealth (1:11).

Zephaniah concludes by reporting that God's judgment will be thorough. God's instruments of invasion will seek out every corner of Jerusalem in carrying away its treasures. If not in theory, at least in practice, the people of Judah behave like full-fledged pagans.

Take It Home

Whereas today's believers may applaud Zephaniah's warning to his fellow countrymen as well given due to the apostasy, immorality, and injustice of that time, we must apply Zephaniah's words to ourselves. A far more insidious danger lurks today: Apathy and inactivity will ultimately take their toll. Those who sit back and do nothing are just as culpable as those who engage in evil.

TEACHINGS CONCERNING THE DAY OF THE LORD

Zephaniah's exhortations based on the surety of the coming judgment are amplified with further information concerning the Day of the Lord (1:14–18). In language bordering on the later apocalyptic genre, he tells of frightful conditions in the natural world and terrible destruction throughout the earth.

Zephaniah declares that the Day of the Lord is near. He previously used that fact to provide grounds for submission to the Lord (1:7). Now he supplies added details to provide a further reason for the citizens of Judah and Jerusalem to repent and submit to God. He describes conditions that will exist primarily in the final stages of the Day of the Lord. But the prophecy must be viewed as one vast event. Some matters that he mentions will soon take place during Jerusalem's fall in 586 BC; others will be repeated in various historical epochs (AD 70), until the whole prophecy finds its ultimate fulfillment in the end times. Keeping such distinctions in mind enables one to keep a clear perspective as to both the meaning of the text and the effect the prophecy must have had upon Zephaniah's hearers. However much the events detailed here may have full reference only to the final phase of the Day of the Lord, they are an integral part of the prophecy and can occur anywhere along the series.

For this section of describing the Day of the Lord, Zephaniah has drawn upon the works of Isaiah, Jeremiah, Ezekiel, and Joel, but he is particularly indebted to Joel (see Joel 2:1–11).

Because of wrath against sin, the earth will experience great distress and anguish. Other prophets report that so severe will be the testing of the eschatological day that it will be called "the time of Jacob's trouble" (Jeremiah 30:7). Zephaniah makes a similar prediction and adds that the day will bring great anguish to all who experience it (Zephaniah 1:15).

Zephaniah goes on to describe conditions in the land and in nature (1:15). Destruction will dot the landscape; everything will be a desolate waste. Once again, Zephaniah draws upon phraseology employed by Job in describing a wasteland (Job 38:27). From the physical world, Zephaniah turns to the socio-political realm in verse 16. That day will be a time of great warfare. Zephaniah concludes by observing the tragic cost in human life and experience that all this will effect (1:17–18).

There is a play on words and ideas in verse 17. Because it is a day of distress and anguish, God will cause distress to mankind. So intense will be the conditions, that people will grope like blind men. How appropriate the punishment, since the charge against them is that they are spiritually blind (Exodus 23:8; Matthew 15:14; Romans 2:19; 11:25; Ephesians 4:18; 1 John 2:11). The effect of these tragic conditions is that human life (flesh and blood) is reduced to a thing of no value, with even corpses being treated as despicable refuse (Jeremiah 9:20–22; 16:1–4; 25:32–33).

The chapter closes with a reiteration of two prominent themes: (1) the self-indulgent greed of the godless wealthy and (2) the certain judgment of all men and nations (1:18).

ZEPHANIAH 2:1–15

DETAILS CONCERNING THE DAY OF THE LORD

Instructions in Light of That Day   2:1–3
Pronouncements of Judgment   2:4–15

Setting Up the Section

In light of the horrifying spectacle of the judgment of the Day of the Lord, Zephaniah presses his fellow countrymen to gather in repentance and humility before God. Utilizing images drawn from the process of separating straw from chaff, Zephaniah gives them a spiritual message designed to achieve the safety and deliverance of those who repent and put their trust in the Lord.

📄 2:1–3

INSTRUCTIONS IN LIGHT OF THAT DAY

In the opening of this section, Zephaniah uses straw and its collection to symbolize the assembling of people (2:1–2). He employs the concept of threshing to point to the necessity of being broken before God. He uses the idea of chaff in connection with the speed and ease with which it is blown away: Like chaff, the Day of Judgment is rapidly approaching; like chaff, wayward sinners will be destroyed in the Day of the Lord.

To *gather together* (2:1) means to come together in genuine repentance and submission to the will of God. Zephaniah's plea is urgent, for God's decree is settled and will soon be put into effect.

The second portion of Zephaniah's prophecies (2:4–3:20) is made up of pronouncements (2:4–3:7), an exhortation (3:8), and teachings (3:9–20). After his preoccupation primarily with the fate of his people in the first part of the book, Zephaniah turns his attention to the foreign nations (2:4–15). He began the first major portion of his prophecy by similarly considering all nations (1:2–3). Here he deals with specific nations that are tied to Judah's situation geographically and politically—Philistia (west), Moab and Ammon (east), Cush (south), and Assyria (north). Some translations refer to Cush as Ethiopia. The Cushites do eventually settle in that area, but for Zephaniah, Cush would have more likely referred to Ethiopia.

📄 2:4–15

PRONOUNCEMENTS OF JUDGMENT

Philistia

Philistine presence in Canaan had been reported since the days of the early patriarchs. The region was made up of city-states—Gaza, Ashkelon, Ashdod, Ekron, and Gath—four of which are mentioned in verse 4.

Zephaniah calls these Philistine settlers *Kerethites*, a name associated with the Philistines (perhaps an early tribe or a branch of the Philistines). According to Zephaniah, the prosperous seacoast district will become pastureland dotted with caves for Israelite shepherds and folds for their flocks. It will belong to the remnant of Judah (2:5–7).

Moab and Ammon

Zephaniah's pronouncements of judgment turn to Judah's eastern neighbors across the Jordan River, the nations of Moab and Ammon. Like the Philistines, these nations are numbered among Israel's traditional foes. Zephaniah's is not the first curse against this people.

Demystifying Zephaniah

According to Genesis 19:30–38, both Moab and Ammon are descendants of Lot, Abraham's nephew. They are conceived incestuously with Lot's daughters through a scheme set by the young women. Later in Israel's history, the Ammonites join the Moabites in hiring Baalam to curse the Israelites. Both nations harass the Israelites in the days of the judges, and Saul and David fight against them.

Zephaniah condemns both nations for their pride and their blasphemous insults against God and His people. He predicts that both nations, who have often worked together, will be treated like Sodom and Gomorrah—the whole area will be turned into a perpetual wasteland, overrun with weeds and pocked by salt pits (2:9).

Cush

Building on the concept of universal judgment in the preceding verse, Zephaniah tacks on the notice that the judgment of Cush, too, is part of the punishment that will overtake all peoples (2:12). Zephaniah's use of the term *Cushites* refers to Ethiopia, a part of Egypt. As the Cushite dynasty had passed, so also will Egypt and, one day, all earthly powers that stand in opposition to the Lord.

Assyria

In verses 13–15, Zephaniah's fourth message against the foreign powers swings around to the north—Assyria's capital city, Nineveh, will be rendered desolate, fit only for animals. Assyria's rapacity, pride, and cruelty demand her destruction. The reason for the demise of Assyria in general and of Nineveh in particular is given in verse 15—haughtiness. Centuries later, the city's ruins are unrecognizable.

ZEPHANIAH 3:1–20

FINAL WORDS

Setting Up the Section

Although the judgments in Zephaniah's prophecy and the pronouncement of woe upon Jerusalem at the opening of this chapter are not encouraging, the prophet's message is not yet complete. Before the final word has been said, his readers will come to understand that the day of the Lord's judgment, however dark, is but the path to a brighter day.

📖 **3:1–7**

JUDGMENT FOR JERUSALEM

Zephaniah concludes his messages on judgment by turning to his own nation and to the holy city in particular. In delivering his pronouncement against Jerusalem, Zephaniah utilizes the form of the woe oracle, including invective (3:1), reason (criticism) for Judah's punishment (3:2–4), and implied threat (3:5–7).

The judgment begins with a woe in which Zephaniah calls Judah's capital a rebellious and defiled city where oppression is the order of the day. These words describe a lifestyle and social structure at variance with God's character and laws. Zephaniah charges God's people with refusing to obey God's commandments and with unwillingness to learn from chastisement (3:2). They have neither concern nor time for God and His standards.

Even the priests of Jerusalem are defiled. They who were charged with the purity of God's house and the sanctity of His law have violated both. With bold metaphors, Zephaniah exposes Jerusalem's leaders for what they are (3:3).

Zephaniah reminds his hearers of Judah's ultimate leader (3:5–7). In contrast to Jerusalem's corrupt leadership, the Lord is righteous. Unlike the wicked who know no shame, He does no iniquity. With the light of each new day, He brings evidence of His unfailing justice.

Take It Home

God's righteousness may also be seen in His merciful dealings with His people in attempting to woo them back to Himself (3:6–7). Yet rather than demonstrating a desire for repentance, Judah and Jerusalem display only an increased bent for shameless corruption. How do we respond today when God calls us back to Himself? In particular, how do we respond if returning to the Lord requires us to leave a life that is comfortable and profitable for us?

📖 3:8–13

ADDITIONAL TEACHINGS CONCERNING THE DAY OF THE LORD

Beginning with verse 9, Zephaniah turns from judgment to its outcome—God's blessing of the people of the world. In a vivid and varied metaphor, the prophet portrays a courtroom scene in which God rises first as witness on His own behalf and before the assemblage, and then presides as judge to deliver His righteous sentence. The double emphasis on judgment and hope is prominent in 3:9–20. Rather than being irreconcilable themes, judgment and hope are two aspects of one divine perspective.

Structurally, verses 9–13 provide a further reason for the exhortation to wait for the Lord (3:8). The first reason has to do with God's determination to gather the nations for the long-awaited judgment. The second deals with God's promises to a humble and purified future remnant. This section thus carries the author's thoughts to information concerning a future day that will provide the grounds for the closing admonitions of the book (3:14–20).

📖 3:14–20

HOPE IN LIGHT OF THAT DAY

Verses 14–20 form a closing unit of instructions concerning the Day of the Lord. For Jerusalem, faced with the divine sentence against her, Zephaniah has words of instruction that will doubtless be carried out: Sing for joy, shout out loud, be glad, and rejoice. The commands are happy ones, heaped up to underscore the great expectation of the joyous times that lay beyond the immediate punishment. Although the command is aimed at the future Jerusalem, the message will not be lost on the godly worshipers of Zephaniah's own day.

The promise of release from fear is accompanied by words of encouragement not to let either fright or anxiety grip their hearts (3:16–17). Such assurances form a striking contrast with Zephaniah's earlier prophecy that the Day of the Lord will be filled with such horror that even the bravest of warriors will cry out bitterly (1:14).

In a climactic finish to all that he has prophesied, Zephaniah reveals the personal promises of Israel's Redeemer. Though from a literary standpoint verses 18–20 provide a further reason for the commands concerning rejoicing in verse 14, their force must not be missed: God Himself is speaking. The Lord's opening assurance here stands in stark contrast to His pronouncements at the beginning of the book (3:18). Unlike the earlier announcement of God's gathering of the nations together so as to sweep them from the face of the earth (1:2–4), the Lord will gather up those who have been driven away from Jerusalem and, therefore, from the opportunity to partake of Israel's periods of festivity. In God's providence, His sinning people had been punished by being carried away into exile as booty to their conquerors. Now judgment has given way to hope. God will regather His chastised and cleansed people in order to lead them home.

A threefold promise follows in verse 19, part of which is repeated in verse 20, emphasizing Israel's own festive future. The certainty of Israel's newly acquired felicity is assured.

Zephaniah closes his prophecy on the highest of notes. Not only is that which he has just recorded (3:18-20) the word of the Lord, but the whole prophecy is as well. God Himself has spoken.

HAGGAI

INTRODUCTION TO HAGGAI

Haggai's message, so effective in shaking the Jews of 520 BC from their lethargy, has an abiding relevance for all who fail to seek first the kingdom of God and His righteousness. The book of Haggai consists of four addresses.

AUTHOR

We know very little about Haggai outside of the four months of ministry described in this writing. He is mentioned in the book of Ezra.

PURPOSE

Haggai's purpose is clear. The exiles who returned to Jerusalem after their captivity in Babylonia have failed to complete the temple. Haggai calls these citizens to repentance and to action.

OCCASION

Haggai dates his first recorded revelation to the first day of the sixth month of the second year of the Persian king Darius Hystaspes (522–486 BC). Haggai's ministry falls between the sixth and eleventh months of Darius's second year. After years of exile in what was first Babylonia and then Persia, some of the Jewish exiles are allowed to return home. Their city is in ruins as is the temple, their center for worship. Throughout their history, the spiritual well-being of these people has been typified by the state of their place of worship. There is much in need of repair.

THEMES

Themes in Haggai include those familiar to other prophets—repentance, obedience, and worship. In Haggai's writings, however, these themes are built around the temple and all it means to the community of Jews.

HISTORICAL CONTEXT

In a day of profound discouragement and misplaced priorities after the Jews' return from Babylonian exile, the prophet Haggai sounds a call of rebuke, exhortation, and encouragement to his contemporaries. They have begun to rebuild their homes and businesses and to establish their statehood as a Jewish community but have been derelict in tending to the construction of the temple and making the Lord the central focus of all their hopes and dreams.

The prophets Haggai and Zechariah were contemporaries in Jerusalem at the end of the sixth century BC. This setting can be precisely identified; no other biblical author, with the exception of Ezekiel, ties his ministries and messages more closely to a chronological framework.

HAGGAI 1:1–15

REBUILDING THE TEMPLE

The Exhortation to Rebuild   1:1–11
The Response of God's People   1:12–15

Setting Up the section

The opening superscription provides the setting for the first oracle of the prophet (1:2–11) and identifies him and the immediate recipients of his message.

Haggai, whose name means something like "festive" or "festival," appears (apart from self-references in this treatise) only in Ezra 5:1 and 6:14. Since the oracle is transmitted on the first day of the month, a festival day (Numbers 10:10; 28:11), the prophet's name itself is revelatory of the occasion.

📖 1:1–11

THE EXHORTATION TO REBUILD

Zerubbabel son of Shealtiel, named in verse 1, is the second in a line of Jewish governors. According to Jeremiah, Gedaliah was the first governor (Jeremiah 40:7). The last mentioned in the Bible was Nehemiah (Nehemiah 8:9). The term *governor* suggests an overseer. Joshua the son of Jehozadak is here designated the high priest.

Verses 2–6 highlight the indifference of the people. The prophet chides the returned exiles and their fellow countrymen for putting their own interests ahead of the Lord and the temple. The result has been calamitous, for the more they seek self-satisfaction, the less they achieve it.

In verse 2, God's reference to the Jews as *these* (or *this*) people (rather than *my* people) implies alienation from God. The real issue is clear: The Jews who have returned from exile in Persia are more concerned for their own well-being than for honoring God by building His dwelling place among them (2:4–9). Throughout their history, establishing

God's dwelling had been an essential religious touchstone.

In verses 3–5, God, speaking through the prophet, shifts His attention from Zerubbabel and Joshua to the people at large, asking if it is appropriate for them to build their own houses even though they have protested building Yahweh's house. He challenges them so they might understand the connection between their negligence of God's house and their lack of success in everyday life (1:6).

Haggai gives four examples of the futility of selfish effort. There may be metaphorical overtones to this statement, but it also has literal meaning. Evidently the crops have failed, and now, when the fall harvest should be underway, prospects are grim.

Critical Observation

In verse 2—and elsewhere in 1:5, 7, 9, 14; 2:4, 6–9, 11, 23—Haggai refers to God in a way that describes His almighty power. This description is particularly important to the prophets, such as Zechariah and Malachi, who minister after the exiles' return and must encourage tiny, defenseless Judah in the face of imperial Persia's enormous might.

The exhortation in verse 5 is repeated in verse 7. In light of the preceding indictment (1:2–6), the people need to reflect on their ways. Their indifference leads to instruction so that the impasse might be resolved and the temple construction begun. The prophet points out that the people have sown much but harvested little and looked for much but received little (1:6, 9). Furthermore, they suffer from a lack of food, drink, clothing, and resources—a condition attributed to the drought the Lord brought upon the land, the effects of which are again listed in the same order: food, drink, protection, and productivity (1:10–11).

The cause of this disastrous condition, hinted at in verse 4, is articulated in verse 9: God's house is in ruins. The command to rebuild (1:8) is in strong antithesis to those who, in verse 2, insist that the time for rebuilding Yahweh's house has not yet come.

In verse 7, after the normal introductory formula, Haggai once more urges Zerubbabel, Joshua, and presumably the people to remember with seriousness their past failures and the remedy about to be announced.

Demystifying Haggai

Lack of any reference to stone or other materials does not mean the temple is a wooden structure, for clearly there is abundant stone from the demolished temple of Solomon lying all about. Ezra records a letter from Tattenai, governor of Trans-Euphrates (western Asia), containing a complaint to King Darius that the Jews, thanks to Haggai and Zechariah, are already rebuilding the temple with stones and timber (Ezra 5:8).

As though to reinforce His point that the promised glory has been frustrated by Judah's indolence and self-centeredness, Yahweh reiterates that the people have sought much for themselves but with meager results (1:9). As long as the temple remains unfinished, the people can continue to expect poverty and lack of fulfillment (1:10–11).

THE RESPONSE OF GOD'S PEOPLE

The first oracle, which ends with this section, consists of an address (1:2–11) and a response (1:12–14), bracketed by an introductory and concluding date formula (1:1, 15).

Haggai's stern rebuke and urgent appeal to the leaders and citizens has the desired effect, for they immediately resume construction on the temple, which had been set aside for sixteen years. Though fear is a factor, more important is Yahweh's pledge to be with them, and the supernatural stirring of their spirits to carry out His mandate (1:12–14). Within a month, they organize themselves, make their plans, marshal their labor force, and begin the work (1:15).

The people here are referred to as a remnant. The notion of a remaining few who will survive both apostasy and judgment to become the nucleus of a restored nation is pervasive in the Old Testament.

Verse 13 is an assurance of God's presence among the people. This assurance finds expression in His supernatural movement among them. Governor, priest, and people alike respond to the kindling of their dormant spirits by setting to work.

The date here reveals a twenty-three day interval between the time the message to rebuild is first proclaimed (1:1) and the time of its execution (1:14). We can't know with certainty the reason for the delay, but it may have been as simple as tending to harvest (1:11).

HAGGAI 2:1–23

LOOKING AHEAD

Setting Up the Section

In this chapter comes the message that the unpromising beginning of a second temple will someday give way to one whose magnificence and glory far transcends that of Solomon's. Yahweh is with His people and will, in line with His ancient covenant promises, reenact the Exodus and restoration to such a degree that the temple will become a place of pilgrimage from all nations. Yahweh will bring in the day of peace.

🔖 **2:1–9**

THE GLORY TO COME

Virtually all students of Haggai agree that 2:1–9 (or 1:15–2:9) constitutes a single and undivided oracle, though opinions differ on its placement in the book. The oracle as a whole contains language that is markedly concerned with end times, especially in verses 6–9.

Critical Observation

Significantly, this word of Yahweh comes on the twenty-first of Tishri (October 17), which is precisely the seventh day of the Feast of Tabernacles. Exactly 440 years earlier (Tishri, 960 BC), Solomon had finished and dedicated his temple (1 Kings 6:38; 8:2), to which the prophet is about to compare the one under present construction. Twenty-six days have passed since construction began, and already the differences are becoming painfully evident.

No one will be more aware of the contrast between Solomon's temple and the structure under construction than those old enough to have experienced the Solomonic temple so ruthlessly destroyed by the Babylonians sixty-six years earlier. To these people, Haggai addresses his question. He concludes that they view the new building as inconsequential compared with the old.

In verses 4–5, Haggai speaks one more word of encouragement to the leaders and the people, urging them to be strong in boldness and confidence. The somewhat veiled allusion to Moses and Joshua in verse 4 (most appropriate in view of the name of the present high priest) becomes more transparent in verse 5, with its reference to the Exodus. Just as Yahweh had been with His people in the ancient days, so He will be with them now.

Haggai thus harks back to the past but also anticipates future redemption and glory. This provides an entry into the end-times message of verses 6–9.

In this first extended apocalyptic vision of the book, Haggai describes the tremendous upheavals that will attend the epiphany of Yahweh in the last days.

In verse 6, the objects of the shaking—heavens, earth, sea, and land—draw attention to Yahweh's violent intervention in the past and suggest that He will do so once more, and in just a little while.

These phenomena will accompany the new exodus and new covenant as well, as both Haggai (2:6–7) and other prophets attest. There will be a shaking of the natural structures and of men and nations. These cataclysmic events will cause the peoples to bring their precious belongings to the holy city and temple. Once this has come to pass, Yahweh will fill the temple with His glory. The house's glory will be greater than before (2:9).

The real glory of the final temple will not consist of material things. This may, in fact, be the primary thrust of verse 8. Haggai affirms that its glory will consist not of silver and gold but of God's presence (2:4–5) in the temple and among His people (2:7).

📖 2:10–19

THE PROMISED BLESSING

Many scholars divide the third oracle (2:10–19) into two sections—2:10–14 and 2:15–19. They do this because of the assumption that "this people" of verse 14 refers not to Judah but to Judah's enemies in the land. However, "this people" is a perfectly appropriate description of the Jews, especially since Haggai has already used this description (1:2).

The third oracle is dated on the twenty-fourth of Kislev (or December 18, 520 BC), about three months after the work on the temple had begun again in earnest (1:15) and two months after its pitifully modest prospect begins to become apparent (2:1, 3). The people have deluded themselves into thinking that holiness is gained merely by association with holy things (2:11–12) and have failed to consider that unholy associations render one unclean (2:13–14).

The specific occasion for the oracle is unclear, but it could well have been delivered as a warning against cooperation with the Samaritans and others in the work of the temple, and the religious influence the non-Jews wielded.

If so, it is clear why the hypothetical set of questions posed by Yahweh are targeted to the priests, the religious leaders. Verse 12 asks if a person can make unholy things into holy things simply by touching them with holy hands. The meats mentioned here, if profane because they are gifts from pagan kings, will remain profane no matter who touches them. The gifts of pagan kings, no matter the spirit in which they are given, cannot become clean and acceptable to Yahweh just because they come in contact with the sacred sites and rituals of the covenant people. Such gifts should, therefore, be politely refused. To fail to do so is to render oneself unclean (2:14).

Verses 13–14 represent a converse case. Granted, unclean things don't become clean by virtue of their association with the clean. However, will things that are clean become contaminated by the unclean? The answer is an unqualified yes. The example is the corruption caused by contact with a corpse. The dead body mentioned here isn't linked with something in the immediate context of this passage. The point is that God's people can pollute, and have polluted, themselves because of their ungodly associations (2:14).

Take It Home

While it is impossible to know precisely what calls forth these words of denunciation, the context of the book suggests that it is the people's self-centeredness and inverted priorities (1:2–4, 9), and their tolerance and acceptance of assistance of their pagan neighbors—assistance that involves even the presentation of sacrificial animals. Haggai's prophecy speaks to us today, not so much in terms of the food we eat, but in terms of the priority we place on our faith and the spiritual practices that sustain that faith.

The community's moral and spiritual defilement described in the previous passage calls for divine discipline (2:10–14). From the very beginning of their postexilic life, before the foundations of the temple were laid some sixteen years earlier, the people had suffered Yahweh's wrath because of their self-service (2:16–17). This chastening marks their whole life until Haggai, called by God, urges them to forsake their shortsighted materialism and resume the work of building a house for Yahweh.

The language of failed expectation here is like that of Haggai 1. Yahweh visited the people with drought, a generic term fleshed out in the blight, mildew, and hail of the present passage (1:11; 2:17).

In verses 18–19, Haggai refers back not to the initial groundbreaking for the temple in 536 BC (2:15) but to the renewal of construction exactly three months earlier. This reference provides a backward glance focused on the refounding of the temple and subsequent events. In spite of this backward glance, however, verses 18–19 relate to the present and future. The date of the laying of the foundation is the date of the oracle, the twenty-fourth day of the ninth month (2:18). The seed has already been sown, and the fruit trees promise rich production in the season to come, but the growing season is a future event. In the midst of December, there is little on which to subsist. Verse 19 contains a promise of better days ahead. Even though the vestiges of the people's previous disobedience remain to make their existence most uncomfortable, all this will change. God will begin a new age of prosperity.

ZERUBBABEL THE CHOSEN ONE

This fourth and final message of Haggai is received and delivered on the very same day as the third, but to Zerubbabel alone. The apocalyptic language focuses on the destruction of all things hostile to the rule of Yahweh, a destruction that cannot be separated from the last clause of 2:19. In verse 19, the promise to bless from that very day finds its expression in the end-times hope outlined in verses 20–23. In terms reminiscent of his second oracle, the prophet speaks of a shaking of heaven and earth and the overthrow and shattering of human kingdoms (2:6–7).

The difference in the two addresses is the results of the shaking. In 2:7 it results in tribute to Yahweh in His temple. Here, it is a defeat of the nations so severe in its results that no one and nothing remains but Yahweh and His own sovereign ruler.

Continuing with His focus on the future, the prophet introduces the climax of his message by relating it to "that day" (2:23). Since the context indisputably is apocalyptic in nature, the Zerubbabel to whom the oracle is directed cannot be the governor whom Haggai has so frequently addressed. Rather, one must see Zerubbabel as a prototype of one to come who will be Yahweh's servant and chosen vessel.

Demystifying Haggai

Zerubbabel the governor is a descendant of Jehoiachin, most likely his grandson (1 Chronicles 3:17–19; Matthew 1:12). Because of this, using his name in this oracle has prophetic significance. Zerubbabel is a link in the Davidic monarchy. It is to this monarchy that God promises eternal reign. When someone of that bloodline became governor of Judah, it must have seemed to the restored community that God's ancient covenant promise—that there would never fail to be a son of David on the throne (2 Samuel 7:16; Psalm 89:24–37)—had come to pass.

ZECHARIAH

INTRODUCTION TO ZECHARIAH

The books of Haggai, Zechariah, and Malachi were composed in the postexilic period of Israel's history to offer hope to a people whose national and personal lives had been shattered by the Babylonian destruction of Jerusalem and captivity of the people. Zechariah goes beyond Haggai's burden for the immediate, earthly situation of the postexilic community and sees, through a vision and dream, the unfolding of divine purpose for all of God's people and for all the ages to come.

AUTHOR

At least thirty people mentioned in the Bible bear the name *Zechariah*, which means "the Lord remembers." The prophet and author of this book, however, is further identified as being the son of Berekiah and grandson of Iddo (1:1). He was born during Judah's captivity in Babylon and returned to Jerusalem with a group led by Zerubbabel. Iddo was a priest during that time (Nehemiah 12:1–7), and Zechariah eventually succeeds his grandfather in that role.

Some people propose that the latter portion of Zechariah (chapters 9–14) likely has a different author. They cite a variation in writing style and the author's inclusion of historical events that span beyond a single lifetime. Yet those variations are not evidence enough to sway the beliefs of other scholars, who continue to maintain that the book has a single author.

PURPOSE

After about seventy years of exile in a foreign land, God's people are released to return to their homeland, only to discover that the walls and temple of Jerusalem have been demolished. Projects are planned for reconstruction, but the people need much encouragement and faith during this period. As both prophet and priest, Zechariah brings assurance of God's faithfulness and hope for the future of His people.

THEMES

Zechariah adopts an already existent apocalyptic tradition of writing from which he draws heavily and to which he makes a significant contribution. The apocalyptic format receives immeasurable momentum from the trauma of the exile, a calamity that not only shook the social and political structures of Judah but also threatened to undermine the covenant faith itself. So Zechariah shifts the focus from the present to the future, from the local to the universal, and from the earthly to the cosmic and heavenly.

HISTORICAL CONTEXT

The release of the people of Judah was in conjunction with the overthrow of the Babylonians by the Medes and Persians. Zechariah begins his ministry in the eighth month of the second year of the Persian king Darius (1:1)—520 BC. Zechariah's final chronological reference (7:1) is to the ninth month of the fourth year of Darius (518 BC). If one accepts that Zechariah is the sole author of the book, the latter date presumably marks the occasion for all the oracles and other messages of chapters 7–14.

The opposition to the rebuilding projects in Judah occurs prior to Darius, and serious antagonism of the Jewish people does not arise again until Xerxes (486 BC). It is safe to assume, therefore, that work on restoring the temple goes unimpeded during the two years of Zechariah's ministry.

CONTRIBUTION TO THE BIBLE

Rich in apocalyptic imagery and packed with messianic prediction and allusion, Zechariah's writings become a favorite of the New Testament evangelists and apostles. No minor prophet excels Zechariah in the clarity and triumph by which he looks to the fulfillment of God's program of redemption.

OUTLINE

ZECHARIAH 1:1–3:10

ZECHARIAH'S NIGHT VISIONS, PART I

Setting Up the Section

The overall message of Zechariah, though occasionally obscure, is largely clear and plain. The prophet seeks to comfort his discouraged and pessimistic compatriots, who are in the process of rebuilding their temple and restructuring their community, yet who view their efforts as making little difference in the present and offering no hope for the future. Zechariah challenges members of the restored remnant to work confidently and to fully expect that what they do will be crowned with success when God, true to His Word, will bring to pass the fulfillment of His ancient promises to their forefathers. This section introduces the book and covers the first four of eight visions the prophet sees in a single night.

📖 1:1–6

INTRODUCTION

The rather lengthy introduction to the book of Zechariah is clearly intended as a preface to all the night visions that follow (chapters 1–6), if not the entire book. This is evident from the fact that 1:7 is also an introduction, perhaps for the first vision only, but more likely for all eight visions that follow.

Zechariah, here identified as the son of Berekiah and grandson of Iddo (1:1), is also mentioned in Ezra (5:1; 6:14) and Nehemiah (12:16). However, both of those citations imply that the prophet is the son of Iddo, and neither mentions Berekiah. It is likely that Zechariah's father died young and Zechariah was raised by his grandfather. This would also explain why Zechariah succeeds Iddo as priest (Nehemiah 12:10–16).

"The second year of Darius" refers to 520 BC, and the "eighth month" is October/November, so Zechariah's visions are only a month prior to Haggai's final vision, which would have been December 18, 520 BC (Haggai 2:10, 20). Zechariah is likely quite young, and his ministry may have extended well beyond his people's return from exile.

Zechariah begins his book with a solemn exhortation to learn from history. God had been extremely displeased with the generations past (1:2) because they had stubbornly refused to heed the appeal of their prophets to turn to the Lord (1:3–4). Ways and practices (deeds) refer not to incidental sins but to a whole pattern of rebellion and disloyalty.

Zechariah next turns his attention to the calamity that overcame their ancestors because of their failure to heed the prophets' warnings. Both they and the prophets who had warned them had long since passed away (1:5), but God's Word had come to pass. The wicked nation had been overthrown according to the terms of the covenant, and those who lived to see it had been forced to admit that God brought to pass everything He had threatened (1:6).

The message of Zechariah will be precisely the same as that of his prophetic predecessors. His people must turn to the Lord in covenant affirmation if they expect God to reciprocate (1:3).

Critical Observation

Zechariah's use of *the LORD Almighty* (NIV) as a title for God (three times in 1:3) is most striking. In this book, the prophet uses the title fifty-three times. Yet such usage coincides with other prophets at work at the same time. Malachi uses the title twenty-four times, and Haggai uses it fourteen times in only thirty-eight verses. In light of the emergence of universal empires at the time, Judah needs to be reminded that the Lord is indeed almighty. He is the Lord of hosts—Lord even of those mighty worldly powers.

📖 1:7–17

VISION ONE: THE FOUR HORSEMEN

The second introduction to the book of Zechariah (1:7) embraces all the visions to follow (1:8–6:16). The next introductory passage does not appear until chapter 7. The date equates to February 15, 519 BC, in the modern calendar—approximately three months after the initial call of Zechariah (1:1) and two months after Haggai's last revelation (Haggai 2:10, 20). Significant events around this time that may have bearing on elements of Zechariah's first vision are (1) the return of Darius to Persia from Egypt (through Palestine) and (2) the approaching New Year's day, a time when Zerubbabel will be crowned as Judah's king, restoring a Davidic successor to the throne (Haggai 2:20–23).

It appears that Zechariah is recounting a series of dream-visions from a single night. These dreams are not random or from his own imagination because they are presented in a historical and chronological sequence on one hand, and in an interlocking literary pattern on the other. Similarities are found between visions #1 and #8, #2 and #7, #3 and #6, and #4 and #5.

Both Zechariah's first and eighth (1:8; 6:1–8) visions feature four kinds of horses. Much effort has been made to connect the two visions, but the colors of the horses are not the same, and there is no reason to assume that the horses in both visions must match. In the first vision, either the man on the red horse dismounts and stands in the ravine, or the horse itself stands there with the rider still on him. Hebrew grammar favors the former, as does the description in 1:10. As for the three horses in the background, it is not certain whether or not they have riders. Presumably they do, because verse 11 indicates more than one speaker.

Critical Observation

The myrtle is a particularly appropriate element of this vision. A fragrant, decorative shrub that sometimes reaches the size of a tree, it is used in connection with the Feast of Tabernacles and in postbiblical times in betrothal celebrations. Its perpetual greenness and aromatic qualities provide a suitable setting for the inauguration of the Lord's domain, which is everlasting and pleasant in every way.

It seems that Zechariah stands with an interpreting messenger-angel and that both of them hear the answer to Zechariah's question as given by the man among the myrtles (the angel of the Lord). His response is confirmed by the riders of the horses. Overwhelmed by his own response, the angel of the Lord addresses the Lord Himself to ask about the conclusion of the seventy years of discipline. The Lord's answer is directed to the messenger/interpreter beside Zechariah, for it is the prophet who had raised the inquiries about the vision he had seen. That messenger in turn speaks to Zechariah, commanding him to deliver the Word of God to his people (1:14).

The mission of the rider of the red horse (and presumably all four horsemen) is to walk across the whole earth (1:10). To walk about on the earth is to assert sovereignty over it (see Genesis 13:17; Job 1:7; Ezekiel 28:14). Here the Lord, through the symbolism of four cavalry charges, announces that He is Lord of all.

The result of the horsemen's roaming the earth is that the land is at rest and quiet (1:11). It is therefore a suitable time for the Lord to end the judgment of the seventy-year exile by displaying His compassion for His elect people (1:12). His jealousy for Judah (1:14) is, after all, an expression of His singular interest in her and His determination to restore His people. The mention of Zion reflects the Davidic reign as part of the messianic program of redemption.

The nations, on the other hand, have become the object of the Lord's judgment. God had indeed been a little angry at His people (1:15), but the enemies of God's people brought about a measure of retribution beyond what God would have imposed.

This vision has clear implications for the end times, but it also relates to the historical circumstances of the late sixth century BC. The peace established by Cyrus strengthened and expanded under Darius, who put down rebellions associated with his ascension to the throne. Cyrus and Darius did not realize, however, that their universal peace was brought about by the Lord, God of Israel. The horses of Darius are, in fact, the horses of the Lord.

Still, the conditions are suitable for the seventy-year exile to be over. Jeremiah first refers to a seventy-year period, dating its end with the demise of the Babylonian (Chaldean) kingdom (Jeremiah 25:11–12). It is clearly understood, however, that the seventy years have a flexible starting and concluding date because their termination is also connected to the completion of the second temple (Zechariah 1:16). It may also be noted that the completion of Jerusalem's second temple takes place in 516 BC, exactly seventy years after the destruction of Solomon's temple in 586 BC.

Demystifying Zechariah

Many of Zechariah's visions, including this first one, are accompanied by oracles. The primary purposes of these oracles are (1) to confirm the message of the vision; (2) to provide further understanding of its meaning; and (3) to exhort the audience to carry out its commands.

Zechariah records in 1:13 that the Lord had spoken "kind and comforting" words to the interpreting angel. Those words are revealed in the oracle that follows the vision (1:16–17). God promises to either *turn* or *return* to Jerusalem (the intended translation is uncertain, as is whether the tense is present or future. But either interpretation would have been good news for the people of God).

We know from Haggai that God promises to bless His people, beginning with the ceremony of laying the temple foundation (Haggai 2:18–19). The work of reconstructing the temple began about five months prior to Zechariah's night visions (Haggai 1:15), but it is far from finished. The good news given to Zechariah is that what had been started will now be brought to fruition. Indeed, not only will the temple be rebuilt, but also the reconstruction will include outlying cities in addition to Jerusalem. They will become abundantly prosperous (1:16–17).

📄 **1:18–21**

VISION TWO: THE FOUR HORNS

Just as Zechariah's first and eighth visions complement each other with similar themes and perspective, so, too, his second and seventh visions are a matched pair. They each have two parts, and both are concerned with the nations. This second vision has no accompanying oracle.

The connections between this vision and the first one are also striking. The fact that the first vision is of four horses and this one describes four horns and four craftsmen is significant. The horses of the first vision are God's instruments of dominion over all the earth (1:10–11); the four craftsmen will reduce the nations to defeat.

Critical Observation

Symbolizing political and military power by the horn of an animal is common not only in the Old Testament but also in other ancient Near Eastern literature. A horn represents power, authority, prestige, and influence. For example, David describes the Lord as his rock, fortress, deliverer, shield, tower, and horn (Psalm 18:2). Other prophets make similar references to horns (Jeremiah 48:25; Daniel 7–8; Micah 4:13).

Zechariah's second vision contains two elements (four horns and four craftsmen), so the interpretation is divided into two parts. In response to the query about the horns (1:19), the angelic interpreter first asserts that they are scatterers of Judah, Israel, and Jerusalem. Under further interrogation, he adds that the horns are associated with the nations. The nations had used their horns (military might) to effect the dispersion of God's people (1:21).

As for the craftsmen, the messenger reports that their task is to bring down those nations, to nullify the effect of their great power (1:21). The ultimate result will presumably reverse the scattering so that the dispersed can return again to their land.

The listed order of those attacked is somewhat puzzling: Judah, Israel, and Jerusalem (1:19). Later, only Judah is mentioned (1:21). If Judah is seen as central, then Israel may denote the nation in its broadest sense and Jerusalem in its narrowest. The order indicates, then, that the scattering is total.

Some people attempt to identify four specific nations or events to associate with the horns. But what is suggested here (and elsewhere) by the number four is the universal character of the persecution of God's people by the nations. Israel's struggle against the nations had persisted from their settlement in Canaan until the fall of Jerusalem to the Babylonians. But the final destruction had been so climactic and irreversible that it stands out in Zechariah's text.

There is no reason to attempt to identify any particular forces to associate with the craftsmen. The word *craftsmen* used can apply to any skilled artisan regardless of his medium. But in this case, the way the word is used in the original language suggests that these four particular craftsmen are also destroyers, or devastators. They have come forth to throw down the arrogant nations that had scattered God's elect. After the Babylonian horn is cut off by the instruments of Darius, the rebuilding promised in Zechariah's first vision can take place.

📖 2:1–13

VISION THREE: THE SURVEYOR

Zechariah's third and sixth visions both have to do with measuring and/or dimensions, with a focus narrowed down from international interests to Jerusalem itself. In this vision, only Zechariah and one other unidentified man are participants.

It was necessary to reestablish the ancient boundary lines of Jerusalem preparatory to the city's full reoccupation. Zechariah witnesses a form of surveying, as the properties are measured out for redistribution.

Critical Observation

Before the fall of Jerusalem, Jeremiah had been told to anticipate the day when houses, fields, and vineyards would once more be bought there (Jeremiah 32:6–15). It had always been God's intent for His people to reclaim the land. Ezekiel, too, had been shown a similar scene, but the surveyor in his vision measured out the land with a reed (rod) rather than a cord (Ezekiel 40:3).

The task of the man in this third vision is to measure Jerusalem by breadth and length (2:2). The reason breadth comes first in this instance may be due to the orientation of the city. In fact, only here and in Ezekiel 40–48 are "breadth and length" designated rather than "length and breadth."

The interpreting messenger-angel appears again, this time to provide further information to Zechariah ("young man") than he had already obtained from the surveyor (2:4). This secondary messenger appears only in the first and third visions. In a sense, he is an interpreter for the interpreter. In this case, he urgently commands the first angel to go to Zechariah and provide the meaning of the vision. What is about to happen is imminent, and those who hear the message cannot be slow to act upon the news.

Zechariah is informed that the surveyor is in the process of laying out allotments in and around Jerusalem in preparation for the burgeoning population that will live there. In the absence of the walls that formerly stood, the old boundary lines will need to be redrawn. Jerusalem will be reoccupied by such a vast population that the walls that once enclosed it will be inadequate (2:4).

This prophecy has definite end-times significance, but it is also relevant for Zechariah's own circumstances. It is impossible to know a great deal about the construction and configuration of the walls about Jerusalem in the postexilic period. For the greater period of time, there were no walls—none sufficient, at least, to provide protection.

Demystifying Zechariah

It should not be assumed that Jerusalem had been continually without walls between the Babylonian conquest (586 BC) and the restoration work overseen by Nehemiah (completed in 445 BC). Ezra refers to walls existing during the time of King Artaxerxes (464–424 BC) that were most likely constructed during the earlier reign of Xerxes (Ezra 4:12). And Nehemiah's appeal to Artaxerxes was that the walls of Jerusalem had been destroyed and needed to be rebuilt (Nehemiah 1:3; 2:4–5). Everyone knew that the Babylonians had leveled the walls of Jerusalem, so Nehemiah's surprise at hearing that the walls were missing suggests that the walls had been replaced for a time and destroyed yet again.

Early Jerusalem housed only six thousand to eight thousand inhabitants. One estimate of the city's population in 700 BC is twenty-four thousand. And it is unlikely that preexilic Jerusalem ever contained as many as forty thousand people. Yet the people who returned from exile in 538 BC numbered 42,360 Jewish citizens, 7,337 slaves, and 200 singers (Ezra 2:64–65). Add to that crowd of people a group of animals exceeding eight thousand (Ezra 2:66–67). Admittedly, not all of them would have settled within the city limits of Jerusalem, but it seems that many did (Ezra 2:70; 4:4).

Eighty years later, Ezra himself leads about five thousand more individuals back to Judah (Ezra 8:1–14), most of whom apparently settle in or about Jerusalem (Ezra 8:31–32). Yet when Nehemiah arrives thirteen years after that, he finds that any former walls have been reduced to rubble. With the ruin of the walls, the population of the city had evidently evacuated (Nehemiah 7:4). After Nehemiah sees to the repairs, he conducts a lottery to repopulate Jerusalem (Nehemiah 11:1–2).

But regardless of the shifting population and varying conditions of the walls of Jerusalem during ancient times, Zechariah learns of a future when there will be no need of walls to protect the great population of the city. The Lord Himself will be a wall of fire and a source of glory for all the inhabitants (2:5).

The oracle following Zechariah's third vision (2:6–13) is a summation of the first three visions as a whole. It serves as both a warning to Babylon (2:6–9) and a promise of blessing to Judah (2:10–13).

The land of the north (2:6) is soon clearly identified as Babylon (2:7). Yet by Zechariah's time, the Babylonian exiles have already returned, so it appears that Zechariah is describing a future, more widespread regathering of God's people. In the language of the prophets, *Zion* (2:7, 10) is a key term used to refer to the end-times kingdom. And *the four winds* (2:6) suggest that exiles will be returning from all directions, not only from the north.

The *apple of God's eye* (2:8) is a reference to either the opening of the eye or the pupil. Either way, the eye is one of the most important and vulnerable parts of the body. This bold metaphor warns that to strike a blow at Zion is equivalent to striking at the Lord, attempting to wound Him in a most sensitive area. God will surely respond to such aggression. Long ago God had told Abraham, "I will bless those who bless you and curse those who treat you with contempt" (Genesis 12:3 NLT). That pledge is never abrogated and proves to be in force even with respect to the postexilic community of Judah.

The warning directed toward Babylon is closely associated with the blessing of Judah. The blessing of God's people can ultimately occur only after all hostile powers have been put down. The two parts of the oracle are also connected by the literary themes of "daughter of Babylon" versus "daughter of Zion" (2:7, 10). The personification of Zion suggests not only the corporate nature of Judah's existence as one people of the Lord but also the tenderness that God feels toward them as their Father. The names *Zion* and *Jerusalem* are frequently used synonymously.

Zion's response to the promised redemption in 2:6–9 is a ringing cry of joy. The reason for such unmitigated joy is that the Lord is coming and will live in Zion's midst (2:10). Both Haggai and Zechariah share this theology of divine presence, a note that was especially meaningful in the days of the regathered community struggling to build a temple worthy of God's dwelling place. But Zechariah is particularly concerned with orienting this theological truth to the age to come, when all nations (not just Israel and Judah) will join themselves to the Lord and be His people (2:11). In addition, God will take the land of Judah as His special allotment in all the created universe. Zechariah's reference to "the holy land" (2:12) is unique to this verse in scripture.

Demystifying Zechariah

One of the major tenets of ancient Israel's faith that distinguishes the nation from the paganism of the ancient world is her concept of the nearness of her God as opposed to the aloofness of the gods of the nations. The Lord is utterly transcendent, but the revolutionary contribution of Israel's theology is the awareness that God also lives among His people, even if invisible. Adam and Eve in the garden, Moses leading the Israelites, the psalmists, and the prophets all recognized the Lord as One who dwelled in their midst. The same message continues in the New Testament. Early in his Gospel, John identifies God's Word as One who becomes flesh and makes His dwelling among us (John 1:14).

Of interest here is the increasingly narrow parameter of the Lord's inheritance, from the whole earth to the Jerusalem temple. This narrowing of compass runs parallel, however, to an increasing broadness of His saving activity. He becomes not just the God of Abraham, Isaac, and Jacob, but the God of the nations.

3:1–10

VISION FOUR: THE PRIEST

Zechariah's fourth vision is quite different from most of the others in a number of ways. Only it and the following one (4:1–4) deal with actual identifiable human beings. The usual introduction formula that precedes a vision is lacking. There is no interpreting messenger in this case. And there appears to be an absence of standard formulaic language in the vision.

The person identified in the vision is Jeshua (3:1), a high priest with whom Zechariah is personally acquainted. The same figure appears later in Zechariah (6:11), in Haggai (Haggai 1:1), and frequently in Ezra (2:2; 3:2, 8; 4:3; 5:2; 10:18) and Nehemiah (7:7; 12:1, 7, 10, 26). He is a direct descendant of Aaron through Zadok, founder of the line of priests established by David and Solomon (1 Chronicles 6:3, 8–15). His father, Jehozadak, had gone into Babylonian exile in 586 BC, so by Zechariah's night visions in 519 BC, Jeshua must certainly have been an old man.

In the vision, Jeshua appears in a state of ritual impurity, so much so that he is being condemned for it by Satan in the presence of the Lord (3:1). The accusation is not stated, but it may be inferred from 3:3: He is unfit for the priestly ministry. The accuser and the accused are both standing, the former at the right side of the latter, not unlike in a modern courtroom. The judge is the messenger/angel of the Lord.

When Satan challenges Jeshua's right to function under these circumstances, the judge speaks up, perhaps even before Satan can open his mouth, and rebukes the accuser to his face (3:2). The rationale for the rebuke is that Satan has overlooked the fact that the Lord, who had chosen Jerusalem, had also declared Jeshua to be a brand snatched from the fire (3:2). When it looked as though all was lost where the covenant community and its worship were concerned, the Lord graciously stepped in and rescued a remnant by which He will reconstitute a believing people.

According to the law, the accusation of Satan is valid; the uncleanness of a priest attempting to minister can lead to his excommunication (Leviticus 22:3). Jeshua (and the entire remnant nation for that matter) may appear impure, but the elective grace of God is still in effect. It is precisely at this point of the priest's need that the Lord speaks, commanding those attending him to remove Jeshua's filthy clothing and replace it with fine garments (Zechariah 3:4). Simultaneously, the Lord verbally absolves Jeshua's iniquity in an act of grace.

Zechariah is also a priest, and he speaks out as he recognizes the need for a proper headdress for Jeshua (3:5; see Exodus 28:36–38). Such interruption of a vision by the one receiving it is not common among other prophets, but it occurs rather frequently in the book of Zechariah.

By investing Jeshua with pure, clean clothes and a spotless turban, the Lord has prepared the priest for a larger role in the covenant community, provided Jeshua responds to God's act of grace by assuming the task to which his reinstatement has called him.

Jeshua must meet two conditions, one having to do with his way of life and the other with his specific vocation as priest. First, he must walk in the ways of the Lord. Second, he must keep the requirements of the particular office to which he has been called (3:7).

Then, with a sharp command, the Lord addresses both Jeshua and his companions who sit before him. It is likely that the seated figures are a sign concerning the coming of the branch and the restoration of Israel as a priestly nation (3:8). Zechariah will later aver that this messianic branch/servant will build the temple of the Lord (6:12–13). It seems likely, then, that the stone placed before Jeshua (3:9) must be taken to be the foundation of the second temple.

It isn't uncommon for a stone to be used as a messianic symbol throughout the Bible (see Isaiah 28:16). But the stone in Zechariah's oracle is unique; it has seven eyes (3:9). In biblical numerology, the number seven signifies fullness or completeness, so the seven eyes suggest omniscience or undimmed vision. In the following vision, Zechariah will identify the seven eyes as the eyes of the Lord that take in everything that is happening on the earth (4:10). And, in addition to the eyes, the stone is about to be inscribed by the Lord.

Demystifying Zechariah

It seems evident that the stone in 3:9 is the cornerstone of a building, most likely the temple of the Lord. In the ancient Near Eastern world, cornerstones frequently bore inscriptions to identify the builder and the purpose of the building. The eyes on the stone are to be the divine signature of the Lord as the architect and builder of the structure. The statement of purpose is a reference to the temple as a place of expiation of sin.

In summary, Zechariah's fourth vision describes a day of redemption in which Jeshua (typical or representative of Israel as a priestly people) will be cleansed of his impurities and reinstalled in his capacity as high priest. This presupposes a temple in which this can take place, so Jeshua will build such a structure. This temple will only be a model for one yet to come, one whose cornerstone is the Lord Himself. That cornerstone contains the glorious promise of the regeneration of the nation, a mighty event of salvation that will be consummated in a single day.

Take It Home

The book of Zechariah is not the simplest portion of scripture to understand and apply. How do you feel about having to work a bit harder to comprehend what is going on? Do you enjoy the challenge of deeper thought and extra study, or do you prefer more clear-cut portions of the Bible? Based on what you've seen in Zechariah so far, how would you describe it to a friend?

ZECHARIAH 4:1–6:15

ZECHARIAH'S NIGHT VISIONS, PART II

Setting Up the Section

This section continues to present the visions of Zechariah. This opening series of visions helps provide a basis for understanding the prophet's writings that follow them.

📖 4:1–14

VISION FIVE: A GOLD LAMPSTAND AND TWO OLIVE TREES

Zechariah's fifth vision forms a matching pair with his fourth, both in juxtaposition and subject matter. Both deal with cultic persons or objects (the high priest and the menorah, respectively), both mention historical persons who were Zechariah's contemporaries (Jeshua and Zerubbabel), both refer to temple building, and both reach their climax on a strong messianic note.

The prophet sees in this vision a golden lampstand (menorah) flanked by two olive trees, the whole of which symbolizes the Spirit of the Lord. The messenger who speaks to Zechariah (4:1), a principal figure in the previous visions (except for the fourth), returns now and awakens the prophet. Since Zechariah continues in a visionary state, he is not waking from sleep, but his sensibilities have been so heightened as to be comparable to a man waking from a slumber.

Zechariah immediately recognizes the golden lampstand, as any priest would. The menorah was traditionally located on the south side of the Holy Place in the temple. Its purpose was to illuminate the interior of the Holy Place (Exodus 25:37), and it also represented the illumination of the presence of the Lord Himself.

However, the lampstand of Zechariah's vision is different from the menorah described in Exodus (4:2–3). First, it appears to have a general vessel for storing the oil located somewhere above its center. The oil for this lampstand is not poured into the lamps by the Levites but comes from the reservoir, a second difference. And finally, its connection to the olive trees is a third difference. The trees directly yield their oil without the need for plucking and crushing olives, and the oil appears to flow from the olive trees to the reservoir and then into the cups with no human hand or effort whatsoever.

Critical Observation

The major source of lamp oil in ancient Palestine was the olive, so it is not surprising that two olive trees appear in Zechariah's vision to provide that fuel. It is important to note that the trees are not to the left and the right of the menorah, but they flank the reservoir. The oil could not go straight to the cups but had to be mediated through the upper container that received it directly from the trees.

Baffled by what he has seen, the prophet proceeds to ask several questions of the interpreting messenger (4:4–6, 11–14). This time the interpretation of the vision is divided by the oracular response section (4:7–10). Zechariah first inquires as to the menorah and then, following the oracle, asks about the two olive trees (4:11). The question from the interpreting messenger (4:5) is not to infer that Zechariah is ignorant, but instead it confirms that the prophet cannot possibly understand what he is seeing without supernatural insight.

Everything Zechariah has seen so far, the messenger explains, is the Word of the Lord to Zerubbabel (4:6). This is the first time that Zerubbabel is mentioned in Zechariah's book, and he is named only three more times, all in the oracle section that immediately follows. In fact, it seems that the reason this vision has its interpretation divided by the oracle is to maintain the emphasis on Zerubbabel.

Critical Observation

Old Testament theology is not clear concerning the person of the Holy Spirit, the third person of the Godhead who is so central to New Testament revelation. Yet we read of the Spirit of God moving over the primordial waters during creation (Genesis 1:2), the tabernacle workers being filled with God's Spirit to do their creative work (Exodus 28:3; 31:3), and the Spirit's power and insight providing for the work of Israel's judges (Judges 3:10; 6:34; 11:29; 13:25; 14:6, 19; 15:14, 19) and prophets (2 Kings 2:15–16; Ezekiel 2:2; 3:12, 14; 8:3; 11:1, 5). Particularly relevant is the reference to the Spirit of the Lord in the commissioning oracle of Isaiah 11:1–5, one recognized by all scholars as messianic and eschatological, or pertaining to end times. The language in that passage is reflected in Zechariah 3–6. The branch in Zechariah 3:8 provides the same messianic allusion as the sprout from the root of Jesse in Isaiah 11:1.

The Spirit of the Lord will empower Zerubbabel, the branch (6:12), to accomplish mighty works, including the completion of the temple (4:7–8), the assumption of rulership (Haggai 2:23; Zechariah 6:13), and the reduction of iniquity and sinful forces (Haggai 2:21–22; Zechariah 3:9).

Zechariah has faithfully described what he has seen, yet he cannot understand its significance (4:11–12). For a second time, the interpreting messenger underlines the prophet's inability to comprehend by asking him if indeed he fails to discern these aspects of the vision (4:13). At this point, the messenger reaches the climax of the dialogue by declaring that the olive trees are the two anointed ones who stand by the Lord of the earth (4:14). It is important to connect these two anointed ones with the trees that symbolize them. They are not just anointed, but they are anointed with the oil of these trees.

Officials who were anointed in Old Testament Israel were the high priest, the king, and, on occasion, prophets. In Zechariah's own time and perspective, the two anointed ones would likely refer to Jeshua and Zerubbabel. Both are direct descendants of the heads of their lines, Aaron and David. Both have already been singled out for their involvement in the restoration of the postexilic community (Haggai 1:1, 12, 14; Zechariah 3; 4:6). And both have been given evidence of having been chosen by God (Haggai 2:23; Zechariah 3:2).

The significance of Zerubbabel is confirmed in the oracle portion of this vision (4:7–10). Zechariah is confident that the mountainous project of rebuilding can be completed with God's help—so much so that he addresses the mountain of obstacles (4:7). He is convinced that Zerubbabel will be able to face the mountain, level it to a plain, and completely achieve the rebuilding committed to his charge (4:9).

As if his message to Zerubbabel is not clear enough so far, Zechariah is most explicit as to what overcoming mountains and raising capstones are all about. He calls to mind that Zerubbabel has already, nearly twenty years earlier, made preparation for the temple foundation. Now the hands that had begun the work will complete it, a promise repeated in 6:12–13 and fulfilled four years later, in 515 BC (Ezra 6:15).

This fifth vision of Zechariah's is seemingly tied to earlier visions. The seven eyes of the Lord that "range throughout the earth" (4:10 NIV) seem connected to the seven eyes on the engraved stone in vision four (3:9). And the reference to running "to and fro" through all the earth conveys a similar image as Zechariah's first vision, where the four horses walk throughout the earth (1:8–11).

5:1–4

VISION SIX: THE FLYING SCROLL

Zechariah's sixth vision has several things in common with his third one. Both have a national focus and highlight the centrality of Judah in the restoration program. In contrast to other visions, a solitary individual is the recipient of these two. Both have an emphasis on length and breadth measurements, be it the city of Jerusalem (2:2) or an unusual scroll (5:1–2). And they both feature movement: The man of vision three is on the move to accomplish his task, and the scroll in this vision is flying.

Critical Observation

Scrolls from this era were typically made of leather or parchment, consisting of single sheets sewn together and rolled around wooden rollers at either end. Writing would ordinarily be on the inside, with only the description of its contents or other brief notations written outside the roll. Usually the length of a scroll would be many times its width, the width being the measurement of a single sheet from top to bottom (seldom exceeding eight to twelve inches). The length of a scroll would rarely be more than twenty-five to thirty feet.

The measurements of the scroll are so different from the norm that one must realize immediately that the dimensions are really not of the scroll itself but of something described within the scroll. Thus the thirty feet by fifteen feet (5:2) either defines an actual area or refers to something or some place whose length is twice its width. Among biblical objects or places that fit such criteria are the Holy Place in the tabernacle (Exodus 26:31–35), the porch of Solomon's temple (1 Kings 6:3), and the great bronze altar of the temple (2 Chronicles 4:2). All three of these options have to do with the sanctuary, the place where the Lord meets with His people.

The connection of the scroll with the dwelling place of the Lord leads to the conclusion that the scroll contains the covenant document that binds God and the nation together. The interpretation of the vision (5:3–4) is filled with covenant terminology and motifs that make it certain that the scroll either is the Jewish Torah or contains covenant texts of the Torah. The unidentified speaker immediately equates the scroll with the *curse*—a technical term referring to the sanctions of covenant documents.

The flying scroll of Zechariah mentions only two of the covenant stipulations (5:3), although those two represent the entire law. One has to do with interpersonal, human relations, and the other deals with the individual's responsibility before God. Someone who steals violates the eighth commandment (Exodus 20:15), a breach, therefore, of the entire second half of the law. He who swears falsely in the name of the Lord violates the third commandment (Exodus 20:7), a statute that is representative of the first part of the law. Whoever breaks either or both parts has sinned grievously, having violated the covenant that the Lord has made.

The purging (banishing) mentioned in 5:3 is explained in 5:4. The scroll, the Lord says, is something He has authored and sent out. It is a message but also a weapon by which He will judge His recalcitrant people. It is His powerful Word that accomplishes the objective for which it is sent, whether that be salvation or condemnation (Isaiah 55:11). Using a verb normally found in situations of hospitality, Zechariah states that the scroll will spend the night in the homes of the thief and of him who swears falsely in the Lord's name. It will remain there until its intended mission is accomplished. The covenant breaker will discover that his sins against God and against others will lead inexorably to utter devastation (Zechariah 5:4).

One more instructive parallel should be drawn between this vision and Zechariah's third one. In the third vision, the surveyor is about the business of building, the result of which is a city with no wall of protection other than the Lord Himself, the "wall of fire" (2:5). Here the scroll does not build but, to the contrary, destroys—leaving no wall, roof, or foundation. In the first case, the remnant people who trust confidently in the Lord will find adequate shelter in His presence among them. In the present case, the thief and blasphemer will know nothing of this protective grace but only the wrath of a holy God whose covenant mercies have been spurned (see Habakkuk 2:9–11).

📖 5:5–11

VISION SEVEN: THE EPHAH

This is one of the most perplexing of the night visions of Zechariah, not only because of the bizarre nature of what is being presented, but also due to conundrums of grammar and syntax. An *ephah* (5:6) was a familiar unit of solid or liquid measure approximately equal to five gallons. But due to the description in the vision, several translations refer instead to the *container* for the measurement ("basket," "vessel," "measuring basket," etc.).

In this vision, as in the fifth one (4:1), the interpreting angel takes the initiative to introduce the scene (5:5). Zechariah sees "the lead cover of the basket" (5:7 CEV). In the context, this can only mean a cover for the ephah (5:8). He then sees one woman within the ephah (to be differentiated from two others mentioned later) (5:9). It is when the cover is raised that the woman therein becomes visible to the prophet.

Because these are visions, Zechariah is not seeing objects necessarily to scale. For a woman to be contained in a five-gallon vessel is, in actual life, impossible. Similarly, the dimensions of the scroll in the previous vision are disproportionate and exaggerated, but they clearly communicate a message.

At last the woman is identified—she is called *Wickedness* (5:8). The woman's danger is most apparent, for no sooner has the interpreting messenger pronounced her name than he slams the heavy cover down upon the ephah to be certain that she cannot escape (5:8). In the original Hebrew, the urgency is magnified: The messenger *threw* the woman into the ephah and *threw* the lead weight upon its top. The ephah has become not only a means of conveyance but also a cage.

Once the woman is secure, the ephah takes flight, supported by two women with stork-like wings (5:9). The fact that the bearers are also women is consistent with the feminine flavor of the entire vision. The reference to the wind in their wings is no doubt intended as a double entendre. The same word translated *wind* also means "spirit." So the same spirit that empowers Zerubbabel in temple building (4:6) is now at work transporting Wickedness to her destination.

Critical Observation

The stork was among the list of unclean birds for the Israelites, one that could not be eaten because it was an abomination (Leviticus 11:13, 19). Yet even people in ancient times recognized its affectionate care for its young and its appropriate name (in the original language, "loving, faithful, constant"). So Zechariah's paradoxical picture of an unclean bird is appropriate considering the cargo and mission of the women with stork-like wings—providing tender care of their charge as they fulfilled the mandate of the Lord.

Wanting to understand the destination of the flying ephah, Zechariah learns that the location is Shinar (Babylonia), where the stork-like women will build Wickedness a house and settle her there (5:10–11). Reference to Shinar is tantamount to Babylon. It was at Babylon, in the land of Shinar, that the rebel human race erected a great ziggurat, or tower, the purpose of which was to frustrate God's mandate to fill the earth (Genesis 11:4; see 1:28; 9:1). From that time, Babylon became synonymous with arrogant human independence.

According to various biblical writers, Babylon—whether past, present, or future—is the paradigm of wickedness and of hostility to the gracious purposes of God. From Zechariah's perspective, Babylon's role must have been exclusively future. By 520 BC, Babylon had been swallowed up by the irrepressible Persian Empire.

Transporting Wickedness to Shinar/Babylon is returning her to where she belongs. She had come from Babylon and had dogged the steps of God's people for centuries, leading at last to their destruction and captivity. But in the day of restoration, she will submit meekly to the Lord of all the earth and settle into the house built especially for her until the day of her final disposition, something Zechariah does not explicitly address.

6:1–8

VISION EIGHT: THE CHARIOTS

Of all Zechariah's visions that appear to complement one another, the first and the last are most similar, effectively serving as bookends that envelop the whole series. Each concerns four principle objects (horses/horsemen in the first, chariots in this one). The objects in both are sent to do the bidding of the Lord. The interpreting messenger is key in both to disclose the vision and explain its meaning. A valley/ravine is present in both (presumed in the final vision, which is set between two mountains). And both visions share a cosmic, universalistic interest.

Various forms of the verb meaning "come forth," or "go forth" (6:1), appear fifteen times in seventy-seven verses, and with increasing frequency. Its first usage is in the third vision, again in the fifth, twice in the sixth, four times in the seventh, and seven times in this final vision. The pattern suggests an intensely heightened sense of activity. This flurry of action throughout the visions, occasioned by the Lord's work of renewal and redemption, comes to a peaceful end at last when His sovereignty is established.

This time what Zechariah sees going forth are four chariots that emerge from between two mountains (6:1–3). In the Old Testament, a chariot was not just a mode of transportation; its primary use was as a war machine. The four chariots in the vision reflect the worldwide extent of their travels. They are sent forth to reclaim all the earth for the Lord, a result that follows the splitting of the mountain in the Day of the Lord (6:1; 14:10). Zechariah witnesses the arrival of the four chariots between the two mountains, having come there from heaven. Once they are sent forth, there will be peace in Jerusalem (14:11) and throughout the whole earth (6:7–8).

Demystifying Zechariah

The chariots are to go throughout the earth, though it doesn't appear that they are dispatched north, south, east, and west. Due to the geography of Palestine, one must go north even to go to the northwest or northeast. Assyria, Babylon, and even Persia were all considered "north" of Palestine, even though they don't appear quite that way on a map.

There can be little doubt that Zechariah's vision pertains to the nations and circumstances of his own times, but it cannot be limited to that era because of the presence of its eschatological and apocalyptic characters. The picture here is one of final and universal dominion of the Lord over His creation. How that will take place is a major part of the message of the oracles of Zechariah in the chapters that follow (7–14).

📖 6:9–15

A CONCLUDING ORACLE

Zechariah records an oracle that appears to serve as a comment on, and climax to, the night visions as a whole. It does not belong with the series that commences with chapter 7, because that collection is dated more than a year later (7:1). The central portion of Zechariah's writing so far, the content of the fourth and fifth visions, focuses on the elevation of Jeshua and Zerubbabel to positions of honor and influence. Not surprisingly, then, those same two persons are the central concern of this final, summarizing oracle.

The identities of the men listed in 6:10 are not clear. There is at least some chance that, in terms of their names, they are priests who were given their assignment here. They are to take silver and gold to fashion a crown for Jeshua the high priest. The word used for *crown* denotes a regal crown rather than the expected headdress for a priest (turban, mitre, diadem, etc.), so this particular crowning of the priest must have had regal implications.

The Word of the Lord through Zechariah is directed specifically to Jeshua (6:12), thus distinguishing him from another man called the branch (6:12). There is no doubt as to the identity of the branch. Converging lines of identification within Zechariah (4:7–10) and elsewhere (Isaiah 11:1; 53:2; Jeremiah 33:15; Haggai 2:23) make it certain that Zerubbabel is in view. As a direct offspring of the line of David, he is well-qualified to sit on the royal throne of Judah, a responsibility clearly stated in 6:13.

Demystifying Zechariah

Translations of Zechariah vary as to whether the presumed priests are instructed to fashion a *crown* (singular) or *crowns* (plural). The plural form seems to be appropriate. Jeshua wears one as priest, and Zerubbabel (the branch) wears another as king.

Priest and king come together in 6:13. The harmony between the two figures clarifies that two separate persons are in view. Jeshua and the branch (Zerubbabel) are both the center of attention. Both are crowned and enthroned, charged with administering, under the Lord, the affairs of their respective civil and religious realms. The two complement each other. The quality of office is anticipated in the fifth vision, where Zerubbabel and Jeshua appear as olive trees and anointed ones of the Lord (4:11–14).

In addition to being important leaders in their own time, Jeshua and Zerubbabel are also symbolic, anointed ones whose messianic significance is unmistakable (Haggai 2:23; Zechariah 3:2–5, 8; 4:14; 6:11–13). They point toward something far more remarkable and transcendent than anyone could have anticipated. Beginning with David is the undeniable presumption that royal and priestly rule will someday merge in one individual. This anointed one of the Lord will reign from Zion and be heir of all the nations (Psalm 2:2, 6–8). As universal ruler, he will also be a priest after the line of Melchizedek (Psalm 110:4).

Apart from Psalm 110, no. Old Testament passage comes as close as this one to uniting the royal and priestly offices. With this in mind, the harmony between the two takes on a greatly enhanced meaning. Jeshua and Zerubbabel are messianic forerunners whose persons and functions prototypically portray the One to come who dies as servant, intercedes as priest, and will return as king.

Take It Home

It can be a struggle to make sense of Zechariah's visions. Part of the difficulty lies in the fact that the visions contain a number of objects that may have had a great significance for his original audience but are quite foreign to modern readers. How might this awareness influence you the next time you are discussing your faith with someone else? For example, could it be that you find yourself using words or phrases that are meaningful to you but unfamiliar to your listener, causing him or her to struggle more than necessary in attempting to comprehend?

ZECHARIAH 7:1–14:21

ZECHARIAH'S ORACLES

Setting Up the Section

A clear break exists between the content of Zechariah 7 and the material that precedes it. Based on the dates Zechariah provides (1:7; 7:1), the oracles of this section begin about twenty-two months later. Unfortunately, the biblical record is silent about the impact of Zechariah's previous visions. Apart from the tantalizingly brief historical references here, there is very little that can be known at all about that period of time. Still, Zechariah has much more relevant information to record.

📖 7:1–8:23

ORACLES CONCERNING HYPOCRITICAL FASTING

This portion of Zechariah lies between the night visions of chapters 1–6 and the self-designated oracles of chapters 9–14. The prophet's topic is fasting, a theme elaborated in both negative and positive manners. Zechariah does not specifically designate this section as an oracle, as he does in following passages, but its formal character defines it as such.

It is evident that progress is well under way on the temple by the date of this oracle (7:3). The priesthood is active there with some degree of formality and legitimacy, although it is also clear that the temple is not completely finished (8:9).

A group of travelers arrives to inquire about a religious matter (7:2–3). For a number of years, the travelers' community had fasted and wept in the fifth month (in observance of the destruction of Solomon's temple, a disaster that had occurred almost exactly seventy years earlier). The next anniversary is just a few months away, and they are asking if it is appropriate to create holy days to observe occasions that had arisen in the post-Mosaic period.

Yet what may have appeared to be an innocent query about the propriety of fasting is instead a question fraught with hypocrisy. In fact, God's response is a sharp rebuke. Their fasting and mourning, not only on the fifth but also during the seventh month, had for seventy long years been an empty exercise designed to enhance not the Lord but rather those who engaged in it in a hypocritical manner. Their religion had become one of outward show with no inner content. God points out that just as they eat and drink for their own satisfaction, so, too, do they fast (7:6). Their religious activity is centered on themselves, not their holy and loving God.

Demystifying Zechariah

The unspecified observance of the seventh month (7:5) evidently dates back to the murder of Gedaliah, the Jewish governor appointed by Nebuchadnezzar after the fall of Jerusalem (Jeremiah 40:5). He had come from an honored family, one that enjoyed the confidence of good King Josiah. However, some anti-Babylonian survivors of Jerusalem's destruction and exile formed a conspiracy to assassinate him (Jeremiah 41:1–2). Gedaliah's death was an extremely traumatic event for the community already crushed nearly to annihilation by the loss of the temple, the ruin of the holy city, and the deportation of most of its leadership.

In 7:7, Zechariah is not asking about the authenticity and accuracy of the earlier prophetic writings but rather if his own contemporaries are willing to obey those words. The Negev was in the south of Judah and consisted largely of desert. For the Negev to be populated, times of unusually suitable climatic conditions and freedom from hostility were necessary. This is even truer of the Shephelah (lowlands, or foothills) between Judah and the western plains. Zechariah's point is very apparent: If mighty and prosperous Jerusalem and Judah had been overthrown for failing to heed the warnings of earlier prophets, it is essential for his own audience to pay strict attention to those words, as their community is struggling for its survival. This is no time for hypocritical self-indulgence.

The Lord then reviews the basis for true worship, including fasting, by appealing to earlier canonical principles that provide its moral and spiritual framework (7:8–10). Such appeals to justice, mercy, compassion, and proper treatment of one another were abundant throughout the texts available to the people of that time, especially in the writings of Moses.

Past generations had responded to the word of witness from the prophets by "giving a shoulder of stubbornness" and "making their ears heavy"—the literal translations of the phrases in 7:11. The result was predictable: The Lord sent great wrath against them (7:12–14). The land had become desolate as a result, so much so that it appeared to be virtually uninhabited (Ezekiel 36:32–36). What had once been a place flowing with milk and honey had become a desert devoid of life and pleasure. Unless Zechariah's audience understands the abhorrence with which the Lord views superficial and self-serving religious observance, they can expect the same calamitous results as those experienced by their forefathers.

Critical Observation

Note the number of times Zechariah uses the name *Lord Almighty* (or *Lord of hosts*) as the name for God in his writing, and particularly throughout this section. As he describes things that appear humanly impossible, each usage of this name is an affirmation that such things can indeed come to pass by the resources of the Almighty One.

But the future appears more positive for Judah. When the Lord makes His abode in Jerusalem, the city will be radically transformed (8:1–3), including a repopulation to fill the city (8:4–5). In anticipation of the skepticism that Zechariah's message will surely elicit, the Lord makes it clear that He is speaking and that nothing is too difficult for Him (8:6).

References to the east and west (8:7) indicate the rising and setting of the sun, suggesting that future immigrants to Jerusalem will come from places throughout the world, not just the nearby surrounding areas. After the Lord has verified that He will dwell in the midst of Jerusalem (8:3), He promises to bring His people back to do the same (8:8).

Therefore it is important for the people to shoulder the responsibilities requisite to the fulfillment of God's promise. Their deliverance and return will depend wholly on God's grace (8:7–8), but present and future prosperity in the land will be directly related to their obedience and hard work. So the section in 8:9–13 is bracketed with the Lord's repeated challenge to "let your hands be strong" (NIV).

The reference here is to the rebuilding that commenced during the second year of Darius and not to the initial attempts at construction in 536 BC (8:10–12). Zechariah alludes to the days of social and economic distress in Judah (unemployment, no payment of wages, social unrest, etc.) before the people rearranged their priorities and began to put the Lord and His temple at the center of their community life. But apparently the preaching of the prophets had been effective (8:11), so the latest generations do not suffer the same consequences that their ancestors faced. The remaining remnant of the nation will possess the land during a peaceful, productive time (8:12).

Israel had been a curse (8:13) to other nations in the sense that the people had failed to engagingly attract those nations to the one true God. But now, the Lord says, they will be a blessing. There is no need to look any further than to the Jewish Messiah, Jesus Christ, to see what untold blessing Israel has been to the world.

The painful experience the Lord had previously brought on Judah had been a disciplinary action to produce consciousness of sin and a desire for repentance, and it had accomplished its intent. The Lord was then able to do good again to Judah, and the people could live where truth and justice were restored and valued (8:14–17).

In yet another example of the careful craftsmanship with which Zechariah arranges his material, the final portion of this oracle (chapters 7–8) comes full circle to the theme with which it began: the concern for fasting. At the beginning, only one city sent its representatives (7:2); but at the end, all the languages of the nations will be represented (8:23). And fasting in sorrow will be turned into feasting for joy (7:3; 8:19).

To begin with, there will be a mass pilgrimage of the people of the earth to seek the Lord at Jerusalem (8:20–22), to beseech His leniency and mercy when He might be inclined otherwise. It is impossible to know what prompts the desire, but the wording indicates a great urgency. Zechariah pictures movement on a universal scale—many peoples and strong nations (8:22).

Critical Observation

The idea of the nations converging at Jerusalem to worship the Lord at His temple is a major eschatological theme. Zechariah has already affirmed this explicitly in the oracle following his third vision (2:11). He will have more to say about the matter in chapter 14. No prophet excels Zechariah in his presentation of the universal pilgrimage of nations and their confession of the Lord's kingship.

At a ten-to-one ratio, other people will outnumber the Jews who return to seek the face of the Lord (8:23). The number *ten* is not to be taken literally but rather is symbolic in the Bible of totality or comprehensiveness. So urgent will be their desire, that they will hold onto the people of God (literally, "clutch at the sleeve" NLT) with no intention of letting go.

It is particularly interesting that the reason the nations will want to join themselves to the Jews is that they will have heard that God is with Israel. As the field of interest becomes much broader than Israel, a different name for God is used. *Yahweh* (the Lord Almighty), which has been used so frequently by Zechariah, is here changed to the generic *Elohim*. It suddenly becomes obvious to all the nations that their god is Israel's God. What they have been seeking through the millennia of human history has at last been found (Philippians 2:11; see Isaiah 45:23).

9:1–11:17

AN ORACLE CONCERNING THE LORD'S SOVEREIGNTY

After Zechariah's night visions (1–6) and his oracles on fasting (7–8), the final chapters (9–14) comprise a final main division. This last section consists of two parts: an oracle concerning the nations (9–11) and an oracle concerning Israel (12–14). Chapter 9 begins with his anticipation of the coming of the true King.

Demystifying Zechariah

Many scholars accept the unity of chapters 9–14, but many disagree that this section originated with Zechariah the prophet, attributing it instead to a "Zecharianic school," or a later addition by someone with no original connection to Zechariah. While true that a careful study reveals a change of mood, outlook, style, and composition compared with the first eight chapters, it is not unreasonable to presume that as Zechariah matures, he chooses a different literary form in which to express the grand and glorious ideas that permeate his thinking.

For the first time in the book (with the possible exception of 5:5–11), the prophet directs a message about or against pagan nations. But he does so to provide a backdrop to the coming of the messianic King who will take His royal throne as a result of conquest.

The Word of the Lord against Israel's enemies is described as a march through those nations that will terminate at the temple in Jerusalem (9:8). No sooner has this march of the Lord commenced than it commands the attention of all the surrounding peoples, including Israel (9:1-2). It is uncertain how Hadrach (the point of origin) is related to Damascus, but Damascus is clearly to the south. Third in line is Hamath, a territory to the west and north of Damascus, roughly the territory of modern-day Lebanon. Tyre and Sidon lay west and northwest of Damascus on the Mediterranean coast, and they may be more familiar than some of the other locations because their names are often symbolic of human pride. Zechariah notes that Tyre has amassed and hoarded great revenues of silver and gold but will soon see its power and possessions taken away (9:3-4).

Next on the list are a series of Philistine city-states: Ashkelon, Gaza, Ekron, and Ashdod (9:5-6). The once-proud Philistia will be shamed and embarrassed. The blood and abominable things (9:7) are references to their religious perversions, which no doubt include slaughtering animals considered by Israelites as unclean and eating meat that has not been properly drained of its blood. However, too little is known of the Philistines to determine precisely what practices are in mind here.

Yet Zechariah declares that Philistia will be thoroughly chastened and purified, becoming a remnant for God, like a clan in Judah (9:7-8). By Zechariah's time, the Jebusites have been totally assimilated into Judah. One day Ekron (perhaps representing all of Philistia) will have the same privilege. The Philistines (and by extension the preceding nations as well) will feel the awesome wrath of the Lord, but those who are left—a small remnant—will then be included within the covenant of God.

The march ends at Jerusalem with the Lord, triumphant in His procession, standing guard over His house (the temple). Then He surrounds it with His presence so that no hostile force can ever again oppress His people (9:8). It is a sure thing. What God sees in advance must surely come to pass.

Demystifying Zechariah

This portion of scripture is eschatological literature. Although it is grounded in the present time of the prophet (and uses well-known place names), Zechariah views the future in very stylized and conventional patterns. His point is that the Lord will manifest Himself in the last days as a vanquishing hero. One should not, therefore, look to precise historical events of which this is an account, nor should one anticipate a future scenario in which God will literally march from Hadrach to Jerusalem, establishing His dominion over all opposition.

The following passage of scripture (9:9-13) is one of the most messianically significant passages in the Bible, in both the Jewish and Christian traditions. Judaism sees in it a basis for a royal messianic expectation, while Christianity sees a prophecy of the triumphal entry of Jesus Christ into Jerusalem on the Sunday before His crucifixion (Matthew 21:5; John 12:15). Both agree that a descendant of David is depicted here, one who, though humble, rides as a victor into his capital city of Jerusalem.

On first reading, it appears that the Christian interpretation does not square exactly with Zechariah's prophecy. Although Jesus is described as entering Jerusalem in precisely the manner envisioned by Zechariah in 9:9, He dies within days of the event, never having made any active claim to the throne of David. The New Testament account shows that the servant who will someday be exalted as King must first suffer and die on behalf of those who will make up His kingdom in the ages to come.

After seeing that Jesus' triumphal entry is a historical prototype of an eschatological event that must yet take place, that distinction can be detected in the Zechariah passage. Zechariah provides a clear difference in tone and emphasis between 9:9 and 9:10. The coming One is first described as humble or lowly (9:9), a most inappropriate way to speak of One whose triumph is complete in every respect. Only in 9:10 is that triumph translated into universal dominion. This is precisely why any devotee of Bible study must consider the backdrop of the entire revelation of God, Old Testament and New Testament alike.

Using the metaphor of imprisonment, the Lord says He will release Zion's prisoners from the waterless pit (9:11). This is a backward reference to the release and restoration of the Babylonian exiles. God had released them because of the covenant He had made with His people long ago, sealed with blood, the sign of the covenant. He had promised to do so in the great blessings sections of the covenant texts of Leviticus 26:40–45 and Deuteronomy 30:1–10.

To return "twice as much" (9:12 NIV) suggests a double portion of blessing. A specific manifestation of that blessing, one much in line with the militaristic theme of the whole oracle, is the use the Lord will make of Judah, Ephraim (Israel), and Zion (9:13). He will bend Judah as one draws a bow, using Ephraim as an arrow. Zion will be stirred up against Yawan (Greece), used as a sword in the Lord's hand. Defended by the Lord of hosts, His chosen ones will both devour and subdue their enemies. Such bold imagery suggests that the death of the Lord's foes is in some sense an offering to Him (9:14–15).

The eschatological character of the oracle is underlined again in 9:16 by the use of the classic phrase *in that day*. Thus, the references to Hadrach, Damascus, and even Greece must be viewed as having end-times significance. At the end of this section of his oracle, the prophet bursts out in an expostulation of praise (9:17).

The focus then shifts to the elect people of the King. In a second exodus, they will come from all the nations to the promised land, where they will share His dominion with Him. Things had been bleak, indeed, as the whole history of Israel and Judah can attest, but there is now hope in light of the restoration from exile and particularly in light of God's gracious promises concerning the age to come.

All the Lord's people need to do is ask for rain, the showers of His blessing (10:1), and it is certain to come. God previously withheld the autumn and spring ("latter") rains, but Judah had adamantly remained in rebellion against Him. The result was the exile, a time of drought and despair, "a waterless dungeon" (9:11 NLT). But it is the Lord who makes thunderstorms, so Zechariah offers hope that the latter rain of prosperity will indeed arrive.

Zechariah is still looking to the future, because in his own day, Judah had suffered a devastating crisis of leadership in both her spiritual and political life. Throughout their history, Israel and Judah had turned to illicit religious channels such as teraphim, augurers, and dreamers (10:2), all of whom delivered nothing but falsehood and emptiness.

Demystifying Zechariah

Teraphim were small household images thought to represent supernatural powers and to be a means of eliciting information from the spirit world (Genesis 31:19, 34–35; 1 Samuel 19:13, 16; Hosea 3:4). Many times, *teraphim* is translated simply as "idols." *Augurers* may also be called "diviners"—people who sought supernatural disclosure by examining animal livers, shaking (casting lots with) arrows, or other methods (Ezekiel 21:21).

Zechariah condemns all forms of divination. The result of such an abysmal search for guidance had been the aimless wandering of the people like sheep (10:2–3). The allusion to sheep afforded the prophet a shift from consideration of *spiritual* leadership to that of the kings in the *political* realm. Kings of the time were commonly described as shepherds, and the Old Testament record is replete with references to the kings of Israel, beginning with Saul (1 Samuel 28:3–7), who seek after illicit channels of revelation and end up leading the people to ruin and dispersion. Because of this history of wicked leadership, the Lord is angry (Zechariah 10:3).

Yet in the middle of 10:3, the focus shifts from past and present to future, and from a negative assessment of Judah's leadership to a positive one. Judah is the Lord's flock, and He will care for it. Then, far from being the meek and easily bullied sheep of the past, they will become a charger on which the Lord can ride to battle.

God foresees Judah as the source of four elements: the cornerstone, the peg, the bow, and the ruler (10:4). These should be interpreted in the context of the warfare that prevails here rather than in terms of construction, architecture, or anything else.

Cornerstone (or *corner tower*) occurs as a metaphor for a leader such as a king or governor. It seems that Zechariah is alluding to a future human figure who will provide the very foundation for a revived kingdom structure. Paul understands this One to be Christ, the chief cornerstone (Ephesians 2:20).

Peg can refer to a tent peg. More likely in this instance, it can also indicate a peg in the wall from which items are hung. A person who bears the weight of responsibility might be said to be a peg (Isaiah 22:20–24). Zechariah is writing of someone to serve as a stout hook on which all of Judah's hopes for the future can be suspended.

Battle bow as a personal epithet is otherwise unknown in the Bible. But a helpful reference is that of 9:13, where the Lord says He will bend Judah as a warrior bends a bow. Since Judah is the *source* (10:3–5), the actual bow must be someone who comes out of Judah—an idea that is consistent with Old Testament messianic theology.

As for the *ruler* to come from Judah, it is somewhat surprising that Zechariah doesn't use the expected word that means king or prince. Instead he uses a term usually reserved for oppressive, tyrannical rule. From the perspective of God's foes, His total and violent domination will cast Him as someone to whom they must submit against their will. This impression gains support in 10:5, where the aforementioned rulers (and perhaps the cornerstone, peg, and battle bow as well) will be like warriors treading down in the mud of the streets. They will prevail over their foes because the Lord will be with them (10:5).

Ephraim (Israel) had previously appeared in a metaphor as an arrow projected by the Lord from the bow of Judah (9:13), and the result had been a lavish celebration of victory. Here again, Ephraim's heart will rejoice as with wine, as will that of Israel's offspring, celebrating God's glorious triumph over all opposition (10:6–7).

Zechariah shares a well-established tradition when he looks at the eschatological deliverance of Israel in terms of exodus (see Isaiah 43:1–7; Haggai 2:4–5). In this case, the process of regathering will begin when the Lord signals (sometimes translated *whistles*) for His people to return (Zechariah 10:8). Once they gather, they will multiply as they did in the days of Moses, and the pitiful postexilic remnant will once more become the mighty and innumerable host of God (2:4; 8:4–5).

The people are compared to a bag of seed sowed among the nations. Alive once more, they will return to the Lord and to the land (10:9). The reference to Egypt and Assyria (10:10) represents the universal distribution of the exiles of all ages. Gilead and Lebanon were both nearby, but they are never designated as falling within the land of promise. They merely accommodate the overflow of refugees that will fill the land of Palestine.

Like the original Exodus, this returning influx of people passes safely through the "sea of distress" (10:11). *Nile* is a name for Egypt. Both Egypt and Assyria will cease to be threats to the people of God.

Demystifying Zechariah

Zechariah 11 is one of the most difficult passages in the entire book. The protagonists are not always identified, the speakers and roles are confusing, and the whole temporal orientation is uncertain. The section opens with a poem filled with symbolism.

As Zechariah continues, it soon becomes apparent that the objects he mentions under the guise of trees and animals are the same as the ones he calls shepherds. The poem in 11:1–3, then, turns out to be a lament for the destruction of the evil shepherds who, as already noted, represent kings (11:8, 17). So the cedar tree of Lebanon, the oak of Bashan, and the fir (pine) tree are symbols of powerful rulers. The fact that three trees are mentioned leads one to suspect that the three shepherds of 11:8 are relevant to the total interpretation.

In a most unusual development, God commands Zechariah to undertake a series of actions, doing so in the place of the Lord Himself (11:4–16). First he is to shepherd the flock of slaughter (11:4). The flock had been bought and sold by strangers (probably foreign kings), and the sheep were unprotected by their own shepherds. In what appears to be an incredibly harsh statement, it seems that even the Lord has withdrawn His compassion (11:6). This, of course, is precisely what had taken place in the last decades of Israel's and Judah's history leading up to their respective captivities by the Assyrians and Babylonians.

Critical Observation

The fact that the Lord completes the chastisement begun by foreign oppressors does not exonerate His people from responsibility for their evil ways. God acts out of a spirit of correction, but they act out of spiteful selfishness and depravity. The Lord, then, can condemn foreign nations for their hostility toward His people even though He may have allowed their aggression as part of a greater purpose.

Shepherding the flock may have meant that Zechariah was reliving the Lord's dealings with His people in allegory (if only in his own mind) so he could report in a fresh way what Israel's history was really all about. An indispensable instrument for the job is the shepherd's staff, so Zechariah takes two of them, one named *Pleasantness* (or *Favor*) and the other *Binders* (or *Union*) (11:7). The former name speaks of the relationship between the Lord and His people (11:10) and the latter of that between Israel and Judah (11:14).

Zechariah also eradicates the three shepherds—another clue that he is reliving the Lord's own experience in Israel's history and that his removal of the leaders is symbolic. *One month* (11:8) is best viewed as meaning a short time rather than a specific point in history when three key leaders all fell within a literal period of thirty days.

The dying, perishing, and cannibalism mentioned in 11:8–9 had been a somber part of history. When God withdrew His compassion, surrounding aggressive nations had shown little mercy to Israel and Judah. Jeremiah had predicted Judah's gruesome resorting to cannibalism (Jeremiah 19:9) and later reflected on its fulfillment (Lamentations 2:20).

To dramatize that the fall of Jerusalem and exile of Judah were tantamount to the breaking of the Lord's covenant, Zechariah takes the staff named Pleasantness and breaks it in two (11:10–11). Yet for God to break His covenant with His people is not to suggest an irreparable breach, for the Old Testament witness pervasively attests to the inviolability of that fundamental relationship. What is meant is that the benefits of the covenant—in this case, the benefit of protection from conquest and deportation—have been withheld.

Zechariah, standing in for the Lord, had been a good shepherd to the flock of Israel and Judah when no one else had. Yet when the time comes for him to be compensated for his services, he is offered thirty pieces of silver (11:12)—the pittance paid for a slave who had been gored to death (Exodus 21:32). This is actually the Lord being appraised, and only His service is considered, not His intrinsic value. Therefore, the silver is like refuse because of the insulting attitude it represents (11:13).

Critical Observation

Potters' shops were usually located near refuse pits, where the shards and other unusable or broken materials were cast (Jeremiah 18:2; 19:1–2). The place of the potter, then, was not only a place of creation and beauty but also one of rejection and ruin. It became a metaphor for a scrap heap.

Thirty pieces of silver being cast down in the house of the Lord brings to mind the incident with Judas recorded in Matthew 27:3–5. Just as the Lord is priced at only thirty silver shekels as far as His service to Israel is concerned, so Jesus is later viewed by Judas and his generation as having no more value than a slave. In this sense, the rejection of the Lord in Zechariah 11:13 is a prophecy fulfilled in Matthew 27:9.

Having accomplished this part of his commission, Zechariah takes the second staff (Binders) and cuts it in two (11:14), signifying the unbinding of the brotherhood of Israel and Judah. Indeed, Israel had ceased to exist as a separate entity at the Babylonian deportation and was not reestablished as a nation until the twentieth century.

Once again the Lord commands Zechariah to dramatize his message by taking up the implements of an unwise shepherd (11:15). Although Zechariah was previously reliving the *history* of his people, at this point his orientation is exclusively *future* in both historical and eschatological terms. It is fruitless to try to identify the foolish shepherd. It is best, perhaps, to see the figure as the whole collective leadership of Israel from Zechariah's time forward, culminating at last in the epitome of godless despotism, the individual identified in the New Testament as the Antichrist (Matthew 24:5, 24; 2 Thessalonians 2:3–4; 1 John 2:18, 22).

Fundamental to the work of a shepherd should be his concern for any sheep that might have separated from the flock and gone their own way (Isaiah 53:6; Matthew 18:12–14). Yet the foolish shepherd will not seek the scattered ones nor heal the broken ones. He will even stop nourishing the healthy sheep. So thorough and cruel will be his disposition of these defenseless ones that he will rip their very hoofs from them (Zechariah 11:15–16).

The Lord is not oblivious to the shepherd who so abuses and exploits his people, however. The woe-judgment that comes upon him will be a sword that wounds his arm and his right eye (11:17). Without the arm to carry the sheep and the eye with which to search and find, the shepherd truly is worthless—not only in a moral sense but in a practical, functional sense as well. Why the shepherd is not killed is unclear, but he is so severely incapacitated that he can no longer function.

Although this particular oracle ends on a pessimistic note, Zechariah's message as a whole has not ended. In the following, final oracle, he offers glorious hope of a triumphant shepherd yet to come.

📖 **12:1–14:21**

AN ORACLE CONCERNING ISRAEL

The final great oracle of Zechariah, embracing all of chapters 12–14, stands in sharp contrast with what has immediately preceded in chapter 11 as it picks up the eschatological themes of chapters 9–10. This section introduces a cosmic, universalistic motif and focuses on the messianic aspect of the end-times redemption, going so far as to identify the Lord Himself as the messianic figure (12:10–14; 13:7–9). One of the clues that the oracle's thrust is eschatological is the focus on *Israel* rather than *Judah*. Israel, from Zechariah's standpoint, is a thing of the past.

The opening description of the Lord is one of Creator (12:1). His grand actions underline His creative and redemptive role. Here at the brink of a new age, it is important to realize that the same God who brought everything into existence is well able to usher in the new creation of a restored people in a renewed and universal kingdom.

The mighty Lord will use His chosen people Judah as an instrument by which He does battle with the nations and brings them under His dominion. This is what is meant in describing Jerusalem as an "intoxicating drink" (12:2 NLT). The nations will drink of Jerusalem—partake of her in hostility and conquest—but they will end up inebriated.

Jerusalem is also a stone of burden (12:3). God's people are likened to pillage being carried off by victors, but they will be heavier than the looters bargained for, so heavy and jagged that they will lacerate the shoulders of those who try to spirit them away. Drunken and scarred, the nations come in for further judgment. The Lord will confuse their horses and cavalrymen. Their horses will be blinded, but God will open His own eyes on behalf of the house of Judah (12:4).

When all this comes to pass, Judah's rulers will realize that the people of Jerusalem have been their greatest strength. The Lord of hosts used them as a discomfit to their enemies and has guaranteed that the nation will survive. The rulers will themselves become a "firepot among pieces of wood" and a "flaming torch among sheaves" (12:5–6 NASB), incinerating all the surrounding woods that threaten Israel.

In addition to Jerusalem, even tents and humble habitations throughout Judah will enjoy pride of place among God's people (12:7). In that day, the Lord will defend the residents of Jerusalem in such a powerful way that even the weakest among them is comparable to the great warrior King David. And in an even more startling hyperbole, the dynasty of David is compared to God (12:8).

Demystifying Zechariah

One must not allow any literary device such as hyperbole (great exaggeration) to determine one's understanding of the theological content in a passage such as 12:8. All that is intended is an argument to magnify the Lord's glorious redemption of His people. The weak become strong and the strong become stronger—as powerful as God Himself if the syllogism requires it to be so.

Once the Lord has accomplished His work of judgment on the nations and secured Judah and Jerusalem from them (12:9), He will begin a work of grace among the redeemed. The spirit of grace will pour out on God's people, though they little deserve it. In fact, the Lord must extend His grace to enable His people to seek it in the first place.

Grace, however, is an abstraction. It must take shape from some occasion or action that produces an awareness of the need for divine favor. Zechariah cites one such action: "They will look on [the Lord], the one they have pierced" (12:10 NIV). But the prophet's references to the Lord shift immediately from me to Him. This is an extremely difficult text within the confines of its Old Testament setting. The most satisfying resolution is to accept a change in pronoun as a grammatical, stylistic feature without a change of the subject. From the Lord's viewpoint, it is me that is the focus; from the standpoint of the people, it is Him.

Yet that raises another question, this one a theological concern. The people of the Old Testament know nothing of a mortal God, One who can be fatally wounded as in this passage. Zechariah's audience likely presumes that the Lord has been pierced in a figurative way, in the sense that they have wounded His holiness and violated His righteousness.

By New Testament times, however, Zechariah 12:10 was considered clearly messianic in both Jewish tradition and Christian theology. The verse anticipates the day when the royal house of David and all Jerusalem will receive from the Lord a spirit of grace, enabling people to seek His forgiveness for millennia of waywardness. They will look to the Lord, the One they have mortally wounded by their heartbreaking behavior, a look that produces in them a sense of great sorrow. The only sorrow comparable is that of the loss of a firstborn son in death (Genesis 22:2), and such sorrow is a sign of genuine repentance.

Critical Observation

The great weeping of Hadad-rimmon (12:11) is believed to be the expression of sorrow that took place after the violent and premature death of King Josiah, when he foolishly interposed his tiny army between the Egyptians and the Assyrians (2 Kings 23:29–30). The tragic event was commemorated from that time on (2 Chronicles 35:25).

Nathan (12:12) was the third son of David. Though the kings of Judah after Solomon until the exile were all descendants of Solomon (1 Chronicles 3:10–16), a change occurred at that point, and royal descent began to be traced through Nathan.

Usually community or corporate repentance is standard, but in this case it appears that each member and entity of the community feels individually culpable and must individually give account before God (12:11–14). Judah's lamentation of repentance will result in their forgiveness, followed by purification and cleansing (13:1) described with the metaphor of an artesian well that gushes forth. The cleansing is widespread and removes sin and iniquity, idols in the land, false prophets, and the underlying spirit of impurity that has been so pervasive (13:1–2).

The charlatan prophets will attempt to downplay any involvement in false prophesying. They will deny having had visions, change their apparel, and lie about their participation. But even after removing the traditional hairy cloak of a prophet (13:4), the false prophets will be exposed by the marks on their chests—incisions made by many Canaanite religious practitioners to impress various deities by their acts of wholesale devotion (13:5–6). Their feeble lies will not be convincing.

Problems in the priesthood (13:1–2) and among the so-called prophets (13:2–6) are followed by Zechariah's attention to the monarchy (13:7–9). Again he refers to Israel's kings as *shepherds*. After a bold assertion by the Lord that the shepherd-king is an associate comes a poignant command to strike the leader so that the flock will become scattered. This action will cause not only the leaders of the community to suffer the blow of the Lord's righteous indignation but also the flock (described as insignificant or "little").

The scattering of the sheep, far from being an accidental consequence of the striking of the shepherd, is for the purpose of ridding the flock of the elements that must be purged (13:7). Afterward, only one-third remain. That remnant will pass through a refining process designed to equip them to have minds and hearts that are open and responsive to the sovereign claims of the Lord (13:8–9).

Demystifying Zechariah

Zechariah's original hearers perhaps considered these statements an eschatological repetition of their exile: The shepherd-kings of Israel will suffer the wrath of God, the flock-people will endure pestilence and sword, and the surviving community will be scattered. Then, from the dispersed population will emerge a purified remnant that knows the Lord. But clearly the New Testament evangelists, and Jesus Himself, regarded the Zechariah text as a messianic testimonial (Matthew 26:31; Mark 14:27). It may be that New Testament usage is intended as a maxim to indicate simply that when shepherds are struck down, sheep invariably scatter. After all, Jesus never says directly that He is fulfilling this prophecy; He simply affirms the aphorism of the cause and effect established by the removal of a shepherd from His flock. More likely, however, this is an instance where messianic truth, communicated by a text, may never have been so intended by the original prophet-author.

This oracle, as well as the entire prophecy of Zechariah, ends on the grand and glorious note of the sovereignty of the Lord and the establishment of His universal and eternal kingdom. Triumph comes through tribulation, so the prophet speaks of the Day of the Lord in the context of struggle and conflict (14:1–2). Restoration and dominion cannot come until all the forces of evil that seek to subvert it are put down once and for all. So the nations of the whole earth come against Jerusalem, defeat her, and divide their spoils of war in her very midst.

It is important to note that it is the Lord who gathers the nations (14:2), not only to purify His people in tribulation, but also to provide an occasion for the destruction of their enemies. Zechariah has already described a scene in which Jerusalem is attacked but suffers no loss (12:1–9). But in chapter 14, the deliverance of Jerusalem will be coincident with the triumphant coming of the Lord. The effect of His coming is not only victory for His people (14:3) but also the establishment of His earthly kingdom (14:9–11). Zechariah thus distinguishes between the kingdom of the Lord's universal, unchallenged dominion and a preliminary one in which His lordship prevails and His people are secure only as He exercises direct and forcible predominance.

Shortly after the defeat and pillaging of Jerusalem, the Lord will go forth to do battle, which will bring about cataclysmic changes in the terrain itself, as well as in the patterns of light and darkness and in the seasons (14:3–7). When all seems lost, the Lord leads His people forth and parts the Mount of Olives by the very act of treading on it (14:4), not unlike the way Moses parted the Red Sea to deliver the Israelites. The splitting of the mountain creates a new valley through which the people will flee (14:5). This is no mere earthquake, however, but a shaking of the whole universe as the Lord comes in judgment. This will occur on a day known only to God (14:7).

One result will be life-giving waters that flow from Jerusalem, half to the Dead Sea and half to the Mediterranean Sea (14:8). The meaning of the Hebrew indicates that these are not waters that give life but waters that are alive—moving, fast-flowing, and sparkling.

The Jewish Shema (Deuteronomy 6:4–5) is the very heart of Israel's covenant faith—a confession of the Lord's self-consistency as well as His uniqueness and exclusivity. Zechariah makes unmistakable reference to the Shema in 14:9. The original statement of monotheism, however, breaks out of an exclusively Jewish viewpoint and speaks of the oneness of God on a universal scale. There is no reference to *our* God because the Lord will be the one and only God of *all* the nations.

However, Jerusalem will continue to be the center from which the grace of God will radiate to all the earth. To express the continued centrality of Israel, Zechariah visualizes the leveling of the remainder of the Holy Land and the elevation of Jerusalem so that the city stands high above in a position of eminence and security (14:10).

Demystifying Zechariah

Geba was in the northernmost extent of Judah, and Rimmon was in the far south (14:10). So the whole land, from northern hill to southern height, would become as level as the Arabah—the southern extension of the Great Rift depression south of the Dead Sea, an area unexcelled for flatness.

The prophet isn't trying to provide precise delineations of the eschatological city, but he does want his generation to understand that the idealism of the future is rooted and grounded in the present, in actual history and geography. People will once more occupy Jerusalem, and the city will never again be destroyed (14:11).

All those who have persecuted and tormented God's people, however, will be inflicted with a horrible plague or pestilence of some kind that attacks both humans and animals (14:12–15). In addition to the plague's grotesque physical consequences, it will trigger a panic among the people, causing them to lash out and destroy one another. It appears that the plague and its related events best fit chronologically with the conflict described in 14:3–8, prior to the elevation of Jerusalem (14:9–11).

After the great fire that marks the beginning of the Lord's reign, the survivors among the nations acknowledge Him as King (14:9) and come regularly to offer Him homage (14:16). This is not to suggest, however, that they have undergone conversion in the religious sense (14:17–19). The word used for *worship* in verse 16 can mean only to bow down or do obeisance.

The particular occasion of pilgrimage is the Feast of Tabernacles, one of the three annual events in Israel's calendar when the Lord's able-bodied people are to appear before Him at the central sanctuary. Immediately after the celebration, the Levites will lead the assembly in a great ceremony of covenant renewal (Nehemiah 9:1–38) that culminates in a solemn commitment by the people to reaffirm their covenant allegiance to the Lord (Nehemiah 9:38; 10:29). It is evident that the Zechariah passage should also be viewed against a covenant background (Zechariah 14:17).

In the Bible, Egypt is frequently a symbol of the world at large (Isaiah 27:13; Revelation 11:8). Therefore, it is not distinguished here from the nations just mentioned but appears as a synonym for them (Zechariah 14:18–19).

In closing, Zechariah describes a number of transformations to take place "in that day" (14:20–21). The horse is considered an unclean animal, yet in the Day of the Lord, horses will wear bells bearing the inscription "HOLY TO THE LORD." Lowly pots used formerly as receptacles for ashes (Exodus 27:3) will be elevated to function as the holy bowls before the altar used for sacrifice. These examples point to the fact that "there will no longer be a Canaanite in the house of the LORD Almighty" (14:21 NIV).

The Canaanite, of course, symbolizes what is most reprehensible to God. The Canaanites are a cursed people (Genesis 9:25) and are to be annihilated by the conquest of Israel (Joshua 3:10). To think of their participation in the worship of God at all is scandalous, and to envision their doing so within the holy precincts of the temple is incomprehensible. Yet in the Day of the Lord, all are welcome because they all will be the people of God.

It is impossible to improve on Paul's assessment of the transformation that will characterize that glorious day: "There is neither Jew nor Greek, there is neither slave nor free man, there is neither male nor female; for you are all one in Christ Jesus" (Galatians 3:28 NASB).

Take It Home

Zechariah makes any number of noteworthy points in his final oracles, but perhaps one of the most relevant to today is the ease with which hypocrisy can infiltrate worship habits. Until such hypocrisy was removed, God would not respond. According to Zechariah, earlier generations had ignored the problem and suffered for it; later generations would repent and receive God's blessings. Do you think hypocrisy is a problem in today's church? Do you detect any instances where people in church settings seem more focused on themselves than on God's presence? What do you think is the best way for individuals and congregations to prevent hypocrisy from becoming a problem?

MALACHI

INTRODUCTION TO MALACHI

The book of Malachi is a summons to repentance and revival. In six disputations, the prophet summons the people to forsake their spiritual doldrums and halfhearted commitment to the Lord and return to an active faith and the practice of devotion to God.

AUTHOR

Some have wondered if Malachi's name, which means "my messenger," could be a title rather than a name. But there is no reason to believe that Malachi is written by anyone other than Malachi himself.

PURPOSE

Malachi addresses his people—the small group of exiled Jews who return from Babylonia. He confronts his people for keeping the best for themselves and leaving their leftovers for God. He calls his people back to their commitment and faith, particularly in light of the future judgment awaiting those who do not repent.

OCCASION

The concerns raised by Ezra and Nehemiah in their work of reformation are some of the same that Malachi mentions: spiritually mixed marriages, the neglect of tithing, disregard for keeping the Sabbath, the corruption of the priesthood, and social injustice. Some scholars suggest that it is likely Malachi preached before the reforms of Ezra and Nehemiah, preparing the way for them.

THEMES

Malachi uses the disputation form: Certain people raise a point, which is then contradicted by the prophet or, better, by the Lord speaking through the prophet. Malachi is not the only prophet to use this device. We find it in one form or another in Amos, Micah, and Ezekiel, as well as in Isaiah and Jeremiah. But only Malachi raises it to the organizing principle of his prophecy.

The covenant that God made with His people in the Pentateuch is fundamental to the message of Malachi. Malachi presumes this covenant is to establish a living relationship between the Lord and His people. Beginning in 1:1, Malachi uses the name *Israel* for the people of God. The covenant name has been applied to what remains of the people of God. The northern tribes, who were specifically referred to as Israel during the days of the divided kingdom, are no more, but Israel lives on in the remnant of the entire nation that returns from exile, primarily the descendants of the tribes of Judah and Benjamin.

HISTORICAL CONTEXT

A small company of Jews returns to Jerusalem from Babylon after the exile. The city is still largely in ruins from its destruction fifty years before. By Malachi's time, any enthusiasm and hopefulness has faded. The people are past believing that God is going to do anything grand on their behalf. It is now a time of spiritual discouragement, complaining, and a growing indifference to God's law of perfunctory worship.

So the situation Malachi faces is the same situation faced by Ezra when he came to Jerusalem in 458 BC, eighty years after the first return of exiles from Babylon, and by Nehemiah when he came to Jerusalem in 445 BC.

OUTLINE

MALACHI 1:1–2:9

ISRAEL AND THE PRIESTS

Setting Up the Section

Malachi opens with a statement about nations rather than individuals. The Israelites, descendants of Jacob, are God's people, as opposed to the Edomites, descendants of Jacob's brother, Esau.

📖 1:1–5

GOD'S CALL ON ISRAEL

Verse 1 identifies this writing as an oracle, one given through Malachi, a name that is Hebrew for "my messenger." The oracle is addressed to the nation of Israel. In this writing, the people who make up that nation are also referred to as *Judah* (2:11; 3:4) and *Jacob* (1:2; 2:12; 3:6).

In the first few verses, the term *hate* probably refers to a rejection. God selected Israel and rejected Edom as His chosen people.

Demystifying Malachi

Edom, though a little country, was often used as an emblem for all the enemies of Israel. At no point in Israel's history is Edom an ally, as are (at one time or another) most of the other nearby nations. Prophets such as Ezekiel and Obadiah speak against Edom (Ezekiel 25:12–14; Obadiah 1:1–7). The region is gradually overrun and by the middle/late fifth century has become a non-nation, but verse 5 indicates that in Malachi's time, the Edomites have not yet been thoroughly destroyed.

📖 1:6–2:9

THE CONTEMPTUOUS PRIESTS

This section, containing Malachi's second disputation, concerns Israel's priests' neglect of their duties. The people are complicit in this neglect, as Malachi will say, but the priests are more responsible. This disputation, the longest in the book, takes up twenty-three of a total fifty-five verses.

As a demonstration that Malachi is not calling Israel to a new set of standards but calling her back to the ancient covenant, three texts from Numbers and Deuteronomy are woven through this disputation: Numbers 6:23–27 (the Aaronic benediction); Numbers 25:12–13 (the Levitical covenant of peace); and Deuteronomy 33:8–11 (Moses' blessing of the tribe of Levi and his enumeration of the priests' responsibilities). Malachi's people would have immediately recognized the ironic comparison that is being made.

Malachi 1:6 credits God with the message. The phrase "says the LORD Almighty" (or "says the LORD of hosts") is used often in this disputation. Malachi is attacking the priests, after all. They would be almost certain to react badly to Malachi's criticism, so it is important for him to emphasize that his message is from the Lord.

According to verse 8, the priests are violating the law that requires the best and the first of all the people's property be given to God. The firstborn, the firstfruits, and the most excellent of one's property belongs to God. This is a test of faith because the best animals are, of course, the best breeding stock, and in order to give that stock away to God, one has to believe it is better to honor the Lord than to seek material prosperity.

Malachi doesn't give a detailed reason the priests consent to let the people bring less than their best. It is to the priests' benefit that the people bring in the appropriate offerings. After all, part of these offerings provides sustenance for the priests, who are forbidden to own land. Ignorance is not the problem. The law is specific and emphatic on this point. The priests and the people would have never considered making these kinds of offerings to a dignitary, yet they are skimping on worship.

The doors mentioned in verse 10 are those to the temple courtyard. The sacrifices are offered outside.

We tend to think that lukewarm is better than cold, and something is better than nothing. But when it comes to worship, this is not God's perspective. He holds His people to a high standard. This is a common theme in the Old Testament Prophets. God doesn't want our worship if we are giving it begrudgingly, halfheartedly, and only out of a sense of duty. He doesn't want our worship if it is not an act of true faith.

Verse 11 describes a time when the whole world will worship the Lord. Malachi is interested in the future fulfillment of the plan of salvation. In contrast, according to verses 13–14, the priests are guilty of doing their jobs in a spirit of boredom, and the people seem to prefer it that way.

The moniker "great king" is a common title in some ancient texts and refers to the king over all the other lesser kings—the emperor (1:14). The Lord is the great King who will enforce the penalties of His covenant upon those who betray its requirements.

Demystifying Malachi

The requirement of giving a male animal—while it certainly foreshadows the greater sacrifice of Christ, who is a male, and is made necessary by the representative role of the male in society—is a kindness on the Lord's part. The females are needed to give milk and bear young, but only a few males are needed for breeding. So in this sense, less is lost to the flock when males are sacrificed.

Verse 1 of chapter 2 begins the curses threatened upon the priests for their unbelief and disobedience. According to verse 2, a primary role of the priests—pronouncing blessing—will become futile. The priests will pronounce blessing, as with the Aaronic benediction (Numbers 6:23–27), but the people will get curses instead.

The first curse is particularly heavy for the priest because a man became a priest by family line only (2:2). If descendants are cut off, the family will lose the right to the sacred office. The second curse is one of degradation and dishonor. Priests had to be cleaner than anyone else, and here God Himself is throwing dung in their faces (2:3).

The text of the covenant in verse 4 is found in Numbers 25:11–13, and its language is spread throughout Malachi 2:1–8, as is the blessing of Levi found in Deuteronomy 33:8–11 (Malachi 2:7). No Israelite would have missed the connection.

We read what kind of preacher and teacher a minister ought to be in 2:6–7—Malachi says that a faithful minister turns many from sin and communicates the knowledge and the instruction of the Lord. He does this, Malachi says, because he himself walks with the Lord. Contrarily, verses 8–9 reveal the hearts of the priests in this day. They teach without power, even tailor their messages to certain people's advantage and to others' disadvantage. These verses make it clear that the people have stumbled and the law is up for sale. Israel is sinking into spiritual doldrums and, from there, might eventually sink into spiritual death.

MALACHI 2:10–3:5

THE SINS OF THE PEOPLE

Rebellion   2:10–16

Self-Deceit   2:17–3:5

Setting Up the Section

Malachi's third disputation returns to the sins of the people, specifically the marital unfaithfulness among the people of God. The same format is followed as in the previous disputations: The Lord asserts through His prophet that His people have violated the covenant (2:10–13). This is followed by the people's questioning reply, the Lord's response (2:14), and the implication (2:15–16).

📖 2:10–16

REBELLION

In verse 10, Malachi reminds the people of their special relationship to God, their Father. Israel must live in obedience to God and in union with one another as brothers and sisters, at least in God's family. In this, the Israelites are breaking faith.

Verse 11 reveals the sin of Malachi's people to be spiritual intermarriage. Jews are marrying outside the faith. The fact that Judah is blamed for the sin suggests that it is a national sin, widespread and generally countenanced. The problem with these marriages is religious, not racial or ethnic. Members of other peoples are welcomed into Israelite life and society and into marriage with Israelites so long as they accept the faith of Israel.

Malachi looks to the Lord to enforce the curses of the covenant upon the violator (2:12). The people may have thought that as long as they continue to offer their sacrifices it didn't matter if they also took part in pagan rituals. But God doesn't need their offerings, and He doesn't want them unless they are symbols of faith and trust.

The tears mentioned in verse 13 probably refer to loud displays of emotion during sacrifices. Many religions of the day believed that these protestations of earnestness would influence God to act. What is scorned here is emotion intended to manipulate God.

In verse 14, the same word is used of two kinds of marital sins—improper intermarriage and improper divorce. Marriage is regarded as a covenant. It takes on features like that of God's covenant with His people; it requires fidelity on the part of the covenant partners.

The wife of one's youth probably reflects the fact that many, if not most, marriages in these days are arranged before the children grow to be adults (2:14). Notice the egalitarian language at the end of verse 14: The wife is referred to as a *partner*, not an underling.

Critical Observation

What is specifically being forbidden in verse 16 is divorce because a husband has lost interest in his wife. Old Testament law permits divorce for indecency on the part of the spouse (such as sexual infidelity), but it does not permit divorce for a lack of affection or romantic attraction.

📖 2:17–3:5

SELF-DECEIT

The failure of the people identified in this sixth disputation is doubt of the Lord's justice. The Lord's reply is a promise of a divine messenger to cleanse His people, to restore true worship, and to enact justice. Malachi again addresses the need for the reform of the priesthood and the purification of Israel's worship.

In verse 17, the statement that those who do evil are good in the eyes of God is a statement of irony. It is not likely that anyone is actually saying or even thinking this. The point is that it doesn't seem that God is doing anything about this evil. Does it matter to Him?

The opening verse of chapter 3 answers the concern of 2:17. God will respond, and His response will be in the form of a messenger. The word translated *messenger* here is the same used in 1:1.

The ministry of the messenger described in 3:2–5 is clearly the ministry of a divine figure. He does the things that only the Lord has the power and the authority to do.

The day of the Lord's coming, mentioned in 3:2, is a concept found frequently in the Old Testament Prophets. It refers broadly to a time when the Lord will appear as a conquering judge to punish the wicked and vindicate the righteous, ushering in a new era of blessing. But here, as elsewhere in the Prophets, there is a surprising reversal. The assumption of the people is that the Day of the Lord will be a great day for them. They will be delivered from their enemies and granted prosperity. But here Malachi asks who will be able to endure this day. For those who have kept the covenant, the Day of the Lord will be welcome deliverance. For those who have broken it, it will be a time of judgment and curses.

Demystifying Malachi

A refiner's fire functions to purify metal. Malachi draws this image from the everyday life of Israel. The prophets often use this image to describe either the Lord's elimination of the impurities from His people or His purifying of them. The launderer's soap was a form of lye used to soak the dirt out of clothes. Both fire and lye are agents by which what deserves to remain is separated from what does not.

Verses 4–5 conclude this disputation with a description of renewed worship and re-formed justice—right worship *and* right living. Verse 5 catalogs some of the sins that are commonplace in Malachi's time. Seven violations of the covenant law are mentioned, a sampling of the way in which the people show contempt for God.

MALACHI 3:6–4:6

THE FUTILITY OF THE PEOPLE

Selfishness	3:6–12
Self-Sufficiency	3:13–4:3
Restoration Ahead	4:4–6

Setting Up the Section

This section contains Malachi's final two disputations. The first one addresses the people's failure to give ample offerings to God. The second one involves the promise of vindication for those who have put their faith in God.

📄 **3:6–12**

SELFISHNESS

Verses 6–12 contain the fifth of Malachi's six disputations. As in the second disputation, we find two questions put by the people instead of just one. The subject in both disputations is broadly the same—Israel's begrudging offerings—though in the second disputation the emphasis falls on the priests' failure, and here it falls on the people's failure.

Verses 6–7 focus on God's immutability. It is God's immutability that explains why Israel, though she has violated God's covenant with her generation after generation, has not been destroyed. The Lord is a merciful God, faithful to His covenant and to the promises He made to be Israel's God.

Verse 8 addresses tithes and offerings. The tithe is the requirement to give a tenth of one's income to the Lord. The offerings are gifts above the tithe. Giving of these things is a symbol of recognition that all one has belongs to God.

Verses 9–11 reveal other failures of the people. Either they are holding back part of what they owe by law or not everyone is giving a tithe. Since the tithes are the allotment of the priests and Levites, the people's disobedience causes them hardship.

The floodgates mentioned in verse 10 are a reference to rain, the lack of which has blighted Israel's crops. But verse 11 reveals another layer of meaning. Rain is a symbol of all manner of blessing. Agricultural abundance is an image frequently employed by the prophets to describe the blessing of the new age.

Take It Home

To some, verses 10–12 sound like promises that if we live righteous lives, we will be rich. The fact is, it is plainly understood by faithful people in the Old Testament that God is not promising riches to the pious, at least not in this world. They struggle, as we do today, with the obvious fact that often we find wicked people richer than godly people.

As Christians, we worship a God who is faithful to His promises. It is our responsibility to trust and obey, no matter how we might calculate the costs and likely benefits. God often makes us trust Him before He will show us His blessing.

📖 3:13–4:3

SELF-SUFFICIENCY

In the sixth and final disputation, the people complain that God is not vindicating them by rewarding the righteous or punishing the wicked. The Lord's reply, through Malachi, is that He will most definitely vindicate His people. That day will come, and any doubts about the importance of trusting the Lord and obeying Him will be forever put to rest.

Given that Malachi has confronted his people about their disobedience, verse 14 seems ironic. The people complain about carrying out requirements, but in light of Malachi's charges against the people, what are all the requirements they have carried out?

The mourning they mention was probably the same kind of ritual mourning mentioned in 2:13. Malachi condemns the people for a show of mourning and penitence before the Lord that is nothing but an attempt to manipulate Him.

In verse 15, the idea of challenging or testing God refers to those who openly do what God forbids. Their actions test to see if God will respond. The people here called *evildoers*, or *wicked*, are simply those who are doing other kinds of evil than the insolent and complaining Israelites are doing.

Verse 16 contains the only narrative in the book of Malachi. The people described here (obviously a distinct minority among Israel as a whole) are pious, faithful, and devout. They stir one another up to love and good deeds, and the Lord takes special notice of their spiritual conversation.

The *scroll* (or *book*) *of remembrance* mentioned in verse 16 is probably a document that contains the names of all those who ascribe to some written commitment to the Lord. Another possibility is that it is a scroll akin to "the books," in which are written the record of the lives of men and women, or even to "the book of life," in which are found the names of those whom God has saved.

Fire, mentioned in the first verse of chapter 4, is an image often used to describe the effects of the Lord's judgment. Malachi has already referred to a refiner's fire in 3:2. This is a metaphor.

The fire renders the wicked stubble (4:1). *Stubble*, used here as a term of agriculture, is what is left when everything valuable has been taken away—the leftovers after the field has been cut down with a scythe.

Verse 2 contains a complex figure of speech in the "sun of righteousness" that "will rise with healing in its wings."

There is the image of reversal of fortune in 4:3. The wicked, who generally ride in triumph over the righteous in this world, will be trampled under the feet of the righteous in the Day of the Lord. This, too, is a frequently employed image of divine judgment. The prosperity of the wicked is overtaken in a moment.

📄 4:4–6

RESTORATION AHEAD

Verse 4 mentions the Law of Moses, which summarizes the focal point of the first three disputations. Verses 5–6 mention the Day of the Lord, which is a focus of the last three.

Demystifying Malachi

Verse 5 contains a promise of the coming of Elijah, the quintessential prophet. Does this mean he will return in person? In Matthew 11:7–10 and 17:10–13, we read Jesus' interpretation of this text. In both cases, Jesus mentions John the Baptist as the "Elijah" of whom Malachi speaks.

The sense of verse 6 is not merely that when the Messiah and the Day of the Lord come they will usher in a new harmony in family relationships. The mention of parents and children is a way of saying that when the Day of the Lord comes, He will turn everyone back to faithfulness to the covenant. This is a promise of great revival.

Take It Home

If God is for us, who can be against us? This is Malachi's point from the beginning. Our enemies cannot prevail, and our Edoms can do us no harm with the Lord on our side. Let us then live for Him and walk with Him in the covenant He has so graciously made with us; let us rest in His love. If we have blessings, they have come from His hand.

CONTRIBUTING EDITORS:

Stan Campbell has a MA from Wheaton College and has been a full-time writer in Christian publishing for over 10 years and active in a church ministry for twenty years. Among his almost three dozen books are *The World's Easiest Guide to Understanding the Bible* and *Bible to Go: Genesis to Revelation in One hour*.

Robert L. Deffinbaugh, Th.M. graduated from Dallas Theological Seminary with his Th.M. in 1971. Bob is a teacher and elder at Community Bible Chapel in Richardson, Texas, and a regular contributor to the online studies found at Bible.org.

Stephen Leston, is pastor of Kishwaukee Bible Church in DeKalb , IL. He is passionate about training people for ministry and has served as a pastor at Grace Church of DuPage (Warrenville, IL) and Petersburg Bible Church (Petersburg, AK).

Eugene H. Merrill is Distinguished Professor of Old Testament Studies at Dallas Theological Seminary where he has served on the faculty since 1975. The author of scores of books and articles, mainly of a historical and exegetical nature, Dr. Merrill holds the PhD in Old Testament studies from Bob Jones University, the MA in Jewish Studies from New York University, and the MPhil and Ph.D. in Middle Eastern Studies from Columbia University. He is an active churchman and preaches and teaches abroad on a regular basis.

Richard D. Patterson was chairman of the Department of Biblical Studies and professor of Semitic Languages and literatures at Liberty University, Lynchburg, Virginia. He contributed to The Expositor's Bible Commentary. He also has written numerous articles for *Grace Theological Journal, the Journal of the Evangelical Theological Society,* and other scholarly journals. (A.B., Wheaton College; M.Div., Northwest Baptist Theological Seminary; Th.M. Talbot Theological Seminary; M.A., Ph.D., University of California Los Angeles)

Robert Rayburn holds a Master of Divinity degree from Covenant Theological Seminary and a doctorate in New Testament from the University of Aberdeen, Scotland. His commentary on Hebrews was published in the *Evangelical Commentary of the Bible*.

CONSULTING EDITOR:

Tremper Longman is the Robert H. Gundry Professor of Biblical Studies at Westmont University. He has taught at Westmont since 1998 and taught before that for 18 years at the Westminster Theological Seminary in Philadelphia. Dr. Longman has degrees from Ohio Wesleyan University (B.A.), Westminster Theological Seminary (M.Div.), and Yale University (M.Phil.; Ph.D.). He has also been active in the area of Bible translation, in particular he serves on the central committee that produced and now monitors the New Living Translation.

WITH SPECIAL THANKS TO BIBLE.ORG

Bible.org is a non-profit (501c3) Christian ministry headquartered in Dallas, Texas. In the last decade, bible.org has grown to serve millions of individuals around the world and provides thousands of trustworthy resources for Bible study including the new NET BIBLE® translation.

Bible.org offers thousands of free resources for:
• Spiritual Formation and Discipleship
• Men's Ministry
• Women's Ministry
• Pastoral Helps
• Small Group Curriculum and much more...

Bible.org can be accessed through www.bible.org